Discrete Mathematical Algorithm, and Data Structure

Major Components of Mathematics, and Computer Science Explained with the help of C, C++, PHP, Java, C#, Python, and Dart

Sanjib Sinha

© 2020-21 Sanjib Sinha

1. Introduction to the Discourse

As you know from the title, this book covers a wide range of three topics, in fact, too wide range of three topics, on which you will find books separately. You will find many good books on Discrete Mathematics, you will find many good books on Algorithm and Data Structures, as well.

Keeping that fact in mind, we are writing a book which tries to discover the relations between three well known topics, and, moreover, how they influence each other.

We can compare this relationship, such as, a relation between the writer and readers. Readers always reconstruct a book while reading, and they write it in a new way in their mind. Each time a book is read, it is actually written again.

We can consider this book as a confluence of the three distinct topics, such as Discrete Mathematics, Algorithm and Data Structures.

Let us start with Discrete Mathematics first.

What is Discrete Mathematics? We need to know that first. Second, we need to know what is the relationship of Discrete Mathematics to Computer Science. Finally, we want to know how we can implement the Discrete Mathematical concepts into various fields of Computer Science, such as Algorithm and Data Structures.

Here, we are primarily concerned with Algorithm and Data Structure. These topics sit at the core of any Computer Science curriculum. Without understanding these two components properly, we can not claim that we are students of Computer Science!

Data Structures are most fundamental and building blocks of computer science. Understanding Data Structures is an essential thing to design and build efficient software. At the same way, we can say, that knowing Algorithm is also compulsory to understand these fundamental blocks of Computer Science.

Therefore, I have chosen these two topics and try to implement Discrete Mathematical concepts into them so that our understanding might take a proper shape.

In this chapter, our first and foremost concern is to know what is Discrete Mathematics. However, before starting the book, there is an important question.

Is Discrete Mathematics enough to study Computer Science?

Our answer is – NO.

There are some other topics that we must know – now, simultaneously, or later, to get a proper understanding of Computer Science. If we love our subject, then we will try to understand how Calculus, Linear Algebra and as a whole, Mathematics is related to Computer Science.

We are not pushing ourselves to become a mathematician. That we are not going to suggest.

We want to study computer science.

Nevertheless, we also want to know all the necessary concepts that are related to computer science.

Before moving on to our real discourse, let us know what the word – Mathematics – means to us. Mathematics includes the topics, such as quantity (number theory), structure (algebra), space (geometry), and change (mathematical analysis).

As we see, as a programmer, we also deal with such topics. We deal with numbers, all types of numbers, so an introduction to number theory should be included in our study. We need to study structures (remember data structures); therefore, a knowledge of algebra is important where calculus and linear algebraic equations might play a vital role.

Therefore we need to know how to find area and volume of two moving objects, how to find the slope of a line, or need to know about linear algebraic concepts like matrices and vectors.

On the other hand, Computer Programming involves tasks like data analysis, generating algorithms, making algorithms more accurate with less resource consumption, and finally we need to implement algorithms in a chosen programming language. These processes, as a whole, are known as coding. Knowledge of specialized algorithms and formal logic may be enough to be a good programmer.

However, if we want to change the word – good – to another word – great – then we must equip ourselves with some mathematical knowledge that are not directly related to Discrete Mathematics.

Although they are not directly related, they are indirectly related. The study of calculus starts with the relationship between velocity and distance; and, they are ordered pair of sets, which is very much a discrete mathematical conceptions.

Calculus is a mathematical study of continuous change; however, computer scientific study is severely discrete, it deals with distinct objects.

Besides, linear algebraic conceptions are fundamental in many areas where line, plane and spaces are involved. We need to know them as well. If not now, then we should know them later, of course.

We should always remember that different branches of mathematical conceptions are key components in computation. We should not forget that truth as long as we think ourselves as a student of computer science.

A short Introduction to Discrete Mathematics

What is Discrete Mathematics? We need to know that first. Second, we need to know what is the relationship of Discrete Mathematics to Computer Science. Finally, we want to know how we can implement the Discrete Mathematical concepts into various fields of Computer Science.

Here, we are primarily concerned with Algorithm and Data Structure. These topics sit at the core of any Computer Science curriculum. Without understanding these two components properly, we can not claim that we are students of Computer Science!

Therefore, I have chosen these two topics and try to implement Discrete Mathematical concepts into them so that our understanding might take a proper shape. In this chapter, our first and foremost concern is to know what is Discrete Mathematics.

What is Discrete Mathematics

Discrete Mathematics is a branch of Mathematics and, to be very particular, it is the study of Mathematical structures, and objects that are discrete.

In that sense, 'people', 'animal', 'chair' and everything we see around us, fall under this mathematical study. Why? Because, they are discrete, distinct. They are not continuous. Think about real numbers that consist of rational and irrational numbers, or a number line, which is continuous; so that is not discrete mathematics. Rather, natural numbers (N), like 0, 1, 2, etc, which are discrete fall under this category.

Discrete Mathematical conceptions handle with distinct and separated values. The opposite of discrete mathematics is continuous mathematics, such as calculus or Euclidean Geometry. However, Euclidean Algorithm that helps us find the greatest common divisor of two positive natural numbers (GCD), is very much discrete mathematics. We will see to an example in a minute.

Have you found any contradiction in the above statement?

I have found one; and before proceeding further, I think, we should make it clear first. We have just said that real numbers, or a number line where between 1 and 2, there are infinite numbers, cannot be discrete. However, when we say, positive natural numbers like 1, 2, 3, which are distinct and separated, belong to discrete mathematics. 1, 2 or 51, every positive natural numbers are also real numbers. Right? They belong to the number line. Right? Then where we stand? We are contradicting ourselves.

Therefore, we can conclude that there is no exact definition of Discrete Mathematics. At best, we can say, that the opposite of continuous mathematics is discrete mathematics.

In Mathematics, there are many things that are not continuous. You may think of Set theory, x co-ordinate and y co-ordinate, that refer to different positions on the quadrants, without joining them. You may think of GCD and LCM. Greatest common divisor and least common multiple. They are always discrete.

Consider the statement in logic. True or False. They are discrete. Consider 0 and 1. The binary code, the core conceptions of Computer Science, they are very much discrete.

Consider objects in any object-oriented-programming language. Every new object is discrete.

That is why, Discrete Mathematical conceptions are closely related to every field of Computer Science. In this book, we will only consider Algorithm and Data Structure part.

In the following part we will compute the number of molecules in a hydrocarbon. First, we will compute this program using Java, after that, we will use C++ to compute the same program.

Notice the algorithm. That is same for two languages, although syntactically there are differences. So the steps of algorithm varies. Let us see the algorithm first.

The algorithm will be like this:

```
1 Step 1: take input and store the mass of hydrocarbon, the number of carbon, and the \
2 number of hydrogen atoms
3 Step 2: find and store the formula weight of one mole
4 Step 3: find the number of molecules in given mass of hydrocarbon using the above f\
5 ormula
6 Step 4: output the stored input values and the result
```

Considering that the algorithm is the same, suppose for both languages, its value is 1. However, the syntactical difference makes the second value change.

If we consider that algorithm is the X axis, and the syntactical difference as Y axis, then the hypothetical value might be (1, 2) and (1, 5). Moreover, they are discrete, distinct and separated.

If we want to connect them drawing a line, that no longer remains discrete. That becomes a continuous mathematical conceptions.

With the help of these two programs, what I would like to point out is a simple mathematical statement. The difference between discrete mathematics and continuous mathematics is paper-thin. It also proves our definition of discrete mathematics. Anything, that is not continuous mathematics, is discrete mathematics.

Let us see the Java program first.

```
1 //code 1.1
2 //Java
3     package fun.sanjibsinha.languagebasics;
4     /*
5     we will compute number of molecules in a hydrocarbon
6     a mole of any substance contains 6.02 * 10^23 molecules
7     this is called Avogadro's number
8     relationship of a mass of a substance and the number of molecules is:
9
10    molecules = mass * 1mole/FormulaWeight * (6.02 * 10^23 molecules)/i mole
```

```
11      */
12      import java.util.Scanner;
13
14      public class HydroCarbonMolecule {
15
16          static float massOfHydrocarbon = 0.00f;
17          static int numberOfCarbonAtoms = 0;
18          static int numberOfHydrogenAtoms = 0;
19
20          public static void main(String[] args) {
21
22              System.out.println("Enter mass of HydroCarbon in a floating point: ");
23              Scanner mh = new Scanner(System.in);
24              massOfHydrocarbon = mh.nextFloat();
25              System.out.println("Enter the number of carbon atoms: ");
26              Scanner nc = new Scanner(System.in);
27              numberOfCarbonAtoms = nc.nextInt();
28              System.out.println("Enter the number of hydrogen atoms: ");
29              Scanner nh = new Scanner(System.in);
30              numberOfHydrogenAtoms = nh.nextInt();
31              final int CarbonAMU = 12;
32              final int HydrogenAMU = 1;
33              long formulaWeightOfOneMole = 111111111111L;
34              formulaWeightOfOneMole = (numberOfCarbonAtoms * CarbonAMU)
35                      + (numberOfHydrogenAtoms * HydrogenAMU);
36              double AvogadroNumber = 6.02 * Math.pow(10, 23);
37              double molecules = (massOfHydrocarbon/formulaWeightOfOneMole) * Avogadro\
38 Number;
39              System.out.println(massOfHydrocarbon + " grams of hydrocarbon with " + n\
40 umberOfCarbonAtoms
41                      + " carbon atoms and " + numberOfHydrogenAtoms + " hydrogen atoms contai\
42 n "
43                      + molecules + " molecules.");
44
45          }
46      }
```

Here goes the output:

```
1 //output of code 1.1
2 Enter mass of HydroCarbon in a floating point:
3 16.00
4 Enter the number of carbon atoms:
```

```
5 1
6 Enter the number of hydrogen atoms:
7 4
8 16.0 grams of hydrocarbon with
9 1 carbon atoms and 4 hydrogen atoms contain 6.019999999999999E23
molecules.
```

I would like to write the Avogadro's number using the scientific notation this way:

```
1 double AvogadroNumber = 6.02e23;
```

The output changes from 6.019999999999999E23 to 6.02E23, although it should not have mattered how you have written the Avogadro's number. In the first case,

I have used the Java pow() method. In the second case, I have used the scientific notation. However, the outputs are discrete.

I would like to show you the same program in C++, where I have used the 'cmath' library's pow() function, the same way I have used pow() method in my Java code.

Let us see the program first.

```
 1 //code 1.2
 2 //C++
 3 #include <iostream>
 4 #include <string>
 5 #include <cmath>
 6
 7 using namespace std;
 8
 9 int main() {
10 /* code */
11 std::cout << "Enter mass of hydrocarbon in decimal point value, like 2.33" << '\n';
12 float massOfHydrocarbon;
13 std::cin >> massOfHydrocarbon;
14 std::cout << "Enter number of carbon atoms in positive integer, like 2" << '\n';
15 int numberOfCarbonAtoms;
16 std::cin >> numberOfCarbonAtoms;
17 std::cout << "Enter the number of hydrogen atoms in positive integer, like 3" << '\n\
18 ';
19 int numberOfHydrogenAtoms;
20 std::cin >> numberOfHydrogenAtoms;
21 const int carbonAMU = 12;
22 const int hydrogenAMU = 1;
23 long formulaWeightOfOneMole = (numberOfCarbonAtoms * carbonAMU) + (numberOfHydrogenA\
24 toms * hydrogenAMU);
25 const double AvogadroNumber = 6.02 * pow(10, 23);
```

```
26 double moleculesInHydrocarbon = (massOfHydrocarbon /
formulaWeightOfOneMole) * Avoga\
27 droNumber;
28 std::cout << massOfHydrocarbon << " grams of hydrocarbon with " <<
numberOfCarbonAto\
29 ms <<
30 " \ncarbon atoms and " << numberOfHydrogenAtoms << " hydrogen atoms
contain " << mol\
31 eculesInHydrocarbon;
32 return 0;
33 }
```

The output is: 6.02e+23. Now, if we change the Avogadro's number to this:

```
1 const double AvogadroNumber = 6.02e23;
```

The output remains the same. In Java, although the value changes.

Now, we can conclude that every programming language is discrete, not only syntactically, but also in their output.

What is the relationship between Discrete Mathematics and Computer Science

We can now understand how discrete mathematics and computer science are related. Through our programming logic and algorithm, we can reproduce continuous mathematics in any programming language, like Java.

Let us see another example in Java.

First the code, then we will discuss the concept.

```
 1 //code 1.3
 2 //Java
 3 package fun.sanjibsinha;
 4
 5 import java.util.Scanner;
 6
 7 /*
 8 Finding the y-coordinate of a point on a line
 9 where x-coordinate is given
10 */
11 public class FindingYCoordinate {
12
13     static int lineSlope = 0;
14     static int yIntercept = 0;
15     static int xCoordinate = 0;
16     static int yCoordinate = 0;
17
18     public static void main(String[] args) {
19
20         System.out.println("Enter the value of the line-slope in
```

```
            positive integer: "\
21 );
22          Scanner slopeOfLine = new Scanner(System.in);
23          lineSlope = slopeOfLine.nextInt();
24          System.out.println("Enter the intercept of y-axis: ");
25          Scanner interceptOfY = new Scanner(System.in);
26          yIntercept = interceptOfY.nextInt();
27          System.out.println("Enter the value of x-coordinate: ");
28          Scanner coordinateOfX = new Scanner(System.in);
29          xCoordinate = coordinateOfX.nextInt();
30          yCoordinate = lineSlope * xCoordinate + yIntercept;
31          //line of slope = rise vertically/run horizontally
32          //yCoordinate = (lineSlope * xCoordinate) + yIntercept;
33          System.out.println("The y-coordinate is: " + yCoordinate +
". When the slope\
34  of line is: "
35                  + lineSlope + ". Intercept of y-axis is: " +
yIntercept + ". X coord\
36 inate is: " + xCoordinate);
37
38      }
39
40 }
```

In the above code, with the help of line-slope and y-intercept, we find the y-coordinate. The value of x-coordinate is given.

A line-slope is the ratio of vertical rise and horizontal run of the line. The y-intercept is a given point on the y axis. If we run the program and provide the values, the output comes out as:

```
1 //output of code 1.3
2 Enter the value of the line-slope in positive integer:
3 6
4 Enter the intercept of y-axis:
5 2
6 Enter the value of x-coordinate:
7 2
8 The y-coordinate is: 14. When the slope of line is: 6. Intercept of
y-axis is: 2. X \
9 coordinate is: 2
```

In the above output it is evident that every number is discrete and computing them is easier with the help of a formula. Here the value of y-coordinate is 14, when x-coordinate is 2.

What makes discrete mathematics different from the continuous mathematical proceedings is its capacity of getting counted, discrete structures are always either countable, or distinct. In the above code, we have seen that each vertical rise and horizontal run are discrete, distinct from others. Each time you run the code, providing distinct values will give you values that are separable from the previous ones.

Introducing necessary conceptions

In the following chapters, we will see plenty of examples where discrete mathematical computations will be used.

To name a few, we will discuss set theory and its implementations in data structures. We will see how permutation and combination work together in algorithm. The role of logical statement or truth table will play a great role in our discussion.

We will see how finite collections of discrete objects are implemented in the data structures. They can not only be counted, but also arranged and placed into sets. Studying Euclidean algorithm, along with finding the GCD and LCM, will be a major part in our discussion.

There are many interesting topics to come. So stay tuned and keep reading on.

I write regularly on Algorithm and Data Structure in

2. Introduction to Programming Language and Boolean Algebra

Programming language is a formal language that contains set of instructions, which produce various kind of output. It can either be imperative or declarative.

Imperative means it has sequence of operations to perform. On the other hand, declarative stands for the specification of desired results, it does not comprise of how to achieve it.

There are thousands of programming languages, many are being created everyday, probably! However, most of them are imperative. They comprise of certain commands or instructions for computers to perform certain tasks, producing various outputs. Let us try to understand this part very clearly.

In natural language, such as in English, we have encountered imperative mood where a verb is used to form a command or request. Consider this example: "do it", or "Leave" and many more. Mostly it is directed towards a second person, but in some certain contexts, it can involve first ot third persons, such as, "Let's do it".

The same way, an imperative programming also comprises of certain commands, set of instructions that focus on how a program should operate. Consider a simple procedural imperative programming example in C programming language.

```
1 //code 2.1
2 //C
3 #include <stdio.h>
4 #include <stdlib.h>
```

```
 5
 6 void doSomething(void){
 7     printf("Do something.");
 8 }
 9
10 int main(int argc, char** argv) {
11
12     doSomething();
13
14     return (EXIT_SUCCESS);
15 }
```

In the above code, we have seen the function (method) declaration that gives us a standard output when the function is invoked. In the main() function area, the compiled code will run the code as we invoke the function doSomething(). It gives us the following output.

Quite simple and straightforward.

```
1 //output of code 2.1
2 Do something.
3 RUN FINISHED; exit value 0; real time: 0ms; user: 0ms; system: 0ms
```

The above code snippet gives us an idea of how procedural programming works. It is a part of imperative programming paradigm. It is called procedural, because, the program is built on one or more procedures or functions. It is sometimes also called subroutines.

Now question is, where does discrete mathematical conceptions stand here? What is the relationship between a procedural programming and discrete mathematics?

The simple answer is, a program should build either successfully or failed miserably. It cannot go on continuously. So a program must be either true or false, 1 or 0, to be more precise.

It should be discrete. We need to compile the code successfully, that is discrete. We give the instructions, that should be discrete. And, finally, we need the output, that should also be discrete. Now, imperative programming does not end with only procedural programming. There is object-oriented-programming paradigms. A C++ program could be a good example.

Let us see the code first.

```
1 //code 2.2
2 //C++
3 #include <iostream>
4 #include <string>
5 #include <cmath>
6 #include <cstdlib>
7 #include <sstream>
8 #include <numeric>
```

```cpp
 9 #include <string>
10 #include <vector>
11 #include <cstddef>
12 #include <limits>
13
14 using namespace std;
15
16 class DoSomething {
17
18 public:
19     string giveInstruction = "Do something";
20
21     void givingInstruction(){
22         cout << giveInstruction << "\n";
23     }
24
25 };
26
27 int main(int argc, char** argv) {
28
29     DoSomething firstObject;
30
31     firstObject.givingInstruction ();
32
33     return 0;
34 }
```

The above guy does the same thing, giving us the same type of output, only in a different manner. This C++ guy does the same thing discretely. In a distinct way. We cannot let it run continuously.

I hope, now it is clear to you why we need to understand discrete mathematical conceptions; it is needed to understand our code in a better way. Discrete mathematics is a part of mathematical conceptions that are not continuous. We cannot let our code run continuously. So we need to understand discrete mathematical conceptions.

I am not going to elaborate this section anymore. There are several other types of imperative programming. There are several other types of declarative programming languages. This is not the place to discuss them.

It is only imperative to know that our code cannot run continuously. Either it should build successfully or fail miserably; whatever the outcome, it should be discrete.

Logic, Mathematics, and Programming Language

Does logic come before mathematics? As long as humans are concerned, the answer is "Yes". A child without knowing any mathematical conceptions, knows that what is hot and what is cold. She develops her logical experience by observation and actions. Is it hot or cold? The answer is yes or no. Accordingly, her actions take place.

Latter in life, she applies her sense of logic in understanding mathematical conceptions. Logic comes before mathematics and after that comes algorithm or steps; finally we write code based on that algorithm.

In programming language, logic plays the greatest role; because it leads to the acceptance of one proposition, the conclusion, on the basis of other propositions or premises. Moreover, the conclusion is discrete. That is why, in programming language, the truth table plays an important role. In programming language, if, if-else, or else conditionals lead us to one inference.

In ordinary life we also apply the same logic by observation.

Let us see a very simple program in Java, to see how this logical inference matters.

```
1 //code 2.3
2 //Java
3 package fun.sanjibsinha;
4
5 import java.util.Scanner;
6
7 public class IfAndElse {
8
9     static int age = 0;
10
11    public static void main(String[] args) {
12        System.out.println("Enter your age: ");
13        Scanner yourAge = new Scanner(System.in);
14        age = yourAge.nextInt();
15
16        if (age >= 1 && age <= 18){
17            System.out.println("Happy birthday!");
18        } else if(age == 21 || age == 50){
19            System.out.println("Important birthday!");
20        } else if(age >= 60){
21            System.out.println("Don't retire. Keep working!");
22        } else {
23            System.out.println("Keep living and help others!");
24        }
25    }
26 }
```

We have entered three different number and got the following output:

```
1 //output of code 2.3
2 //output 1
3
4 Enter your age:
5 45
```

```
 6 Keep living and help others!
 7
 8 //output 2
 9 Enter your age:
10 18
11 Happy birthday!
12
13 //output 3
14 Enter your age:
15 61
16 Don't retire. Keep working!
```

The above Java code, is based on a few principles that we can call 'truth table', based on which we build our algorithm. These logical steps are universal. It is not only true for the Java guy, but also applicable to every single programming paradigm. What is that?

There are three logical operators; they are '&&' symbol that stands for 'and'; '||' symbol that stands for 'or'; finally, we have a '!' symbol that just converts true into false and vice versa.

In case of '&&' symbol, if both statements are true, it comes out as TRUE. For the '||' symbol, if any one of the statement is true, it comes out as TRUE. And you have already known about the nature of '!' symbol.

These logical operations are dependent on conditional operators; they also have different symbols, such as '==', '!=', '<', '>', '>=', and '<='; when two conditions are '==', (equal), we perform some operations and so on.

We can conclude that, logic, mathematics, algorithm and code are inter-dependent; and, they should be discrete, as well.

Introduction to Boolean Algebra

George Boole, the founder of Boolean algebra, is considered to be one of the founder of Computer Science also. In 1847, when he wrote his famous book "The Mathematical Analysis of Logic", he had not thought about PC, mobile or tabs. I don't want to say that. But in his second book, "An Investigation of the Laws of Thought" that he wrote in 1854, he clearly set the path for future computations. His great idea started a new branch of algebra, Boolean algebra, where the values of the variables are the truth values: true or false. They are usually denoted by 1 and 0 respectively. In elementary algebra the values of variables are numbers. There are several operations we can do on that like addition or multiplication.

In Boolean algebra, there are only three operations we can do: conjunction (and), disjunction (or) and negation (not). Now we are able to the logical operations as we use to do the numerical operations in elementary algebra.

Moreover, it helps programmers to create a formal description of logical operations with the help of conditionals like "if, else if and else", and in some cases using "switch-cases".

Now it adds great impetus to every modern programming language.

Not only that, with the help of this 'truth table', we can build a very complex decision trees. Let us start with a simple example.

Let us see the code first.

```
1 //code 2.4
2 //Java
3 package fun.sanjibsinha;
4
5 public class IfAndElseSimple {
6     static boolean isTrue = true;
7     static boolean isFalse;
8     public static void main(String[] args) {
9
10         if(isTrue){
11             System.out.println("It's true.");
12             isTrue = false;
13             if(isTrue && isTrue){
14                 System.out.println("It's again true.");
15             } else if(isTrue || isFalse){
16                 System.out.println("It's very much true.");
17             } else {
18                 System.out.println("True is false, so it's false now.");
19             }
20         } else {
21             System.out.println("It's false.");
22         }
23
24     }
25 }
```

Watch the output:

```
1 //output of code 2.4
2 It's true.
3 True is false, so it's false now.
```

Globally we have made the boolean variable 'isTrue' true. Therefore, the first 'if' block allows us to enter into the block. Next, we have made the 'isTrue' false.

Now according to the boolean algebra and truth table, 'false and false' is 'false'; and, 'false or false' is also 'false.' For that reason, we get the above output.

Now, we would like to change this code a little bit.

```
1  //code 2.5
2  //Java
3  package fun.sanjibsinha;
4
5  public class IfAndElseSimple {
6      static boolean isTrue = true;
7      static boolean isFalse;
8
9      public static void main(String[] args) {
10
11         if(isTrue){
12             System.out.println("It's true.");
13             if(isTrue && isTrue){
14                 System.out.println("It's again true.");
15             } else if(isTrue || isFalse){
16                 System.out.println("It's very much true.");
17             } else {
18                 System.out.println("True is false, so it's false now.");
19             }
20         } else {
21             System.out.println("It's false.");
22         }
23
24     }
25 }
```

Watch the output now:

```
1  //output of code 2.5
2  It's true.
3  It's again true.
```

Now, in the second conditional, 'true and true' is 'true'. So, we get the above output.

Let us see more examples and watch the output one after another to comprehend how this truth table works.

```
1  //code 2.6
2  //Java
3  package fun.sanjibsinha;
4
5  public class IfAndElseSimple {
6      static boolean isTrue = true;
7      static boolean isFalse;
8
9      public static void main(String[] args) {
10
11         if(isTrue){
12             System.out.println("It's true.");
13             if(((isTrue && isTrue) || isFalse) && isFalse){
```

```
14                    System.out.println("It's not true any more true.");
15                } else if(((isTrue && isTrue) || isFalse) || isFalse){
16                    System.out.println("It's very much true because we
check between tru\
17 e or false.");
18                } else {
19                    System.out.println("True is false, so it's false
now.");
20                }
21            } else {
22                System.out.println("It's false.");
23            }
24
25      }
26 }
```

It's quite obvious that very first conditional is true, so we enter the block. However, the next conditional comes out as false, because in the truth table 'true and false' will come out as false. Therefore, the code will check the next conditional, which is true.

So the output will be as the following:

```
1 //output of code 2.6
2 It's true.
3 It's very much true because because we check between true or false.
```

As the above code snippets, we can apply the same truth table on other data types using the logical operators. Here is an example:

```
1 //code 2.7
2 //Java
3 package fun.sanjibsinha;
4
5 import java.util.Scanner;
6
7 public class IfAndElse {
8
9     static int age = 0;
10
11    public static void main(String[] args) {
12        System.out.println("Enter your age: ");
13        Scanner yourAge = new Scanner(System.in);
14        age = yourAge.nextInt();
15
16        if (age >= 1 && age <= 18){
17            System.out.println("Happy birthday!");
18        } else if(age == 21 || age == 50){
19            System.out.println("Important birthday!");
20        } else if(age >= 60){
21            System.out.println("Don't retire. Keep working!");
```

```
22          } else {
23              System.out.println("Keep living and help others!");
24          }
25      }
26 }
```

Let us give different types of 'age' to check how our code works.

```
1 //output of code 2.7
2 //output 1
3
4 Enter your age:
5 45
6 Keep living and help others!
7
8 //output 2
9 Enter your age:
10 18
11 Happy birthday!
12
13 //output 3
14 Enter your age:
15 61
16 Don't retire. Keep working!
```

Let us make this example a little bit complex, so we can have an idea about how complicated this combinations might become.

```
1  //code 2.8
2  //Java
3  package fun.sanjibsinha;
4
5  import java.util.Scanner;
6
7  public class MoreIfAndElse {
8
9      static boolean isCold = false;
10     static boolean isRaining = false;
11     static boolean isTakingCar = false;
12
13     public static void main(String[] args) {
14
15         System.out.println("When asked, enter only true or false.");
16         System.out.println("Is it cold outside?");
17         Scanner cold = new Scanner(System.in);
18         isCold = cold.nextBoolean();
19         System.out.println("Is it raining?");
20         Scanner raining = new Scanner(System.in);
21         isRaining = raining.nextBoolean();
22         System.out.println("Are you taking car?");
23         Scanner takingCar = new Scanner(System.in);
```

```
24              isTakingCar = takingCar.nextBoolean();
25
26          if((isCold == true && isRaining == true) || isTakingCar == false){
27              System.out.println("I wear Windcheater jacket with hood.");
28          } else if((isCold == true && isRaining == false) || isTakingCar == true){
29              System.out.println("I wear Windcheater jacket without hood.");
30          } else {
31              System.out.println("I won't wear Windcheater of any kind!");
32          }
33
34      }
35 }
```

Let us give some different types of input as 'true' or 'false' and see how our code responds.

```
 1 //output of code 2.8
 2
 3 //output 1
 4
 5 When asked, enter only true or false.
 6 Is it cold outside?
 7 true
 8 Is it raining?
 9 true
10 Are you taking car?
11 false
12 I wear Windcheater jacket with hood.
13
14 //output 2
15
16 When asked, enter only true or false.
17 Is it cold outside?
18 true
19 Is it raining?
20 true
21 Are you taking car?
22 true
23 I wear Windcheater jacket with hood.
24
25 //output 3
26
27 When asked, enter only true or false.
28 Is it cold outside?
29 true
```

```
30 Is it raining?
31 false
32 Are you taking car?
33 true
34 I wear Windcheater jacket without hood.
```

Like to make the combinations more complex? Well, we can try the following code snippets.

```
1 //code 2.9
2 //Java
3 package fun.sanjibsinha;
4
5 import java.util.Scanner;
6
7 public class AnotherIfAndElse {
8
9      static int age = 0;
10     static boolean isAllowed = false;
11
12     public static void main(String[] args) {
13
14         System.out.println("When asked, enter only true or false.");
15         System.out.println("Enter your age");
16         Scanner yourAge = new Scanner(System.in);
17         age = yourAge.nextInt();
18         System.out.println("Is allowed? Answer either true or false!");
19         Scanner allowed = new Scanner(System.in);
20         isAllowed = allowed.nextBoolean();
21
22         if(age <= 10 || age >= 70){
23             if(isAllowed == true){
24                 System.out.println("You can go free!");
25             } else {
26                 System.out.println("You can go free!");
27             }
28         } else {
29             System.out.println("Your entrance fee is 10 Euro.");
30         }
31     }
32 }
```

As usual, we will give different types of age to test how this combination works by maintaining the truth table rules.

```
1 //output of code 2.9
2 // output 1
3
4 When asked, enter only true or false.
```

```
 5 Enter your age
 6 80
 7 Is allowed? Answer either true or false!
 8 true
 9 You can go free!
10
11 // output 2
12
13 When asked, enter only true or false.
14 Enter your age
15 56
16 Is allowed? Answer either true or false!
17 true
18 Your entrance fee is 10 Euro.
19
20 // output 3
21
22 When asked, enter only true or false.
23 Enter your age
24 2
25 Is allowed? Answer either true or false!
26 false
27 You can go free!
28
29 // output 4
30
31 When asked, enter only true or false.
32 Enter your age
33 85
34 Is allowed? Answer either true or false!
35 false
36 You can go free!
```

The above code establishes one thing, by implementing the proper usage of the truth table, we can stop the middle conditional to override the basic rule that has been defined earlier. The above code snippets check the entry to some places. In between there is a boolean value called 'isAllowed'; you may think this guy as the gatekeeper who can override the entry with a special power. In fact that happens in the real life.

However, through the proper usage of the truth table we have limited his power to override the main conditional that says, for the age range of less than equal to 10 and greater than equal to 70, the entrance fee is zero.

Now if the gatekeeper wants to take price from that age range, he cannot do that.

As we progress, we will see more examples of boolean algebra in the future course of our book. So stay tuned and keep reading.

I write regularly on Algorithm and Data Structure in

3. De Morgan's Laws on Boolean Algebra, Logical Expression, and Algorithm

In this chapter we will learn about basic algorithm, which has its roots in De Morgan's laws on Boolean algebra, and logical expression. After learning about basic algorithmic steps and sequences, we will discuss data structures in the next chapter.

To build complex algorithm, we need to understand the core concepts about data structures (chapter 4); we will come back to more advanced concepts of algorithm again in chapter five.

Let us start this chapter with Boolean algebra.

Augustus De Morgan was a contemporary mathematician of George Boole. Although he did not create the laws using his name, yet it is credited to him, since he was the creator.

De Morgan's laws are based on Boolean algebra, and in every programming language, it is widely applied and equally true.

What the rule states, we can write this way, where 'a' and 'b' are two boolean values (true or false):

```
1 1. not (a and b) is the same as (not a) or (not b)
2 2. not (a or b) is the same as (not a) and (not b)
```

Let us apply this laws in PHP. We have stored the first law in 'DeMorganOne.php' file. Let us see the code first:

```
 1 // code 3.1
 2 // DeMorganOne.php
 3 <?php
 4
 5 /*
 6  * not (a and b) is the same as (not a) or (not b)
 7  */
 8
 9 class DeMorganOne {
10
11     public $numOne;
12     public $numTwo;
13
14     public function notAandB($paramOne, $paramTwo) {
15
16         $this->numOne = $paramOne;
17         $this->numTwo = $paramTwo;
18         $additionOfTwoNumbers = $paramOne + $paramTwo;
19
```

```
20          //not(paramOne and paramTwo)
21          if(!($paramOne >= 10 && $paramTwo <= 15)){
22              echo "Addition of two numbers : $additionOfTwoNumbers";
23          } else {
24              echo "The number is neither less than equal to 10 nor greater than equal\
25  to 15";
26          }
27      }
28
29      public function notAORnotB($paramOne, $paramTwo) {
30
31          $this->numOne = $paramOne;
32          $this->numTwo = $paramTwo;
33          $additionOfTwoNumbers = $paramOne + $paramTwo;
34
35          //(not paramOne) or (not paramTwo)
36          if(!($paramOne >= 10) || !($paramTwo <= 15)){
37              echo "Addition of two numbers : $additionOfTwoNumbers";
38          } else {
39              echo "The number is neither less than equal to 10 nor greater than equal\
40  to 15";
41          }
42      }
43 }
44
45 $firstCase = new DeMorganOne();
46 $secondCase = new DeMorganOne();
47
48 $firstCase->notAandB(11, 14);
49 echo '<br>';
50 $firstCase->notAandB(1, 140);
51 echo '<br>';
52 $secondCase->notAORnotB(11, 14);
53 echo '<br>';
54 $secondCase->notAORnotB(1, 140);
```

We have tested the first law by passing the same value through two class variables and methods; we have obtained the same result.

```
1 // output of code 3.1
2 The number is neither less than equal to 10 nor greater than equal to 15
3 Addition of two numbers : 141
4 The number is neither less than equal to 10 nor greater than equal to 15
5 Addition of two numbers : 141
```

Now, you can play around by passing different types of value to see how this law works. Whatever the values you pass, they must be same for two member methods and you will get the same result.

To test the second law, we have created another PHP file 'DeMorganTwo.php', where we have done the same thing, except that the logical expressions have been changed.

```php
1  // code 3.2
2
3  // DeMorganTwo.php
4
5  <?php
6
7  /*
8   * not (a or b) is the same as (not a) and (not b)
9   */
10
11 class DeMorganOne {
12
13     public $numOne;
14     public $numTwo;
15
16     public function notAandB($paramOne, $paramTwo) {
17
18         $this->numOne = $paramOne;
19         $this->numTwo = $paramTwo;
20         $additionOfTwoNumbers = $paramOne + $paramTwo;
21
22         //not(paramOne and paramTwo)
23         if(!($paramOne >= 10 || $paramTwo <= 15)){
24             echo "Addition of two numbers : $additionOfTwoNumbers";
25         } else {
26             echo "The number is neither less than equal to 10 nor greater than equal\
27  to 15";
28         }
29     }
30
31     public function notAORnotB($paramOne, $paramTwo) {
32
33         $this->numOne = $paramOne;
34         $this->numTwo = $paramTwo;
35         $additionOfTwoNumbers = $paramOne + $paramTwo;
36
37         //(not paramOne) or (not paramTwo)
38         if(!($paramOne >= 10) && !($paramTwo <= 15)){
39             echo "Addition of two numbers : $additionOfTwoNumbers";
40         } else {
41             echo "The number is neither less than equal to 10 nor
```

```
   greater than equal\
42   to 15";
43         }
44     }
45 }
46
47 $firstCase = new DeMorganOne();
48 $secondCase = new DeMorganOne();
49
50 $firstCase->notAandB(11, 14);
51 echo '<br>';
52 $firstCase->notAandB(1, 140);
53 echo '<br>';
54 $secondCase->notAORnotB(11, 14);
55 echo '<br>';
56 $secondCase->notAORnotB(1, 140);
```

We have tested the second law by passing the same value through the class variables and methods. Watch the output, it gives us the same value for two different methods.

```
1 // output of code 3.2
2
3 The number is neither less than equal to 10 nor greater than equal to 15
4 Addition of two numbers : 141
5 The number is neither less than equal to 10 nor greater than equal to 15
6 Addition of two numbers : 141
```

In Java, or C++, you can apply the same logic to test that the laws work. Consider the following Java file where we can comment out the entire process, because we need to test the same code separately.

```
 1 // code 3.3
 2 //Java
 3
 4 package fun.sanjibsinha;
 5
 6 /*
 7 not (a and b) is the same as (not a) or (not b)
 8 not (a or b) is the same as (not a) and (not b)
 9 */
10
11 import java.util.Scanner;
12
13 public class DeMorganslaw {
14     static int numOne = 0;
15     static int numTwo = 0;
16     static int additionOfTwoNumbers = 0;
```

```
17      public static void main(String[] args) {
18          System.out.println("Enter a positive number: ");
19          Scanner one = new Scanner(System.in);
20          numOne = one.nextInt();
21          System.out.println("Enter another positive number: ");
22          Scanner two = new Scanner(System.in);
23          numTwo = two.nextInt();
24 /*
25 These two are same:
26 not (a and b) is the same as (not a) or (not b)
27
28          if(!(numOne >= 10 && numTwo <= 15)){
29              additionOfTwoNumbers = numOne + numTwo;
30              System.out.println("Addition of two numbers is : " + additionOfTwoNumber\
31 s);
32          } else {
33              System.out.println("The number is neither less than equal to 10 " +
34                      "nor greater than equal to 15");
35          }
36
37 Enter a positive number:
38 11
39 Enter another positive number:
40 14
41 The number is neither less than equal to 10 nor greater than equal to 15
42
43 Enter a positive number:
44 1
45 Enter another positive number:
46 140
47 Addition of two numbers is : 141
48
49
50          if(!(numOne >= 10) || !(numTwo <= 15)){
51              additionOfTwoNumbers = numOne + numTwo;
52              System.out.println("Addition of two numbers is : " + additionOfTwoNumber\
53 s);
54          } else {
55              System.out.println("The number is neither less than equal to 10 " +
56                      "nor greater than equal to 15");
57          }
58 Enter a positive number:
59 11
60 Enter another positive number:
61 14
```

```
The number is neither less than equal to 10 nor greater than equal to 15

Enter a positive number:
1
Enter another positive number:
140
Addition of two numbers is : 141

*/

/*
These two are same:
not (a or b) is the same as (not a) and (not b)

        if(!(numOne >= 10 || numTwo <= 15)){
            additionOfTwoNumbers = numOne + numTwo;
            System.out.println("Addition of two numbers is : " + additionOfTwoNumber\
s);
        } else {
            System.out.println("The number is neither less than equal to 10 " +
                    "nor greater than equal to 15");
        }
Enter a positive number:
11
Enter another positive number:
14
The number is neither less than equal to 10 nor greater than equal to 15

Enter a positive number:
1
Enter another positive number:
140
Addition of two numbers is : 141


        if(!(numOne >= 10) && !(numTwo <= 15)){
            additionOfTwoNumbers = numOne + numTwo;
            System.out.println("Addition of two numbers is : " + additionOfTwoNumber\
s);
        } else {
            System.out.println("The number is neither less than equal to 10 " +
                    "nor greater than equal to 15");
        }
```

```
106 Enter a positive number:
107 11
108 Enter another positive number:
109 14
110 The number is neither less than equal to 10 nor greater than equal
to 15
111
112 Enter a positive number:
113 1
114 Enter another positive number:
115 140
116 Addition of two numbers is : 141
117
118
119 */
120
121     }
122 }
```

Inside the commented out sections we have kept the code and output together. In Java, you need to test each law separately. In PHP, we could have used a form inputs to build a web application where we can pass two values to see the result dynamically.

Logical Expression

We can create compound expression by combining logical operations. De Morgan's laws are based on this paradigm. Consider the following expression:

```
1 not(a or b)
```

Whether the above compound expression is 'true' or 'false', depends on different types of combinations. If 'a' and 'b' are both false, the negation of sub-expression (a or b) is true. If any one of them is 'true', then the value will be 'false', and this combination may take different shapes according to the 'truth table', which we have seen before.

A major part of Discrete Mathematical operations is based on Boolean Algebra and the associated logical expressions. Just to recapitulate, we need to remember that there are three logical operators; they are '&&' (and), '||' (or), and '!' (negation). The 'truth table' is based on them.

Logical operators manipulate the logical values. The same way, 'relational operators' also manipulate the logical values.

There are two kinds of relational operators: equality and ordering.

The two equality operators are: '==' and '!='. The '==' operation is true when the two operands have the same value. The same way, '!=' operation is true when two operands have different values.

The ordering operators test the relative size of two values. They are: '<' (less than), '>' (greater than), '>=' (greater than or equal to) and '<=' (less than or equal to).

```
1 Tips: For complicated expressions, operator precedence is important. Arithmetic oper\
2 ators have greater precedence than the relational and logical operators. However, re\
3 lational and logical operators have greater precedence than assignment operators. Ag\
4 ain, relational operators have greater precedence than logical operators.
```

Short Circuit Evaluation

Before all the operands have been considered in the evaluation of any logical expression, we sometimes know the value of the expression. Consider a situation, where two operands are using 'and' operation. If any one of the operands is known to be false, we instantly know that the result is 'false'. On the other hand, when two operands use the 'or' operation and any one of the operands is known to be true, then we know that the value of the expression is true.

A programming language requires that the left operand (the first one) be evaluated before the right (the second one) operand. If the value of the logical expression is determined from the first operand, the second operand is not evaluated.

This type of evaluation is known as short circuit evaluation and bot 'and' and 'or' operations use this kind of special evaluation. To make long story short, the second condition is not checked, depending on what type of operations take place, whether you are using 'and' or 'or'; moreover, what is the value of the first condition. We will check the both cases, using Python. We are going to use Python 3.6.

```
1 // code 3.4
2 // Python 3.6
3
4 print("hello")
5
6 numOne = 10
7 numTwo = 0
8
9 if(numTwo == 10 and (numOne / numTwo == 3)):
10     print("It won't give any error!")
11     # since the first condition is false, it won't execute the second one
12     # it goes to the else bock
13 else:
14     print("It didn't give any error because of short circuit evaluation!")
15
16 if(numTwo == 0 or (numOne / numTwo == 3)):
17     print("It won't give any error!")
```

```
18      # since the first condition is true, it won't execute the second one
19 else:
20      print("It didn't give any error because of short circuit evaluation!")
```

Read the comment section. Besides, we can get the idea from the output:

```
1 // output of code 3.4
2
3 hello
4 It didn't give any error becuase of short circuit evaluation!
5 It won't give any error!
```

Syntax, Semantics and Conditional Execution

So far we have seen many usages of 'if' statement. In a program, when the 'if' statement is reached, it first checks whether the operation is true or not. If it is true,it is executed, the code between the 'if block' is acted upon. Otherwise, if the 'action' is not acted upon inside the 'if block', program execution continues with the next statement in the program.

The description of the execution part of any 'if' statement, is called 'semantic' definition.

Syntax and Semantics

We need to take a very quick look at these two guys – syntax and semantics. They are very essential in every programming language.

Here the rule of natural language follows. Syntax describes the rules by which the words can be combined into sentences. On the other hand, semantics describes what they mean.

Consider a simple example.

```
1 Here is my friend, Emilia.
```

In the above sentence, the syntax and semantics are both flawless. There is no syntactical error and the semantic definition is meaningful.

However, what about the next sentence?

```
1 Here is my chair, Emilia.
```

It is also syntactically correct. There is no syntax error. But, is that sentence meaningful? Semantics describes what the sentence means, and it means nothing. We neither give name to our chairs, nor we introduce them like this.

In a programming language, syntactical rules are important. We should not miss a semicolon after an expression in many languages like C++, Java, PHP, etc. But we should not use semicolon in Python, in the same situation. That is syntax. We should maintain those rules.

We cannot use the keywords or reserved words as variable or function name. That part is OK. But what about the semantics?

That is equally important. If our logical expression is wrong, the program is not meaningful anymore, it takes inputs and gives us erratic output.

In the next two programs, we will see how this syntax and semantics work together in two different programming languages.

We have used Python to create a base of calculation using the 'if-else' logic.

```
// code 3.5
// python 3.6

# base of calculation with the help of if-else logic

print("Enter a number: ")
left = int(input())
print("Enter another number: ")
right = int(input())
result = 0
print("Enter any arithmetic operator like +, -, * and / for "
                        "addition, subtraction, multiplication and division respecti\
vely: ")
arithmeticOperator = str(input())

if(arithmeticOperator == '+'):
    result = left + right
elif(arithmeticOperator == '-'):
    result = left - right
elif(arithmeticOperator == '*'):
    result = left * right
elif(arithmeticOperator == '/'):
    if(right != 0):
        result = left / right
    else:
        print("Denominator is zero.")
else:
    print(arithmeticOperator + " is not recognized!")

if(arithmeticOperator == '/' and right == 0):
    print("The result is undefined.")
else:
    print(str(left) + " " + str(arithmeticOperator) + " " + str(right) + " = " + str\
(result))
```

We have only used one option to test that the program runs fine, when the denominator is zero.

```
 1 // output of code 3.5
 2
 3 Enter a number:
 4 2
 5 Enter another number:
 6 0
 7 Enter any arithmetic operator like +, -, * and / for addition, subtraction, multipli\
 8 cation and division respectively:
 9 /
10 Denominator is zero.
11 The result is undefined.
```

In the next program, we have used the same logic for base of calculation, in a slight different way, in C++, using the 'switch-case' statement. Compare the syntax between these two programs, semantically they are equal, rather meaningful.

```
 1 // code 3.6
 2 // C++
 3
 4 /*
 5 * Creating a base calculator with the help of switch-case logic
 6 */
 7
 8 #include <iostream>
 9 #include <string>
10 #include <cmath>
11 #include <cstdlib>
12 #include <sstream>
13 #include <numeric>
14 #include <string>
15 #include <vector>
16 #include <cstddef>
17 #include <limits>
18
19 int main(){
20
21     std::cout << "Enter a number: " << "\n";
22     int left = 0;
23     std::cin >> left;
24     std::cout << "Enter another number: " << "\n";
25     int right = 0;
26     std::cin >> right;
27     std::cout << "Enter any arithmetic operator like +, -, * and / for "
28              << "addition, subtraction, multiplication and division respectively:: " \
```

```
29        << "\n";
30        char arithmeticOperator;
31        std::cin >> arithmeticOperator;
32
33        int result = 0;
34
35        switch(arithmeticOperator){
36            case '+':
37                result = left + right;
38                break;
39            case '-':
40                result = left - right;
41                break;
42            case '*':
43                result = left * right;
44                break;
45            case '/':
46                if(right != 0){
47                    result = left / right;
48                } else {
49                    std::cout << "The denominator is zero. The value is undefined." << "\
50 \n";
51                    return 1;
52                }
53                break;
54            default:
55                std::cout << arithmeticOperator << " is not recognized." << "\n";
56                return 1;
57
58        }
59        std::cout << left << " " << arithmeticOperator << " " << right << " = "
60                  << result << "\n" ;
61
62        return 0;
63 }
```

We have tested the code in various ways, to find out the semantics is meaningful and the code runs in every possible situation.

```
1 // output of code 3.6
2
3 Enter a number:
4 12
5 Enter another number:
6 12
7 Enter any arithmetic operator like +, -, * and / for addition, subtraction, multipli\
```

```
 8 cation and division respectively::
 9 *
10 12 * 12 = 144
11
12 RUN FINISHED; exit value 0; real time: 5s; user: 0ms; system: 0ms
13
14
15 Enter a number:
16 12
17 Enter another number:
18 0
19 Enter any arithmetic operator like +, -, * and / for addition, subtraction, multipli\
20 cation and division respectively::
21 /
22 The denominator is zero. The value is undefined.
23
24 RUN FINISHED; exit value 1; real time: 8s; user: 0ms; system: 0ms
25
26
27 Enter a number:
28 12
29 Enter another number:
30 2
31 Enter any arithmetic operator like +, -, * and / for addition, subtraction, multipli\
32 cation and division respectively::
33 ===
34 = is not recognized.
35
36 RUN FINISHED; exit value 1; real time: 10s; user: 0ms; system: 0ms
```

From previous code snippets we have learned two important lessons. A program should be syntactically correct, as well as semantically correct. If we write a same program in two different languages, their syntax may be different but semantics is same. There are also two types of semantics – one is known as 'static semantics' and another known simply as 'semantics'.

By the term static semantics, we mean program runs well, gives us no errors, but at the end of the day it is not meaningful. It gives us outputs that were not intended while we wrote the code.

Full semantics, on the other hand, may run the loop for ever or simple crash the program, while we try to run it. In the next program, we are going to sort three numbers in ascending order. Here semantics plays a very vital role.

Why? We will see in a minute.

```
1 // code 3.7
2 //Python 3.6
```

```
 3
 4 # take three numbers and sort them in ascending order
 5
 6 print("Enter first number: ")
 7 first = int(input())
 8 print("Enter second number: ")
 9 second = int(input())
10 print("Enter third number: ")
11 third = int(input())
12 outputOne = 0
13 outputTwo = 0
14 outputThree = 0
15
16 if((first <= second) and (second <= third)):
17     outputOne = first
18     outputTwo = second
19     outputThree = third
20 elif((first <= third) and (third <= second)):
21     outputOne = first
22     outputTwo = third
23     outputThree = second
24 elif((second <= first) and (first <= third)):
25     outputOne = second
26     outputTwo = first
27     outputThree = third
28 elif((second <= third) and (third <= first)):
29     outputOne = second
30     outputTwo = third
31     outputThree = first
32 elif((third <= first) and (first <= second)):
33     outputOne = third
34     outputTwo = first
35     outputThree = second
36 else:
37     outputOne = third
38     outputTwo = second
39     outputThree = first
40
41 print("The numbers in ascending order: " + str(outputOne) + ", "
42 + str(outputTwo) + ", and " + str(outputThree))
```

Syntactically and semantically this program is clean and it reflects in the output:

```
1 // output of code 3.7
2
3 Enter first number:
4 200
5 Enter second number:
6 1
7 Enter third number:
```

```
8 500
9 The numbers in ascending order: 1, 200, and 500
```

In the above program, you can change the static semantics just by changing the positions of the variables; in that case, your code snippets is syntactically correct, and it is built successfully and runs correctly without crashing the program. However, the output will be erratic, because the static semantics is incorrect.

The role of semantics as a whole becomes increasingly important as the logical expressions get complicated. Not only that we always write code with the help of 'if-else' or 'switch-case'; we need control constructs, different types of looping, we need to write complex algorithm, etc.

While write our program that way, we need to keep one thing in mind, what we write should make sense, it should be meaningful. The concept of semantics need to be understood for that reason.

Why we need Control Constructs

We need it because computational thinking gives us enough power to write sequence of steps or recipe for doing any repetitive job. Suppose we need to find out average of a finite set of different numbers. We might imagine doing this for 5, 6 or 10. However, when the list grows and reaches 100000, it becomes impossible.

We need to find out some solution to do that. Suppose our application is programmed to take 100000 inputs from a file where the numbers are stored. Can we enter them manually and see what would be the output?

Consider a program like the following one:

```
1  // code of 3.8
2  // python 3.6
3
4  # we will compute average of six numbers by manual addition
5
6  print("Enter first number: ")
7  first = int(input())
8  print("Enter second number: ")
9  second = int(input())
10 print("Enter third number: ")
11 third = int(input())
12 print("Enter fourth number: ")
13 fourth = int(input())
14 print("Enter fifth number: ")
15 fifth = int(input())
16 print("Enter sixth number: ")
17 sixth = int(input())
18 result = 0.00
19 result = (first + second + third + fourth + fifth + sixth) / 6
20 print("The average of six numbers is : " + str(result))
```

For 6 numbers it is OK. The output gives us the proper value.

```
1 // output of code 3.8
2
3 Enter first number:
4 1
5 Enter second number:
6 2
7 Enter third number:
8 3
9 Enter fourth number:
10 4
11 Enter fifth number:
12 5
13 Enter sixth number:
14 6
15 The average of six numbers is : 3.5
```

However, this type of operations is better handled by iteration using the 'while' statement. What we have seen in the above code makes us believe that we need an action that should be repeatedly executed. We add two numbers and get a total. Next, we add the third number with the running total. It will go on as long as the number of values processed is less than the finite set of numbers that we want to add and then divide by that number to find the average.

Now we need to map that problem to our program domain with the help of 'while' statement. Because the 'while' statement deals execution of any repetitive action better than any other statement, we can write it using 'natural language' this way:

```
1 while(the number of values processed is less than the number of finite set of number\
2 s)
3
4 we take input
5
6 the running total is adding more input numbers as long as the loop continues
7
8 after each cycle the number of values processed is increased by 1
9
10 the loop ends as the  number of values processed is equal to the number of finite se\
11 t of numbers
12
13 now we have the grand total of all the numbers belonging to the finite set of numbers
14
15 to get the average we divide the total by the the number of finite set of numbers
```

Now the time has come to map this problem on our program domain, this way:

```
// code of 3.9
// python 3.6

# we will compute average of six numbers by iteration using while loop

totalNumberToCompute = 6

# since number of iteration yet to be taken
numberOfIteration = 0
# we have not got the total addition of all numbers
total = 0.00
print("Please enter " + str(totalNumberToCompute) + " numbers : ")
print()

while(numberOfIteration < totalNumberToCompute):
    value = 0.00
    value = float(input())
    total += value
    numberOfIteration += 1

averageOfSixNumbers = 0.00
averageOfSixNumbers = total / numberOfIteration
print("The average of six numbers is : " + str(averageOfSixNumbers))
```

And here goes the same output that we have seen in the previous code (3.8).

```
// output of code 3.9

Please enter 6 numbers :

1
2
3
4
5
6
The average of six numbers is : 3.5
```

In this section, we have learned many important concepts. You have probably noticed that we are handling with discrete numbers. We are also talking about a finite set of numbers. It is an integral part of discrete mathematical operations.

In discrete mathematics, we almost always quantify. We always check the 'existential' logical expression like 'if there is' or 'if there exists', etc. Moreover, we also check for 'global' values that is meant 'for all'. For all the numbers inside the finite set of numbers, we are adding them one after another; that leads us to a grand total. We also count how many numbers are there and divide the grand total by the total numbers present inside the finite set.

As we progress, we will see how these concepts come handy for the functions. How set theory is pertinent for collections or data structure, etc. There are a lot of things to cover and we are afraid that we won't be able to cover everything. However, we will try our best to learn a few things, so that in future we can take that knowledge forward.

And by the way, we have also learned what algorithm means actually! To make the long story short, it is a sequence of instructions to solve a problem.

In the next section, we will cut into the subject and turn over the topic to learn more!

Discrete Mathematical Notations and Algorithm

One of the main branches of computer science is algorithm. One of the main branches of discrete mathematics is also algorithm. That is why we use concepts and notations from discrete mathematics in computational algorithm. We can map any problem from the mathematical domain to program domain with the help of same algorithm.

When you combine mathematics and computation, algorithm means a well-defined instructions that are computer-implementable. Yet, mathematics is a separate domain, when we try to map one mathematical problem into computational domain, we need a sequence of instructions that should be unequivocal, which means the algorithm should exhibit a single clearly defined meaning. A distinct meaningful output should come out from the inputs.

Now, we have learned, what algorithm is, however, we must know why we need it.

The question is why we needed algorithm four thousand five hundred years ago in Babylon? Why we needed it three thousand five hundred years ago in Egypt, or later in Greece?

The answer is: to decide something. When we travel by one car and come to a road-divider that indicates two ways, we cannot go to two ways simultaneously. Our decision should be discrete. 1 or 0. True or false.

In contrast, if we have two or more cars, the decision might be something else.

Although ancient Babylonian, Egyptian or Greek mathematicians started using the concepts of algorithm since antiquity, the very term 'algorithm' is derived from the

name of the ninth century Persian mathematician Muḥammad ibn Mūsā al-Khwārizmī. Much before that, Greek mathematicians used sieve of Eratosthenes to find prime numbers; they also used Euclidean algorithm to find greatest common divisors (GCD).

Decision making very heavily depends on effective calculation. In the last century, many renowned mathematicians worked on that and still it goes on. High level programming languages have to come to terms with that. They have to do that, because as time passes by, the size of data has increased, and it will increase with the passage of the time.

We have enough theoretical discussion, let us plunge into code to understand how we can map our problems from mathematical domain to our computational domain. Let us start with prime numbers. In ancient time, Greek mathematicians used sieve of Eratosthenes to find prime numbers. We have plenty of other solutions at our hand now. Still, we need to know what does a prime number actually mean.

A prime number is a natural number that has exactly two discrete natural divisors. Consider this example: 2 is a prime number, because there are exactly two divisors: 1 and 2. The same way, 11 is a prime number, because there are exactly two divisors: 1 and 11.

Based on that concept, we can write our algorithm in natural language, this way:

```
1 take input of any natural number
2
3 process to find how many factors are there
4
5 count the number of factors
6
7 if the number of factors is equal to two, then the number is prime
8
9 if the number is greater than two, then the number is not prime
```

Let us tale that algorithm to our computational domain using Java programming language.

```
1 // code 3.10
2 // Java
3
4 package fun.sanjibsinha;
5
6 import java.util.*;
7 import java.math.*;
8 public class TryingToFindPrime {
9
10     private static Scanner sc;
11
12     public static void main(String[] args) {
13
14         int numOne, integerOne;
15         sc = new Scanner(System.in);
16
17         System.out.println("Please Enter any number to Find Factors: ");
```

```
18              numOne = sc.nextInt();
19
20              int controOne = 0;
21              for (integerOne = 1; integerOne <= Math.sqrt(numOne); integerOne++)
22              {
23                  if (numOne % integerOne == 0) {
24                      if (numOne / integerOne == integerOne){
25                          controOne++;
26                      } else {
27                          controOne = controOne + 2;
28                      }
29                  }
30              }
31              if(controOne == 2){
32                  System.out.println(numOne + " is prime.");
33              } else {
34                  System.out.println(numOne + " is not prime.");
35              }
36          }
37 }
```

We can test the program by giving two inputs like 49 and 47.

```
1 // output of code 3.10
2
3 Please Enter any number to Find Factors:
4 49
5 49 is not prime.
6
7 Please Enter any number to Find Factors:
8 47
9 47 is prime.
```

Here, in the above code, the algorithm is one of the simplest. We have counted the number of factors of any number and test the condition, whether that number crosses 2 or not.

Let us solve the same problem with the help of a different algorithm.

First, we see the code, then we will discuss the algorithm used in it.

```
1 //code 3.11
2 // Java
3
4 package fun.sanjibsinha;
5 import java.util.*;
6 import java.math.*;
7 public class FindingPrime {
8
9     private static Scanner sc;
```

```
10      static int input = 0;
11
12      static boolean isPrime(int num)
13      {
14          if (num <= 1)
15              return false;
16          if (num <= 3)
17              return true;
18          if (num % 2 == 0 || num % 3 == 0)
19              return false;
20          for (int i = 5; i * i <= num; i = i + 6)
21              if (num % i == 0 || num % (i + 2) == 0)
22                  return false;
23          return true;
24      }
25
26      public static void main(String[] args) {
27
28          System.out.println("Enter a number to test whether it is prime or not? ");
29          sc = new Scanner(System.in);
30          input = sc.nextInt();
31          if(isPrime(input)){
32              System.out.println(input + " is prime.");
33          } else {
34              System.out.println(input + " is not prime.");
35          }
36      }
37 }
```

In the above code, we have used a boolean method that uses one parameter; now we can pass any number to test whether that number is prime or not.

We have used the trial and division method to find out whether the output is true or false.

```
1 // output of code 3.11
2
3 Enter a number to test whether it is prime or not?
4 47
5 47 is prime.
6
7 Enter a number to test whether it is prime or not?
8 49
9 49 is not prime.
```

The sieve of Eratosthenes algorithm works on a different type of algorithm. Let us first write the algorithm in natural language. By the way, we should remember that the sieve of Eratosthenes algorithm is used to find out prime numbers in a range of numbers, such as we can test how many primes are there between 2 and 30. Usually the end number is denoted by 'n'; for the sake of simplicity, we consider an integer. The algorithm goes like the following:

```
 1  1. First we need to create a list of consecutive integers from 2 through a certain n\
 2  umber like 30, as we have seen in the above statement: (2, 3, 4, …, 30); we do this,\
 3   because 2 is the smallest prime number
 4
 5  2. Therefore, we can initialize a variable like this: startingNUmber = 2
 6
 7  3. Now, we can specify the multiples of the 'startingNUmber' by counting in incremen\
 8  ts of 'startingNUmber' from (2 *  startingNUmber) to 30, and mark them in the list, \
 9  like this:
10  (2 *  startingNUmber), (3 *  startingNUmber), (4 *  startingNUmber), and so on.
11
12  4. It is not to be mentioned that multiples of 2 will never be the primes, because t\
13  he number of factors becomes greater than 2.
14
15  5. Next, we will find the first number that is greater than the 'startingNUmber'; if\
16   there is no such number, then we stop. Otherwise, let 'startingNUmber' equal the ne\
17  w number, which is the next prime and repeat from the step 3.
18
19  6. When the algorithm ends, the numbers not marked in the list below 30, are all pri\
20  mes.
```

Let us build our program based on this algorithm. This time we have used python 3.6, to get the result. Each step is mentioned inside the comments, we have used in this case.

```
 1  // code 3.12
 2  // python 3.6
 3
 4  # Sieve Of Eratosthenes
 5
 6  def SieveOfEratosthenes(rangeOfNumbers):
 7      # let us create a boolean array "primeArray[...]" that takes a range of any numb\
 8  ers
 9      # next we initialize the array with the entries as true
10      # now if primeArray[anyNUmber] is false if it is not prime, else the number is p\
```

```
11 rime
12     # the startingNumber is 2, because 1 is not prime
13     primeArray = [True for anyNumber in range(rangeOfNumbers + 1)]
14     # we have added 1 with the rangeOfNumbers, so that the endNumber is included
15     startingNUmber = 2
16     while (startingNUmber * startingNUmber <= rangeOfNumbers):
17         # logically if primeArray[startingNumber] is not changed, then it is a prime
18         # in fact, 2 is prime
19         if (primeArray[startingNUmber] == True):
20             # all multiples of startingNumber is not prime
21             # the factors of the multiples are greater than 2
22             for anyNumber in range(startingNUmber * 2, rangeOfNumbers + 1, startingN\
23 Umber):
24                 # in such cases, those numbers are not prime
25                 primeArray[anyNumber] = False
26         startingNUmber += 1
27     primeArray[0] = False
28     primeArray[1] = False
29     # now we can print all prime numbers belonging to that range of numbers
30     for startingNUmber in range(rangeOfNumbers + 1):
31         if primeArray[startingNUmber]:
32             print(startingNUmber)
33
34 SieveOfEratosthenes(20)
```

Here is the output of the above code where we have passed 20, to get all the primes below 20.

```
1 // output of code 3.12
2
3 2
4 3
5 5
6 7
7 11
8 13
9 17
10 19
```

In this algorithm some numbers are marked more than once, like 8, for 2 and 4, both. The main idea is when the number is composite, that is, when it is a multiple of some prime numbers, it is marked.

Since, every even integers are marked out we list odd numbers only (3, 5, ..., n), and count in increments of (2 * startingNUmber), thus marking out only odd multiples of 'startingNUmber'.

After that, multiple of primes becomes composite, having more than two factors, making them composite.

The same way, thousand years ago Greek mathematicians used Euclidean algorithm to find the greatest common divisors of two numbers. Originally it was subtraction based, later the same algorithm had been written numerous way, re-modeling the original one.

We will see those versions later when we will discuss Euclidean algorithm in detail. However, we can take a quick look at the original Euclidean algorithm in a Java program, as shown in the following code snippets.

```java
1 // code 3.13
2 // Java
3
4 package fun.sanjibsinha.gcd;
5
6 import java.util.Scanner;
7
8 public class EuclidAlgorithm {
9
10     static int numOne = 0;
11     static int numTwo = 0;
12
13     //this is Euclid's original version
14     static int subtractionBased(int numOne, int numTwo){
15         while (numOne != numTwo){
16             if(numOne > numTwo)
17                 numOne = numOne - numTwo;
18             else
19                 numTwo = numTwo - numOne;
20         }
21         return numOne;
22     }
23
24     public static void main(String[] args) {
25         System.out.println("Enter a number: ");
26         Scanner num1 = new Scanner(System.in);
27         numOne = num1.nextInt();
28         System.out.println("Enter another number: ");
29         Scanner num2 = new Scanner(System.in);
30         numTwo = num2.nextInt();
31         System.out.println("You have entered " + numOne + " and " + numTwo);
32         System.out.println("The GCD is: " + subtractionBased(numOne, numTwo));
33     }
34 }
```

We can take any two numbers and see how this algorithm works.

```
1 // output of code 3.13
2
3 Enter a number:
4 1071
5 Enter another number:
6 462
7 You have entered 1071 and 462
8 The GCD is: 21
```

The Euclid's Algorithm is one of the oldest algorithms that is still relevant to, not only discrete mathematical conceptions, but also in the computational world of 1 and 0.

In the above program, we have seen that the effectiveness of the algorithm has been proved by the correct output from given inputs.

Now, many things depend on algorithm. Like hardware, algorithm is also considered to be technology for one reason. Every algorithm has its own time-complexity. When an algorithm takes higher time to produce an intended result, it is considered to be non-optimal. On the contrary, less the time-complexity, higher is the desirability.

Therefore, these two parts are very critical while we consider an algorithm. How much time it takes to perform the algorithm, is a big issue. On the other hand, adaptability of the algorithm to computers is another big issue.

As far as Euclidean algorithm is concerned, we can make this algorithm faster by making it recursive based. We can also write the same program in different ways, using Python 3.6 in this case.

```
1  // code 3.14
2  // python 3.6
3
4  # finding greatest common divisor by two different methods
5
6  def GCDOne(numOne, numTwo):
7      if(numTwo == 0):
8          return numOne
9      else:
10         temp = numOne % numTwo
11         return GCDOne(numTwo, temp)
12
13
14 def GCDTwo(num1, num2):
15     if(num2 == 0):
16         return num1
17     elif(num1 > num2):
18         return GCDTwo((num1 - num2), num2)
19     else:
20         return GCDTwo((num2 - num1), num1)
21
```

```
22
23 print(GCDOne(1071, 462))
24 print(GCDTwo(1071, 462))
```

The output is quite expected:

```
1 // output of code 3.14
2
3 21
4 21
```

We always face a trade-off between elegance and speed. Some computer scientists feel, the smallest possible program for producing the output is the most 'elegant'. The most optimal algorithm is the most desirable. Speed matters.

One criterion is definitely the time taken to perform the algorithm, another is its simplicity, which is also termed as elegance.

While we write any kind of program, we need to keep those things in mind.

We have learned that the time taken for running an algorithm is important. It is measured by the 'Time Complexity'. Our final goal is to improve the performance of any algorithm. To do that, we need to count the number of elementary operations performed by the algorithm. 'Time Complexity' does the same thing.

We will cover these concepts in great detail in chapter 5, after understanding data structures. Understanding data structures is needed for one reason: for building complex algorithm, we use various types of data structures. To understand basic algorithm, we have used array, a basic collection of a definite set of elements. Before concluding this chapter, we will take a look at three code snippets, where we have sorted a definite set of discrete integers and arrange them in ascending order.

To make this operation successful, we have used Quicksort algorithm.

The Quicksort algorithm is a popular sorting algorithm that is often used not only for sorting numbers, but also objects from any custom class. Furthermore, there are many other sorting algorithm, which are complex, and we will learn them in the coming chapters.

Before we present the first code snippet, using Python 3.6, we need to know one more thing about Quicksort algorithm. It is of an average 'Time Complexity' and it is represented by Big O notation, as O(nlogn).

For the beginners, it may appear intimidating at first, yet it is not, when you understand the principles behind this Asymptotic notations. Again, to remind you, we will cover this in great detail in chapter 5.

Let us see the first Quicksort algorithm example.

```
1 // code 3.15
2 // python 3.6
```

```python
# Quick Sort Algorithm

def smallerToGreater(array, startingNUmber, endingNUmber):
    searchingIndex = array[startingNUmber]
    lowIndex = startingNUmber + 1
    highIndex = endingNUmber

    while True:
        # we have a collection of numbers; we need to place those numbers in ascending order
        # in that collection there should be a low index number and high index number
        # we need to find the numbers that are larger than the rest amd send it to the right
        # first we need a searching index number that will check the current value
        # if the current value is larger than the searching index,
        # then we should send to the right side of the searching index and we can move left
        # to the next element.
        # the low index number should remain always lower than others,
        # and the numbers larger than the searching index should remain on the right side
        while lowIndex <= highIndex and array[highIndex] >= searchingIndex:
            highIndex = highIndex - 1

        # we also need to traverse the collection in the opposite process
        while lowIndex <= highIndex and array[lowIndex] <= searchingIndex:
            lowIndex = lowIndex + 1

        # if our above algorithm does not work, we exit the loop
        if lowIndex <= highIndex:
            array[lowIndex], array[highIndex] = array[highIndex], array[lowIndex]
        # else the loop continues
        else:
            # and we exit out of the loop
            break

    array[startingNUmber], array[highIndex] = array[highIndex], array[startingNUmber]
```

```
41
42     return highIndex
43
44 def quickSort(arrayOfNumbers, startingNumber, endingNumber):
45     if startingNumber >= endingNumber:
46         return
47
48     partitioningIndex = smallerToGreater(arrayOfNumbers, startingNumber, endingNumbe\
49 r)
50     quickSort(arrayOfNumbers, startingNumber, partitioningIndex - 1)
51     quickSort(arrayOfNumbers, partitioningIndex + 1, endingNumber)
52
53 arrayOfNUmbers = [100, 45, 1, 8, 47895, 5, 56, 23, 0, 89]
54
55 quickSort(arrayOfNUmbers, 0, len(arrayOfNUmbers) - 1)
56 print("The above random array of numbers in ascending order: " + str(arrayOfNUmbers))
```

Let us first see the output first, after that we will discuss the Quicksort algorithm.

```
1 // output of code 3.15
2
3 /home/ss/IdeaProjects/discretemathsdatastructures/PythonDiscrete/venv/bin/python /ho\
4 me/ss/IdeaProjects/discretemathsdatastructures/PythonDiscrete/QuickSort/QucikSortExa\
5 mpleOne.py
6
7 The above random array of numbers in ascending order: [0, 1, 5, 8, 23, 45, 56, 89, 1\
8 00, 47895]
9
10 Process finished with exit code 0
```

In the above code snippets, if you go through the comments, you will get the idea. We need a collection that has a definite set of elements, here integers. We can think it as 'input' or 'n', which is a variable. Now as the value of 'n' increases, the 'Time Complexity' varies.

In the above algorithm, we keep testing the value of the integer with respect to the search index number, and keep the larger number on the right side. It arranges the collection in an ascending order.

Now, almost same thing we are going to do using C language. In the first case, we will have a definite set of integers, just like above. In the second case, we will take input from the users and apply the Quicksort algorithm.

Let us see the first code snippet that handles definite set of integers.

```
1  // code 3.16
2  //C
3
4  #include<stdio.h>
5
6  // we need an utility function to swap two numbers
7  // we will use this function later
8  void swappingNumber(int* numOne, int* numTwo){
9      int temp = *numOne;
10     *numOne = *numTwo;
11     *numTwo = temp;
12 }
13 /*
14 * this function will place a random collection of numbers
15 * in an ascending order
16 * first we assume the last element of an array is the pivot index,
17 * such that all the smaller numbers will be on the left side
18 * of pivot index, and all the higher numbers will be on
19 * the right side of the pivot index
20 */
21 int arrangeNumbers (int arrayOfNumbers[], int lowIndex, int highIndex){
22     int pivotIndex = arrayOfNumbers[highIndex];
23     int indexNumber = (lowIndex - 1);
24     for (int initialNUmber = lowIndex; initialNUmber <= highIndex - 1; initialNUmber\
25 ++){
26         if (arrayOfNumbers[initialNUmber] <= pivotIndex){
27             indexNumber++;
28             swappingNumber(&arrayOfNumbers[indexNumber], &arrayOfNumbers[initialNUmb\
29 er]);
30         }
31     }
32     swappingNumber(&arrayOfNumbers[indexNumber + 1], &arrayOfNumbers[highIndex]);
33     return (indexNumber + 1);
34 }
35
36 void quickSortTheCollection(int arrayOfNumbers[], int lowIndex, int highIndex){
37     if (lowIndex < highIndex){
38         int pivotIndex = arrangeNumbers(arrayOfNumbers, lowIndex, highIndex);
39         quickSortTheCollection(arrayOfNumbers, lowIndex, pivotIndex - 1);
40         quickSortTheCollection(arrayOfNumbers, pivotIndex + 1, highIndex);
```

```
41      }
42 }
43
44 void displayInAscendingOrder(int arrayOfNumbers[], int
sizeOfCollection){
45      int initialNUmber;
46      for (initialNUmber = 0; initialNUmber < sizeOfCollection;
initialNUmber++)
47          printf("%d ", arrayOfNumbers[initialNUmber]);
48      printf("\n");
49 }
50
51
52 int main(int argc, char** argv){
53
54      int arrayOfNumbers[] = {22, 17, -8, 9, 11, 5};
55      int numberOfNUmbers =
sizeof(arrayOfNumbers)/sizeof(arrayOfNumbers[0]);
56      quickSortTheCollection(arrayOfNumbers, 0, numberOfNUmbers - 1);
57      printf("The sorted array is: ");
58      displayInAscendingOrder(arrayOfNumbers, numberOfNUmbers);
59
60      return 0;
61 }
```

Again, we have written our sequence of steps in the comments. Just go through it and you will get the idea. We have solved the same problem, only in a different way.

The next Quicksort algorithm will take inputs from the users. However, there is a limit that we can control. Crossing that limit will give you an error, although a simple 'if-else' statement will solve the problem for us. The four different output shows how we have changed the program to fit the Quicksort algorithm.

```
1 // code 3.17
2 // C
3
4 #include<stdio.h>
5
6 void quicksortInOneFunction(int arrayOfNumbers[25], int firstIndex,
int lastIndex){
7      int firstStorage, secondStorage, pivotIndex, temporaryStorage;
8      if(firstIndex < lastIndex){
9          pivotIndex = firstIndex;
10         firstStorage = firstIndex;
11         secondStorage = lastIndex;
12         while(firstStorage < secondStorage){
13             while(arrayOfNumbers[firstStorage] <=
arrayOfNumbers[pivotIndex]
14                     && firstStorage < lastIndex)
15                 firstStorage++;
```

```
16              while(arrayOfNumbers[secondStorage] > arrayOfNumbers[pivotIndex])
17                  secondStorage--;
18              if(firstStorage < secondStorage){
19                  temporaryStorage = arrayOfNumbers[firstStorage];
20                  arrayOfNumbers[firstStorage] = arrayOfNumbers[secondStorage];
21                  arrayOfNumbers[secondStorage] = temporaryStorage;
22              }
23          }
24          temporaryStorage = arrayOfNumbers[pivotIndex];
25          arrayOfNumbers[pivotIndex] = arrayOfNumbers[secondStorage];
26          arrayOfNumbers[secondStorage] = temporaryStorage;
27          quicksortInOneFunction(arrayOfNumbers, firstIndex, secondStorage - 1);
28          quicksortInOneFunction(arrayOfNumbers, secondStorage + 1, lastIndex);
29      }
30 }
31
32 int main(){
33     int initialNumber, countingLimit, collectionOfNumber[6];
34     printf("How many integers you want for for quick sorting?"
35            " (Maximum value you can enter: 6): ");
36     scanf("%d", &countingLimit);
37     printf("Enter %d elements: ", countingLimit);
38     for(initialNumber = 0; initialNumber < countingLimit; initialNumber++)
39         scanf("%d", &collectionOfNumber[initialNumber]);
40     quicksortInOneFunction(collectionOfNumber, 0, countingLimit - 1);
41     printf("The Sorted Order is: ");
42     for(initialNumber = 0; initialNumber < countingLimit; initialNumber++)
43         printf(" %d", collectionOfNumber[initialNumber]);
44     return 0;
45 }
```

First we will take a look at the output, that will explain why we need to change this code a little bit to get it done perfectly.

```
1 // output of code 3.17
2
3 How many integers you want for for quick sorting? (Maximum value you can enter: 6): 6
4 Enter 6 elements:
5 478
6 2
7 0
8 365894
```

```
 9 25478
10 12
11 The Sorted Order is:  0 2 12 478 25478 365894
12 RUN FINISHED; exit value 0; real time: 16s; user: 0ms; system: 0ms
```

Here in the above code, we have set the limit of inputs to 6. Initially we have followed the rule and entered 6 integer value and we have got the perfect ascending order.

However, what happens, if someone breaks that limit and decides to enter 8 elements?

Here is the output:

```
 1 How many integers you want for for quick sorting? (Maximum value you can enter: 6): 8
 2 Enter 8 elements:
 3 1
 4 2
 5 3
 6 6
 7 5
 8 4
 9 89
10 78
11 *** stack smashing detected ***: <unknown> terminated
12
13 RUN FINISHED; Aborted; core dumped; real time: 17s; user: 0ms; system: 0ms
```

We have entered 8 elements and it breaks the code. The code is not working anymore.

To avoid such incidents, we need to change the algorithm a little bit.

```
 1 // code 3.18
 2 // C
 3
 4 #include<stdio.h>
 5
 6 void quicksortInOneFunction(int arrayOfNumbers[25], int firstIndex, int lastIndex){
 7     int firstStorage, secondStorage, pivotIndex, temporaryStorage;
 8     if(firstIndex < lastIndex){
 9         pivotIndex = firstIndex;
10         firstStorage = firstIndex;
11         secondStorage = lastIndex;
12         while(firstStorage < secondStorage){
13             while(arrayOfNumbers[firstStorage] <= arrayOfNumbers[pivotIndex]
14                     && firstStorage < lastIndex)
```

```
15                    firstStorage++;
16                while(arrayOfNumbers[secondStorage] > arrayOfNumbers[pivotIndex])
17                    secondStorage--;
18                if(firstStorage < secondStorage){
19                    temporaryStorage = arrayOfNumbers[firstStorage];
20                    arrayOfNumbers[firstStorage] = arrayOfNumbers[secondStorage];
21                    arrayOfNumbers[secondStorage] = temporaryStorage;
22                }
23            }
24            temporaryStorage = arrayOfNumbers[pivotIndex];
25            arrayOfNumbers[pivotIndex] = arrayOfNumbers[secondStorage];
26            arrayOfNumbers[secondStorage] = temporaryStorage;
27            quicksortInOneFunction(arrayOfNumbers, firstIndex, secondStorage - 1);
28            quicksortInOneFunction(arrayOfNumbers, secondStorage + 1, lastIndex);
29        }
30 }
31
32 int main(){
33     int initialNumber, countingLimit, collectionOfNumber[6];
34     printf("How many integers you want for for quick sorting?"
35             " (Maximum value you can enter: 6): ");
36     scanf("%d", &countingLimit);
37
38     if(countingLimit <= 6){
39         printf("Enter %d elements: ", countingLimit);
40         for(initialNumber = 0; initialNumber < countingLimit; initialNumber++)
41             scanf("%d", &collectionOfNumber[initialNumber]);
42         quicksortInOneFunction(collectionOfNumber, 0, countingLimit - 1);
43         printf("The Sorted Order is: ");
44         for(initialNumber = 0; initialNumber < countingLimit; initialNumber++)
45             printf(" %d", collectionOfNumber[initialNumber]);
46     } else {
47         printf("You crossed the maximum value limit, try again!");
48     }
49
50     return 0;
51 }
```

Now, we are ready to face the worst case, where users will cross the limit of inputs and get the warning.

```
1 // output of code 3.18
2
```

```
3 How many integers you want for for quick sorting? (Maximum value you
can enter: 6): 8
4 You crossed the maximum value limit, try again!
5 RUN FINISHED; exit value 0; real time: 3s; user: 0ms; system: 0ms
```

Now, once the user crosses the limit, the warning gets displayed on the screen.

If the user follows the rule, it works perfectly again.

```
1 How many integers you want for for quick sorting? (Maximum value you
can enter: 6): 5
2 Enter 5 elements:
3 45
4 56
5 36
6 23
7 12
8 The Sorted Order is:   12 23 36 45 56
9 RUN FINISHED; exit value 0; real time: 8s; user: 0ms; system: 0ms
```

In this chapter, we won't go any further about algorithm. In the next chapter, we will learn about data structures.

After that, in the following chapter, we will follow up complex types of algorithm using data structures.

I write regularly on Algorithm and Data Structure in

4. Data Structures in different Programming languages

The core concepts of data structures in different programming languages are almost same, although the implementation varies syntactically.

Moreover, algorithm or sequence of instructions is deeply associated with the core concepts of data structures. We will see to that in a minute. Before that we need to know a few elementary discrete mathematical algebraic concepts, which are also associated with data structures.

Before cutting into the core concepts of data structures, theoretically we need to understand one key concept. The concepts of data structures in various programming language inherit its roots largely from discrete mathematical algebraic conceptions that are known as date set.

What is data set? A collection of integers.

We can write it like this:

```
1 {14, 1, 58, 3, 85} or {1, 2, 2, 4, 5, 6}
```

We started storing data and started doing operations on them much before any programming languages' forays into data structures. In that sense, we have implemented those old concepts of algebraic data set quite recently into programming languages.

We are, rather forced to do that. The volume of data is increasing faster than ever. Effective means of algorithm to sort those big data is getting more attention than ever.

In programming languages, we had thought of 'array' first; then, we found 'array' was not enough. Therefore, we implemented conceptions like Stack, Queue, Linked List, Trees, Hashing, etc. Data structures are now used in in every programming language to to store data in an organized and efficient manner. And to do that, we need efficient algorithm. That is the basic concept. Moreover, discrete mathematical algebraic data set, algorithm and data structures are twisted and entwined into a meaningful entity.

Let us clear some algebraic concepts about data set. After that, slowly we will enter into the world of complex data structures.

Stay tuned and read on.

Mean, Median and Mode

You have probably noticed that in discrete mathematics, there are always two conceptions go together. One is 'order of operation', and the other is 'distributive property'.

Consider some factors like this:

```
1  x = 3 * (4 + 6)
2  x = 3 * 10
3  x = 30
```

Now, we can rearrange the same factors like this:

```
1  x = 3 * (4 + 6)
2  x = 3*4 + 3*6
3  x = 12 + 18
4  x = 30
```

Therefore, order of operations and distributive property works pretty well with addition and subtraction. However, this will not work with multiplication and division. Just try it.

Any algebraic operation is nothing but a kind of algorithm. In the above case, our algorithm fails for two separate cases. Our algorithm works very well with addition and subtraction; but, it does not work with multiplication and division.

The same thing might happen for a data set. In a collection of numbers, we might try to apply the same algorithm. Consider a data set like this:

1 {14, 5, {78, 1, 56}, 8, 96, 0, 6}

A data set inside a data set. We cannot apply our algorithm here as well. We need to use of 'order of operation' rule to get the addition done inside the sub-data set first.

Now, we understand one thing, what we can do with discrete integers, we cannot always do with a collection of integers. We need to invent some different algorithm.

In any algebraic data set, there is always an average of the collection. Consider this data set:

1 {6, 2, 3, 8, 1}

The average of this data set is : (6 + 2 + 3 + 8 + 1) / 5, or 20.

This is also called 'Mean' of a data set. In mathematics there is other 'mean' as well. The geometric mean, we may have heard of that.

The word 'mean' means many things in our natural language also; but, in algebraic data set, it means the average. No lexical disambiguation, please.

On the other hand, in any algebraic data set, the Median represents the middle value of the data set. In any collection of integers, which is odd in numbers, finding the Median is quite easy.

In the above data set, 3 is the Median or middle value. But it is not true when the number of integers in a collection is even.

Consider the following data set:

1 {1, 2, 3, 4}

Finding the Mean is quite easy. It is not related to the odd or even numbers of the collection. But, in the above data set, finding the Median is not that easy. To find the Median we need to find the middle value of 2 and 3; because they are in the middle.

The middle value of 2 and 3 is 2.5. Therefore, that is the Median of the above data set.

Another important thing of a data set is the Mode. In some data sets, one value or more than one values most often appear. Consider this data set:

1 {1, 56, 7, 89, 7, 3, 56, 2, 1, 7, 8, 9, 3, 45, 3, 96, 3, 78, 5, 3}

In the above data set, there are more than one values that repeatedly appear. Right? We can see that 1 and 56 repeatedly appear two times, 7 appears three times; moreover, the integer 3 repeats five times. Therefore, the most often appeared integer is 3. It is the Mode of the data set.

Reading so far, we may ask ourselves, why we need to know this before studying data structures?

Well, there is an answer.

The sum of a collection of numbers divided by the count of numbers in the collection means the arithmetic mean; it is true for mathematics and statistics, as well. So the 'Mean' of a data set is often referenced as 'arithmetic mean' for lexical disambiguation. As we have learned before there are 'geometric mean' or 'harmonic mean'.

As far as programming language is concerned, sometimes we need to find out the arithmetic average income of a nation's population, which is known as per capita income.

Now, we can logically guess that by using 'Mean' of a data set, we cannot represent the central tendencies of a data set. Consider a data set, where a people's income is much, much greater than most people's income. Theoretically, the nation's per capita income shows a very good central tendencies, which is a false statement; in reality, in that country, 70 percent of people live under poverty line.

In such situation, the 'Median' may be a better description of central tendencies.

Why? Because, the 'Median' separates the higher half from the lower half of a data sample. For a data set, we have seen that it represents the middle value.

Whereas the 'Mean' can be skewed and twisted to give a false representation of central tendencies, here is the basic advantage of the 'Mean'. It may give a better idea of a typical central tendencies. It cannot be skewed using a small portions of extremely large values, compared to a large portions of extremely small values. If only more than half the data are represented by false, and extremely large values, the 'Median' will give an arbitrarily large or small result.

Array, the First Step to Data Structure

We know that an array is a sequential collection of elements. These elements are of same type. They are stored in memory sequentially. An element of an array can be obtained through its respective index. An array element in Java is treated as an object, that is not true in C.

As a definition, we can say that an array is a data structure that holds a similar type of elements. On the other hand, it can represent a large collection of algebraic data set. We can generate a random set of elements in an array like this:

```
1 //code 4.1
2 //Java
3 package fun.sanjibsinha.datastructures;
4
5 public class ManipulatingArray {
6
7     private int arrayOfRandomNumbers[] = new int[20];
8
9     private int sizeOfArray = 5;
```

```java
10
11      public void getRandomElements(){
12          for (int i = 0; i <= sizeOfArray; i++){
13              arrayOfRandomNumbers[i] = (int)(Math.random()*121)+121;
14              System.out.println(arrayOfRandomNumbers[i]);
15          }
16      }
17
18      public static void main(String[] args) {
19          ManipulatingArray manArray = new ManipulatingArray();
20          manArray.getRandomElements();
21      }
22
23 }
```

The above code is a sample of code snippets that can generate a random data set of big integers. Here we have produced only five specimens.

```
1 // output of code 4.1
2
3 185
4 198
5 158
6 146
7 139
8 132
```

We have an idea of how we can manipulate data in a big way. It is just a very small sample.

We can search any value in the random output, like this:

```java
1 // code 4.2
2 // Java
3
4 package fun.sanjibsinha.datastructures;
5
6 public class ManipulatingArray {
7
8      private int arrayOfRandomNumbers[] = new int[20];
9
10     private int sizeOfArray = 5;
11
12     public void getRandomElements(){
13         for (int i = 0; i <= sizeOfArray; i++){
14             arrayOfRandomNumbers[i] = (int)(Math.random()*121)+121;
15             System.out.println(arrayOfRandomNumbers[i]);
16         }
17     }
18
19     public boolean getValueInArray(int findTheValue){
```

```
20          boolean theValue = false;
21          for(int i = 0; i < sizeOfArray; i++){
22              if(arrayOfRandomNumbers[i] == findTheValue){
23                  theValue = true;
24              }
25          }
26          return theValue;
27      }
28
29      public static void main(String[] args) {
30          ManipulatingArray manArray = new ManipulatingArray();
31          manArray.getRandomElements();
32          System.out.println("**********");
33          System.out.println(manArray.getValueInArray(121));
34      }
35 }
```

We are trying to find whether 121 belongs to the randomly generated array of integers. The answer will come out as 'false'. You have probably noticed that we have used this line in our code while generating the random integers.

```
1 arrayOfRandomNumbers[i] = (int)(Math.random()*121)+121;
```

Because 'Math.random()' method produces 'double' data type, we have to cast it to a round figure by using 'int' data type. Each time you run the code, you will get the same output. If you change the value from 121 to a higher value, the output will be higher.

Therefore, the output is quite expected.

```
 1 // output of code 4.2
 2
 3 136
 4 227
 5 157
 6 143
 7 233
 8 195
 9 **********
10 false
```

The element 121 does not belong to the randomly generated collection of integers.

As an object-oriented-programming language, Java treats this type of collection differently than C. In Java an array is a container object that holds a fixed number of values of a single type. Whenever we create an array, the length of the array is established. After creation, the length of an array is fixed.

In Java, whenever we want to create an array object, we write something like this:

```
1 private int arrayOfRandomNumbers[] = new int[20];
```

However, in C, this is different. According to some computer scientists, C stands between problem oriented high level languages like Fortran, Basic and Pascal, and the low level machine languages like Assembly language or Machine language.

Any C programs consists of one or more distinct units called 'functions'.

In C, like in the above code, we declare array, this way:

```
1 // declaring array
2 int individualMarks[10];
```

Whatever be the language type, function based or object-oriented-programming based, the accessing of an array element is the same. This is done with 'subscript'; all the array elements are numbered, starting with 0. In C,what is known as subscript, in Java the same is known as numerical index. In Java each item in an array is called an element. In C it is also known as 'dimension'.

The Mean, Median and Mode of algebraic data set is widely used while we manipulate any array. Consider the following example where we have calculated the average marks of 10 students. The user is asked to give inputs and the program calculates the Mean of the data set.

```
1 // code 4.3
2 // C
3
4 /*
5 * an array is a collective name given to a group of similar quantities
6 * find average marks obtained by a class of 10 students
7 */
8
9 int main(int argc, char** argv) {
10
11 float averageNumber, sumOfNumbers = 0;
12
13 int indexNumber;
14
15 // declaring array
16 int individualMarks[10];
17
18 for(indexNumber = 0; indexNumber <= 9; indexNumber++){
19
20     printf("Enter marks: ");
21     // storing data in array
22     scanf("%d", &individualMarks[indexNumber]);
23
24 }
25
26 for(indexNumber = 0; indexNumber <= 9; indexNumber++){
27     sumOfNumbers = sumOfNumbers + individualMarks[indexNumber];
```

```
28 }
29
30 averageNumber = sumOfNumbers / 10;
31
32 printf("Average number = %f", averageNumber);
33
34
35     return 0;
36 }
```

Let us see the output of the above code.

```
1 // output of code 4.3
2
3 Enter marks: 35
4 Enter marks: 65
5 Enter marks: 98
6 Enter marks: 99
7 Enter marks: 48
8 Enter marks: 75
9 Enter marks: 67
10 Enter marks: 54
11 Enter marks: 89
12 Enter marks: 36
13 Average number = 66.599998
14 RUN FINISHED; exit value 0; real time: 33s; user: 0ms; system: 0ms
```

In the above code, this line is important:

```
1 printf("Average number = %f", averageNumber);
```

We have expected that the output would be a floating point value. In every language, we use all types of primitive data types to declare the type of the array.

In Java, we can declare arrays of many types, this way:

```
1 byte[] anArrayOfBytes;
2 int[] anArray;
3 short[] anArrayOfShorts;
4 long[] anArrayOfLongs;
5 float[] anArrayOfFloats;
6 double[] anArrayOfDoubles;
7 boolean[] anArrayOfBooleans;
8 char[] anArrayOfChars;
9 String[] anArrayOfStrings;
```

We can use the shortcut syntax to create and initialize an array, almost the same way.

In Java, we use the shortcut syntax this way:

```
1 int[] anArrayDeclaration = {
2     100, 200, 300,
3     400, 500, 600,
4     700, 800, 900, 1000
5 };
```

In C, we can use the shortcut syntax almost the same way. Sometimes, if the array is initialized where it is declared, we need not mention the dimension.

```
1 int numArray[] = {1, 21, 3, 45, 7};
```

Whatever language we use, the main advantage of array is it helps us to save the memory of the system. We can allocate memory dynamically; when the memory allocation is not dynamic, it stores the data in contiguous memory locations. This process makes the program faster than other data structures.

The idea of algebraic data set and the conceptions regarding the Mean, Median and Mode will also help us understanding the manipulations of complex arrays. Before going to that section, let us understand some simple features of arrays. To do that we will use Java language, as it is one of the easiest languages to learn.

Let us understand some Array features

In Java, array is an object. However, we also need the help of primitive data types to declare and initialize an array object.

As we have seen earlier, whenever we create an array object with the help of 'new' keyword, the memory is allocated.

Inside the comments in the following code snippet, we will see the relation between the numerical index and the element of an array.

```
1  // code 4.4
2  // Java
3
4  package fun.sanjibsinha.arrayexamples;
5  /*
6  Introduction to array object
7  Primitive data types are not objects created from a class. They are special data typ\
8  es built into the language.
9  To build an array object we need to take help from primitive data types.
10 The only exception is String
11 What features will distinguish array from primitive data types?
12 Let us see to that problem
13 */
14
15 public class ArrayExampleOne {
16
17     public static void main(String[] args){
```

```
18          //an example of primitive data type
19          //a variable is a container that contains a value or a
primitive data types
20          int myAge = 54;
21          System.out.println("An example of primitive data type : " +
myAge);
22          //in case of array we declare and allocate memory with a new
keyword
23          //the following array container holds a fixed number of
value of data type i\
24 nt
25          //the length of the array is established
26          //here the length is 2, this container has 2 elements
27          int[] myBasket = new int[2];
28          //each item or element has a corresponding numerical index
that starts with 0
29          myBasket[0] = 2;
30          myBasket[1] = 3;
31          //each element can be accessed by its corresponding
numerical index
32          System.out.println("The first element of my basket : " +
myBasket[0]);
33          System.out.println("The second element of my basket : " +
myBasket[1]);
34      }
35
36 }
37
38 OUTPUT:
39 -------
40
41 An example of primitive data type : 54
42 The first element of my basket : 2
43 The second element of my basket : 3
```

In this section we will give the output along with the code snippet to understand how the program works.

In Java, while we declare an array we usually take help from the primitive data types. That sounds logical as we need to tell the compiler what type of array we are going to create. According to our declaration, the memory will be allocated. One single exception is the non-primitive data type 'String'. The following example will show you how we can handle that.

```
1 // code 4.5
2 // Java
3
4 package fun.sanjibsinha.arrayexamples;
5 /*
6 How to declare a variable to refer to an array
```

```java
7  */
8
9  public class ArrayExampleTwo {
10
11     public static void main(String[] args){
12         //to declare and create an array of integer type
13         int[] studentClasses = new int[2];
14         //to declare an array of String, a non-primitive data type
15         String[] studentNames = new String[4];
16         //the brackets after the data type indicate it's an array
17         //an array has two parts : data type and name
18         //the data type also indicates what type of elements the array will contain
19         //the next line will give an error of incompatible type
20         /*
21         studentNames[0] = 12;
22         */
23         studentNames[0] = "John"; //this is OK with the compiler
24         System.out.println("The name of the student who has come out first : " + stu\
25 dentNames[0]);
26     }
27 }
28
29 OUTPUT
30 ------
31
32 The name of the student who has come out first : John
```

Read the comments carefully, we will learn many interesting things about an array. The proper initialization of an array varies from one programming language to another.

Java allows two types of initialization. However, one type is strongly discouraged by the official documentation.

Watch the next example, it will show you the proper way of initialization in Java.

```java
1  // code 4.6
2  // Java
3
4  package fun.sanjibsinha.arrayexamples;
5  /*
6  The proper initialization of an array
7  */
8
9  public class ArrayExampleThree {
10
11     public static void main(String[] args){
12         //we can also create and initialize an array like this
```

```
13          int schoolSections[] = new int[4];
14          schoolSections[0] = 1;
15          schoolSections[1] = 2;
16          schoolSections[2] = 3;
17          schoolSections[3] = 4;
18          System.out.println("We want section 1 : " + schoolSections[0]);
19          /*
20          However this above type of initialization is highly discouraged
21          */
22          int[] schoolSection = new int[4]; // it is OK
23
24      }
25 }
26
27
28 OUTPUT:
29 -------
30
31 We want section 1 : 1
```

We have compiled and run the code successfully with the help of improper initialization. However, the proper initialization is shown below:

```
1 int[] schoolSection = new int[4]; // it is OK
```

As long as we use the Java, we will keep using the proper initialization of array.

In C language, we have seen the shortcut syntax before, the next Java program has used the shortcut syntax to create and initialize the array.

```
 1 // code 4.7
 2 // Java
 3
 4 package fun.sanjibsinha.arrayexamples;
 5 /*
 6 The shortcut syntax to create and initialize an array
 7 */
 8
 9 public class ArrayExampleFour {
10
11     public static void main(String[] args){
12
13         String[] nameCollection = {
14                 "John Smith", "Chicago", "good gunner."
15         };
16         System.out.println("He is " + nameCollection[0] + ", from " + nameCollection\
17 [1]
18                 + ". And he is a " + nameCollection[2]);
```

```
19     }
20 }
21
22
23 OUTPUT
24 ------
25
26 He is John Smith, from Chicago. And he is a good gunner.
```

An array can contain another array, or sometimes, in some special cases, multiple arrays. We call them multidimensional array. The components of a multidimensional array are themselves arrays. The following example will show you how we can use multidimensional array.

```
 1 // code 4.8
 2 // Java
 3
 4
 5 package fun.sanjibsinha.arrayexamples;
 6 /*
 7 In multidimensional array components are themselves arrays
 8 The rows can vary in length
 9 */
10 public class ArrayExampleFive {
11
12     public static void main(String[] args){
13         //you may imagine it as columns and rows
14         String[][] nameCollections = {
15                 {"Name", "Location", "Occupation"}, //[0][0] => Name
16                 {"John Smith", "Chicago", "Gunner"}, //[1][0] =>
John ...
17                 {"Ernest Hemingway", "Writer"}, //[2][0] =>
Ernest...
18                 {"Don Juan", "Paris", "Artist"} //[3][0] => Don...
19         };
20         //the first column name represents the first index as
[0][0], and moves on
21
22         System.out.println(nameCollections[0][0] + " : " +
nameCollections[1][0]);
23         System.out.println(nameCollections[0][1] + " : " +
nameCollections[1][1]);
24         System.out.println(nameCollections[0][2] + " : " +
nameCollections[1][2]);
25         System.out.println("+++++++++++++++");
26         System.out.println(nameCollections[0][0] + " : " +
nameCollections[2][0]);
27         System.out.println(nameCollections[0][2] + " : " +
nameCollections[2][1]);
28         System.out.println("+++++++++++++++");
```

```
29          System.out.println(nameCollections[0][0] + " : " + nameCollections[3][0]);
30          System.out.println(nameCollections[0][2] + " : " + nameCollections[3][1]);
31          System.out.println(nameCollections[0][2] + " : " + nameCollections[3][2]);
32      }
33 }
34
35 OUTPUT:
36 -------
37
38 Name : John Smith
39 Location : Chicago
40 Occupation : Gunner
41 +++++++++++++++
42 Name : Ernest Hemingway
43 Occupation : Writer
44 +++++++++++++++
45 Name : Don Juan
46 Occupation : Paris
47 Occupation : Artist
```

When we work with multidimensional arrays, the built-in length property helps us to determine the size of an insider array component. In that case, the numerical index points to the built-in array like the following code snippet.

```
1 // code 4.9
2 // Java
3
4
5 package fun.sanjibsinha.arrayexamples;
6 /*
7 The built-in length property helps us to determine the size of any array
8 */
9 public class ArrayExampleSix {
10
11     public static void main(String[] args){
12
13         String[][] nameCollections = {
14                 {"Name", "Location", "Occupation"}, //[0][0] => Name
15                 {"John Smith", "Chicago", "Gunner"}, //[1][0] => John ...
16                 {"Ernest Hemingway", "Writer"}, //[2][0] => Ernest...
17                 {"Don Juan", "Paris", "Artist"} //[3][0] => Don...
18         };
19         System.out.println("The length of the first array is : " + nameCollections.l\
```

```
20 ength);
21         System.out.println("The length of the index 2 of the first
array is : " + na\
22 meCollections[2].length);
23     }
24 }
25
26
27 OUTPUT
28 ------
29
30 The length of the first array is : 4
31 The length of the index 2 of the first array is : 2
```

The arrays with numerical indexes 0 and 1 have length 3, while the array having numerical index 3, is of length 2. In case of multidimensional arrays, we can easily point them out and do any kind of operations.

Java allows us to copy all or a part of components of any array to another array. In the following example we can clearly see that the first 'String' type array has components that do not mean anything. We can rearrange the components of that array to another array, so that it becomes a meaningful sentence while we give an output.

```
 1 // code 4.10
 2 // Java
 3
 4
 5 package fun.sanjibsinha.arrayexamples;
 6 /*
 7 System class has a method called 'arraycopy()' that has five
parameters
 8 arraycopy(Object source, int source-position, Object destination,
int destination po\
 9 sition, int length)
10 */
11
12 import java.util.Arrays;
13
14 public class ArrayExampleSeven {
15
16     public static void main(String[] args){
17
18         String[] notAMeaningfulSentence = {"My ", "I ", "am ", "not
", "a ", "Robot"\
19 };
20         String[] aMeaningfulSentence = new String[5];
21         System.arraycopy(notAMeaningfulSentence, 1,
aMeaningfulSentence, 0, 5);
22         System.out.println(aMeaningfulSentence[0]
```

```
23                          + aMeaningfulSentence[1] + aMeaningfulSentence[2] + aMeaningfulSente\
24 nce[3]
25                          + aMeaningfulSentence[4]);
26     }
27 }
28
29 OUTPUT
30 ------
31
32 I am not a Robot
```

While we give an output, we can do the same operation in a completely different way. In the above code we have used the numerical indices to get the individual elements. The following example has used 'for' loop to iterate through the same numerical indices and extract the string output.

```
1 // code 4.11
2 // Java
3
4
5 package fun.sanjibsinha.arrayexamples;
6
7 public class ArrayExampleEight {
8
9     public static void main(String[] args){
10
11        String[] notAMeaningfulSentence = {"My ", "I ", "am ", "not ", "a ", "Robot"\
12 };
13        String[] aMeaningfulSentence = new String[5];
14        System.arraycopy(notAMeaningfulSentence, 1, aMeaningfulSentence, 0, 5);
15        for (int i = 0; i<=4; i++){
16            System.out.print(aMeaningfulSentence[i]);
17        }
18     }
19 }
20
21
22 OUTPUT
23 ------
24
25 I am not a Robot
```

One of the most common advantages of any array is we can iterate through that array and the process of iteration helps us to get all the components out of any type of array.

```
 1  // code 4.12
 2  // Java
 3
 4
 5  package fun.sanjibsinha.arrayexamples;
 6  /*
 7  We can perform some of the most common manipulations related to arrays
 8  */
 9
10  public class ArrayExampleNine {
11
12      public static void main(String[] args){
13
14          String[] notAMeaningfulSentence = {"My ", "I ", "am ", "not ", "a ", "Robot"\
15  };
16          String[] aMeaningfulSentence = java.util.Arrays.copyOfRange(notAMeaningfulSe\
17  ntence, 1, 6);
18          for (int i = 0; i <= (aMeaningfulSentence.length - 1); i++){
19              System.out.print(aMeaningfulSentence[i]);
20          }
21      }
22  }
23
24  OUTPUT
25  ------
26
27  I am not a Robot
```

So far we have learned one key concept of array. The elements of any array should belong to the same data type. On that principle, the multidimensional array also works.

Inside an array we have components that also contain one or more arrays. However, the components of multidimensional array should be of the same data type for one reason. We need to declare the data type well before the initialization.

Whatever be the nature of any array, it always works on the same principle: we get the element through the numerical index.

```
 1  // code 4.13
 2  // Java
 3
 4
 5  package fun.sanjibsinha.arrayexamples;
 6
 7  /*
 8  How array works : index=>element
```

```
 9 */
10
11 public class ArrayExampleTen {
12     public static void main (String[] args)
13     {
14         //declaring a certain type of array, we choose data type int
15         int[] ageCollection;
16
17         //the next step deals with allocating memory for elements, we choose 5
18         ageCollection = new int[5];
19
20         //the initialization process begins with the first element
21         for (int i = 0; i <= 4; i ++){
22             int j = 18;
23             j = j + i;
24             ageCollection[i] = j;
25             System.out.println("Element at index " + i + " => " + ageCollection[i]);
26         }
27     }
28 }
29
30
31 OUTPUT
32 ------
33 Element at index 0 => 18
34 Element at index 1 => 19
35 Element at index 2 => 20
36 Element at index 3 => 21
37 Element at index 4 => 22
```

Another important factor we should always keep in our mind. According to the depth of the multidimensional array, we can always use the nested 'for' loop. Consider the following example, where we have a two dimensional arrays.

According to its dimension, we have used one nested 'for' loop.

```
 1 // code 4.14
 2 // Java
 3
 4
 5 package fun.sanjibsinha.arrayexamples;
 6
 7 /*
 8 Multidimensional array using nested for loop
 9 */
10
11 public class ArrayExampleEleven {
12
```

```java
13      public static void main(String[] args){
14
15          int[][] myArray = {
16              {1, 2, 3},
17              {4, 5, 6},
18              {7, 8, 9}
19          };
20
21          for (int i = 0; i < 3; i++){
22              System.out.print(i + " => ");
23              for (int j = 0; j < 3; j++){
24                  System.out.print(myArray[i][j] + " ");
25              }
26              System.out.println();
27          }
28
29      }
30 }
31
32
33 OUTPUT
34 ------
35
36 0 => 1 2 3
37 1 => 4 5 6
38 2 => 7 8 9
```

In Java, we have many built-in array methods. We can import those class methods and use them to manipulate any type of arrays.

```java
1  // code 4.15
2  // Java
3
4  package fun.sanjibsinha;
5
6  import java.util.Arrays;
7
8  /*
9  Testing a few built-in array methods
10 */
11 public class Array12 {
12
13     public static void main(String[] args){
14         //array declaration
15         int[] myNumber = new int[5];
16         //now we need to add elements
17         myNumber[0] = 50;
18         myNumber[1] = 60;
19         myNumber[2] = 70;
20         //etc
```

```
21          int[] anotherNumber = {1, 2, 3};
22          //we can print any array value this way
23          System.out.println(Arrays.toString(myNumber));
24          System.out.println(Arrays.toString(anotherNumber));
25      }
26 }
27
28 OUTPUT
29 ------
30 [50, 60, 70, 0, 0]
31 [1, 2, 3]
```

In Java, an array object is created by using a 'new' keyword; it is needless to say that each array object creates a reference value along with it. We can easily get that reference value just by printing it out. The next code snippet shows us the same example.

```
1  // code 4.16
2  // Java
3
4  package fun.sanjibsinha;
5  /*
6  There are few basic rules we should remember about an array
7  */
8
9  public class A13 {
10
11     public static void main(String[] args){
12         //array declaration
13         int[] myNumber = new int[5];
14         //now we need to add elements
15         myNumber[0] = 50;
16         myNumber[1] = 60;
17         myNumber[2] = 70;
18         //etc
19         int[] anotherNumber = {1, 2, 3};
20         //printing the value of an array like this
21         //gives us reference value : [I@5ba23b66
22         System.out.println(myNumber);
23         //we can print out the individual value of element by index
24         System.out.println(myNumber[0] + " => " + anotherNumber[0]);
25         //we can also use for loop
26         for (int i = 0; i <= 2; i++){
27             System.out.println(myNumber[i]);
28         }
29     }
30 }
31
32 OUTPUT
33 ------
```

```
34
35 [I@5ba23b66
36 50 => 1
37 50
38 60
39 70
```

We can check whether an array has a certain value or not. We can create our own method, or we can use the built-in methods like the following code snippet.

```
1  // code 4.17
2  // Java
3
4  package fun.sanjibsinha;
5
6  import java.util.Arrays;
7
8  /*
9  We can check if any array has a certain value
10 */
11 public class A14 {
12
13     public static void main(String[] args){
14         //array declaration
15         int[] myNumber = new int[3];
16         //now we need to add elements
17         myNumber[0] = 50;
18         myNumber[1] = 60;
19         myNumber[2] = 70;
20         //etc
21         int[] anotherNumber = {1, 2, 3};
22         String[] nameColection = {"John", "Bob", "Mary"};
23
24         System.out.println("Does array nameCollection contains this element? "
25                 + Arrays.asList(nameColection).contains(2));
26         System.out.println("Does array nameCollection contains this element? "
27                 + Arrays.asList(nameColection).contains("John"));
28
29     }
30 }
31
32
33 OUTPUT
34 ------
35 Does array nameCollection contains this element? false
36 Does array nameCollection contains this element? true
```

When we pass an array as a parameter of a method, it adds a lot of flexibility in our code. It also reduces the excess code baggage. Manipulations of array by passing it as a parameter lets us do many types of operations.

```
// code 4.18
// Java

package fun.sanjibsinha;
/*
We can pass array as parameter and we can manipulate that feature in many ways
In this problem we have solved how to add a collection of numbers
*/

import java.util.*;

import java.util.Arrays;

public class A15 {

    public static void main(String[] args){

        int[] anotherNumber = {10, 25, 300};
        addingAColectionOfNUmbers(anotherNumber);
    }
    public static void addingAColectionOfNUmbers(int[] aCollectionOfNumbers){
        int sum = 0;
        for (int i = 0; i < aCollectionOfNumbers.length; i++){
            sum += aCollectionOfNumbers[i];
        }
        System.out.println(sum);
    }
}

OUTPUT
------
335
```

Like any primitive data type, we can return any array object using a method. As always, we need to use the 'new' keyword.

```
// code 4.19
// Java

package fun.sanjibsinha;
/*
we can return any array value using a method
*/
```

```
8
9  public class A16 {
10
11     public static void main(String args[]){
12         int newArray[] = returningArrayMethod();
13
14         for (int i = 0; i < newArray.length; i++){
15             System.out.print(newArray[i] + " ");
16         }
17     }
18
19     public static int[] returningArrayMethod(){
20         //returning any array from a method
21         return new int[] {111,222,3333, 456897};
22     }
23 }
24
25
26 OUTPUT
27 ------
28 111 222 3333 456897
```

We have given the output by accessing each numerical index.

Not only internal libraries, there are extremely useful external libraries too, Apache commons is such external libraries that help us to manipulate any array.

```
1  // code 4.20
2  // Java
3
4  package fun.sanjibsinha;
5  /*
6  In this problem we will see how we can manipulate different type of
7  Array methods using internal and external libraries
8  */
9
10 import org.apache.commons.lang3.ArrayUtils;
11
12 import java.lang.reflect.Array;
13 import java.util.Arrays;
14
15 public class A17 {
16
17     public static void main(String[] args){
18
19         int[] numberCollection = {1, 2};
20         //we can get a particular value through index
21         System.out.println(Array.get(numberCollection, 1));
22         //we can get the length of the array
23         System.out.println(Array.getLength(numberCollection));
```

```
24
25          /*
26          Using external libraries is required in some situations where we want to
27          manipulate array values. Please consult the related texts and associated lin\
28 ks
29          written in the book
30          */
31          //using apache commons lang3 external library
32          int[] cartOne = {1, 2, 3, 4};
33          System.out.println("The length of the first cart : " + cartOne.length);
34          int[] cartTwo = {5, 200, 36, 4, 78, 123};
35          System.out.println("The length of the second cart : " + cartTwo.length);
36          int[] addingCart = ArrayUtils.addAll(cartOne, cartTwo);
37          System.out.println("Combining two carts the length has changed : " + addingC\
38 art.length);
39          //we can also see the final output
40          System.out.println("The adding cart looks like this : " + Arrays.toString(ad\
41 dingCart));
42
43      }
44 }
45
46 OUTPUT
47 ------
48
49 2
50 2
51 The length of the first cart : 4
52 The length of the second cart : 6
53 Combining two carts the length has changed : 10
54 The adding cart looks like this : [1, 2, 3, 4, 5, 200, 36, 4, 78, 123]
```

With the help of these external libraries we can reverse any array components; in usual case, we need to write extra code to get the same result.

```
1 // code 4.21
2 // Java
3
4 package fun.sanjibsinha;
5 /*
6 Some more Array methods using external apache commons lang3
7 */
8
```

```
 9 import org.apache.commons.lang3.ArrayUtils;
10
11 public class A18 {
12
13     public static void main(String[] args){
14         //we can reverse an Array
15         char[] myName = {'s', 'a', 'n', 'j', 'i', 'b'};
16         //now we can just add this characters to get my name
17         System.out.println("My name : " + new String(myName));
18         //let us reverse thsi character to see how my name looks in the mirror
19         ArrayUtils.reverse(myName);
20         System.out.println("My name on the mirror : " + new String(myName));
21     }
22 }
23
24 OUTPUT
25 ------
26
27 My name : sanjib
28 My name on the mirror : bijnas
```

The Apache commons array utility libraries have many other features, which help us to get other benefits; we can remove any array element using the external libraries.

```
 1 // code 4.22
 2 // Java
 3
 4
 5 package fun.sanjibsinha;
 6
 7 /*
 8 We can remove any element of an array using apache commons lang library
 9 */
10
11 import org.apache.commons.lang3.ArrayUtils;
12
13 import java.util.Arrays;
14
15 public class A19 {
16
17     public static void main(String[] args){
18         //declaring an array
19         int[] myNumber = {1, 58, 23, 45, 47, 13, 35};
20         //the length of the array and the output
21         System.out.println("The length of the array : " + myNumber.length);
22         System.out.println("The array before removing any element :
```

```
                              " + Arrays.toStr\
23 ing(myNumber));
24           //removing an element in the array
25           int[] newArrayOfMyNumber = ArrayUtils.remove(myNumber, 2);
26           System.out.println("The length of the new array after
   removel of index 2 : "\
27   + newArrayOfMyNumber.length);
28           System.out.println("The array after removing element 3,
   index 2 : "
29                   + Arrays.toString(newArrayOfMyNumber));
30           System.out.println("The index 2 and element 3, that is
   number " + myNumber[2\
31 ] + " is missing in the new array.");
32       }
33 }
34
35
36 OUTPUT
37 ------
38
39 The length of the array : 7
40 The array before removing any element : [1, 58, 23, 45, 47, 13, 35]
41 The length of the new array after removel of index 2 : 6
42 The array after removing element 3, index 2 : [1, 58, 45, 47, 13,
   35]
43 The index 2 and element 3, that is number 23 is missing in the new
   array.
```

In Java, the data type of any array may be user defined. Not only primitive or non-primitive data types, but we can also use the user defined data type like the following code snippet.

```
 1 // code 4.23
 2 // Java
 3
 4
 5 package fun.sanjibsinha;
 6
 7 class Person{
 8     int age;
 9 }
10
11
12 public class A20 {
13
14     public static void main(String[] args){
15
16         Person onePerson = new Person();
17         onePerson.age = 10;
18         Person twoPerson = new Person();
```

```
19          twoPerson.age = 20;
20          Person threePerson = new Person();
21          threePerson.age = 30;
22          Person[] persons = new Person[3];
23          persons[0] = onePerson;
24          persons[1] = twoPerson;
25          persons[2] = threePerson;
26          System.out.println("The age of three Persons : " + persons[0].age +
27                  ", " + persons[1].age + ", " + persons[2].age);
28
29      }
30
31 }
32
33
34 OUTPUT
35 -------
36
37 The age of three Persons : 10, 20, 30
```

We can create and initialize more user defined array objects to make our program more robust. Consider the next problem.

```
1 // code 4.24
2 // Java
3
4 package fun.sanjibsinha;
5
6 class Mobile{
7      int modelNumber;
8      String modelName;
9      public void displayModels(int model, String name){
10         this.modelName = name;
11         this.modelNumber = model;
12         System.out.println("The model number : " + model + ". The model name :  " + \
13 name);
14     }
15
16 }
17
18 public class A21 {
19
20     public static void main(String[] args) {
21         //we are creating three mobile objects in heap
22         //three reference variables from stack point to the heap
23         Mobile sam = new Mobile();
24         Mobile red = new Mobile();
25         Mobile zen = new Mobile();
```

```
26          //an array of objects can be created just like any primitive data type
27          Mobile[] mobiles = {sam, red, zen};
28          for (int i = 0; i < mobiles.length; i ++){
29              //we want model number starts from 10
30              int j = 10;
31              j += i;
32              if(i == 0){
33                  mobiles[i].displayModels(j, "Sam");
34              }
35              else if(i == 1){
36                  mobiles[i].displayModels(j, "Red");
37              }
38              else {
39                  mobiles[i].displayModels(j, "Zen");
40              }
41          }
42      }
43 }
44
45 OUTPUT
46 ------
47
48 The model number : 10. The model name :   Sam
49 The model number : 11. The model name :   Red
50 The model number : 12. The model name :   Zen
```

Finally, we are going to conclude this section with a special Java feature. We can take out the elements directly from the array like the following code.

```
1  // code 4.25
2  // Java
3
4
5  package fun.sanjibsinha;
6
7  public class A22 {
8
9      public static void main(String[] args) {
10
11         int[] myNUmbers = {12, 18, 36, 6, 24};
12         //enhanced for loop
13         //it takes out the value directly from the array
14         for (int i : myNUmbers){
15             System.out.println(i);
16         }
17
18     }
19 }
20
```

```
21
22  OUTPUT
23  -------
24
25  12
26  18
27  36
28  6
29  24
```

In this section, we have learned many simple features of array using Java language. We can use the same algorithm for any other language as long as we use the iteration or numerical indices.

In the coming sections we will see how we can relate algebraic data set properties like the Mean, Median and Mode with arrays. We will also see how we can connect discrete mathematical conceptions like Set theory, Probability and programming conceptions arrays in our mind.

Let us start with Set theory and Probability.

Set Theory, Probability and Array

In discrete mathematics studying 'Sets' is mandatory. Have you ever thought why? It is because Set theory is only concerned about distinct numbers. Quite naturally it has widespread applications in Computer Science.

Literally we can translate every single property of Set theory into computer programming. And, yes, with the help of simple arrays. We don't need complex data structures, algorithm, classes, or any collection hierarchy.

Set theory conceptions are distributed over a considerable amount in computer science as a whole. We will see that later, in detail, how Set theoretical conceptions are applied in Declarative programming language like SQL. With all types of set operations we can make declarative statements in any SQL query. You will find typical 'union','intersection', 'difference', 'complementary', and many more.

Moreover, we can do the same thing in our array world, also.

A Set in discrete mathematics is a list of well defined collection of unique integers. Do you find any similarity with an Array? An array is also a well defined collection of similar quantities. It could be integers, any kind of decimal values, or even Strings, characters. The main difference is an array does not always contain unique items.

As a result we can manipulate arrays in some diverse ways, and that was intended when the conceptions of arrays had been incorporated in programming languages. An array allows duplicate values, and that is important when Probability comes into pictures. We will see to that in a minute.

We can say an Array is basically a Set with indexes. Both are data structures and both contain a list of items. In particular, both have similar types of operations that can be performed, such as Union, Intersection, etc.

Before going to connect them we need to have a clear conceptions about the differences. A Set does not allow duplicate items, but an Array does. A Set does not have any index attached with its items, but an Array does. In an Array we can take out a specific item and traverse the whole Array structure until it is found. In a Set, we cannot do that.

The major advantage of an Array is we can take out any value with the help of the index.

As a matter of fact, we can conclude that they have more similarities than differences. Therefore let us immerse briefly into some code snippets that will show how we can connect them in reality.

According to the Set theory, the Union occurs between two Sets and the output omits the common value. Let us do the same with a PHP code.

```
1  // code 4.26
2  // PHP
3
4  <?php
5
6  /*
7   * They have similarities and differences
8   * Set theory of Discrete mathematics and PHP has many similarities
9   * Both represent data sets
10  Both hold a list of similar elements
11  We can operate on both by performing union, intersection etc
12  */
13
14  // consider two separate arrays
15
16  $arrayOne = [11, 12, 13];
17  $arrayTwo = [11, 12, 13, 14, 15];
18
19  // consider one universal array that contain elements of both arrays
20
21  $universalArray = [11, 12, 13, 14, 15, 16, 17, 18, 19, 20];
22
23  /*
24   * According to the set theory, the union occurs as
25   * $arrayOne + $arrayTwo
26   * the output omits the common value
27   * we can do the same using PHP
28   */
29
30  $unionOfTwoArrays = $arrayOne + $arrayTwo;
```

```php
echo "Union of two arrays : [" . implode(", ", $unionOfTwoArrays) . "]<br>";

/*
 * We can do the difference operation using the same technique
 * we can use the PHP default methods
 */

$differenceOfTwoArrays = array_diff($arrayTwo, $arrayOne);

echo "Difference of two arrays : [" . implode(", ", $differenceOfTwoArrays) . "]<br>\
";


/*
 * We can do the intersection operation using the same technique
 * it keeps the same elements
 * we can use the PHP default methods
 */

$intersectionOfTwoArrays = array_intersect($arrayOne, $arrayTwo);

echo "Intersection of two arrays : [" . implode(", ", $intersectionOfTwoArrays) . "]\
<br>";

/*
 * We can do the complement operation on two arrays
 * we can use the PHP default methods
 */

$arrayOneComplement = array_diff($universalArray, $arrayOne);

echo "Complement of arrayOne : [" . implode(", ", $arrayOneComplement) . "]<br>";

$arrayTwoComplement = array_diff($universalArray, $arrayTwo);

echo "Complement of arrayTwo : [" . implode(", ", $arrayTwoComplement) . "]<br>";
```

In the above code, we have done most common Set operations, such as Union, Differences, Intersection, and Complement.

```
// output of code 4.26

Union of two arrays : [11, 12, 13, 14, 15]
Difference of two arrays : [14, 15]
```

```
5 Intersection of two arrays : [11, 12, 13]
6 Complement of arrayOne : [14, 15, 16, 17, 18, 19, 20]
7 Complement of arrayTwo : [16, 17, 18, 19, 20]
```

We can use the language of set theory to define nearly all mathematical objects, as well as every kind of possible programming operations. The major reason behind that is the Set theory deals with a diverse collection of topics, ranging from the structure of the real number line to the study of the consistency of large cardinals. We will discuss those topics, in great detail, later.

After a brief display of Set theory in programming, we will switch over to Probability, another important concept of discrete mathematical operations. Just like the Set theoretical conceptions, the Probability concepts are also applied diversely into computer science and programming world.

Before dipping our toes into code, let us discuss what exactly probability means. Consider heads and tails. If you throw it up, there is 50-50 probability to either get heads or tails. But the equation changes when you throw a 'dice' or 'die' up in the air.

What is the probability of getting a '2' when you throw a dice? The favorable outcome is 1, as the dice has one '2'. On the contrary, the possible outcome is 6. Because there are 6 sides in a dice. Although a dice is a three dimensional object, we can write the 6 elements in a data set. To speak more frankly, we can create and initialize an array with the 6 integers and calculate all the probabilities.

The Probability theory is not limited to dice only, we can explore a range of huge data and calculate all types of probabilities.

Let us check the next code snippet.

```
1 // code 4.27
2 // Python 3.6
3
4 # we are to find the probability of finding an element in an array
5 # it depends on two factors
6
7 # Probability = number of favorable outcome / number of possible outcomes
8 # number of possible outcomes is the length of the array
9 # number of favourable outcome is the total number of the element in the list
10 # Probability = total number of the element present / size or length of the array.
11
12 # define the function to find the probability
13 def findTheProbability(theArray, theLenghtOfArray, theElement):
14     count = theArray.count(theElement)
15
16     # find probability up to 4 decimal places
17     return round(count / theLenghtOfArray, 4)
```

```
18
19 theArrayVariable = [22, 22, 22, 22, 22, 22, 22]
20 theElementToFind = 22
21 theLenghtOfTheArrayVariable = len(theArrayVariable)
22
23 print(findTheProbability(theArrayVariable,
theLenghtOfTheArrayVariable, theElementTo\
24 Find))
```

In the above code, you can guess what will be the outcome. Since every element of the array is the same, the probability is 100 percent.

```
1 // output of code 4.27
2
3 1.0
```

The Probability goes down extensively with the reduction in the numbers. When the total number of a particular integer reduces, and the number of other integers increases, the Probability plunges. Watch the next code snippet, where we have used the same code as above, but we have changed the elements of the array.

```
 1 // code 4.28
 2 // python 3.6
 3
 4 # we are to find the probability of finding an element in an array
 5 # it depends on two factors
 6
 7 # Probability = number of favorable outcome / number of possible outcomes
 8 # number of possible outcomes is the length of the array
 9 # number of favourable outcome is the total number of the element in the list
10 # Probability = total number of the element present / size or length of the array.
11
12 # define the function to find the probability
13 def findTheProbability(theArray, theLenghtOfArray, theElement):
14     count = theArray.count(theElement)
15
16     # find probability up to 4 decimal places
17     return round(count / theLenghtOfArray, 4)
18
19 theArrayVariable = [45, 22, 62, 72, 82, 92, 122]
20 theElementToFind = 22
21 theLenghtOfTheArrayVariable = len(theArrayVariable)
22
23 print(findTheProbability(theArrayVariable,
theLenghtOfTheArrayVariable, theElementTo\
24 Find))
```

Look at the output, the Probability dips drastically compared to the before code snippets.

```
1 // output of code 4.28
2 0.1429
```

While calculating the Probability, we have used the Python default class methods that makes our life simpler to calculate the Probability. In other languages, we are not that lucky. Take Java for instance, we need to build some function using control constructs to calculate the same Probability.

```java
1 // code 4.29
2 // Java
3
4 package fun.sanjibsinha.setprobability;
5
6 import java.util.Arrays;
7 public class ProbabilityAndArray {
8
9     static float totalNumberOfTheElement;
10    static float theProbability;
11
12    static float findTheProbableElementInArray(int[] theArray, int theLengthOfArray, \
13  int theElement){
14
15        for(int i = 0; i < theLengthOfArray; i ++){
16            if(theArray[i] == theElement){
17                totalNumberOfTheElement++;
18            }
19        }
20        theProbability = totalNumberOfTheElement / theLengthOfArray;
21        return theProbability;
22
23    }
24
25    public static void main(String[] args) {
26        int[] theArray = {25, 25, 25, 25, 25, 25};
27        int theElement = 25;
28        int lengthOfArray = theArray.length;
29        theProbability = findTheProbableElementInArray(theArray, lengthOfArray, theE\
30 lement);
31        System.out.println(theProbability);
32    }
33
34 }
```

Yet, that is interesting side of programming; we can explore many possibilities. We can find solutions to given set of a problem in many different ways.

In the above code, you can guess the outcome.

```
// output of code 4.29
1.0
```

Let us change the above code a little bit by rearranging the array elements, we will get a different outcome.

```java
// code 4.30
// Java

package fun.sanjibsinha.setprobability;

import java.util.Arrays;
public class ProbabilityAndArray {

    static float totalNumberOfTheElement;
    static float theProbability;

    static float findTheProbableElementInArray(int[] theArray, int theLengthOfArray,\
    int theElement){

        for(int i = 0; i < theLengthOfArray; i ++){
            if(theArray[i] == theElement){
                totalNumberOfTheElement++;
            }
        }
        theProbability = totalNumberOfTheElement / theLengthOfArray;
        return theProbability;

    }

    public static void main(String[] args) {
        int[] theArray = {255, 2523, 25, 725, 7825, 245};
        int theElement = 25;
        int lengthOfArray = theArray.length;
        theProbability = findTheProbableElementInArray(theArray, lengthOfArray, theE\
lement);
        System.out.println(theProbability);
    }

}
```

The Probability plunges drastically.

```
// output of code 4.30
0.16666667
```

The same code semantically changes when we write it in PHP 7. We can use some default class methods and try some other tricks, as well.

```php
// code 4.31
// PHP 7.3

<?php

/*
 * how much probability is there to find an element in a given array
 */

class ProbabilityClass {

    public function countNumberOfValuesInArray($theArray, $matchTheElement){
        $countNumbers = 0;
        foreach ($theArray as $key => $value){
            if ($value == $matchTheElement){
                $countNumbers++;
            }
        }
        return $countNumbers;
    }

}

$theProbable = new ProbabilityClass();

$theDice = [1, 2, 3, 4, 5, 6];
$theElement = 2;
$theLength = sizeof($theDice);
$totalNumbersOfValues = $theProbable->countNumberOfValuesInArray($theDice, $theEleme\
nt);
$theProbability = (floatval($totalNumbersOfValues / $theLength));
echo "The probability is: " . $theProbability;
```

We have tried to calculate the Probability of outcomes using the example of a dice, theoretically we have discussed it earlier.

You can watch the outcome.

```
// output of code 4.31
The probability is: 0.16666666666667
```

Now, just for fun, we can play around the same algorithm using a more object-oriented-programming approach. We have tried to rewrite the above code in a different way to get the same result.

```php
// code 4.32
// PHP 7.3

<?php

class Dice{

    public $sidesOfDice = [1, 2, 3, 4, 5, 6];

    // Probability = total number of the element present / size or length of the arr\
ay.
    public function throwDice($sidesOfDice, $totalSides) {
        $this->sidesOfDice = $sidesOfDice;
        $lengthOfDice = sizeof($sidesOfDice);
        $theProbability = $totalSides / $lengthOfDice;
        return $theProbability;
    }
}

class TotalSides{

    public function getSide($sidesOfDice, $theSide) {
        $count = 0;
        foreach ($sidesOfDice as $value) {
            if($value == $theSide){
                $count++;
            }
        }
        return $count;
    }
}

$numberOfSides = new TotalSides();
$theProbability = new Dice();
echo "The probability of getting 2 when you throw the dice is: " . $theProbability->\
throwDice($theProbability->sidesOfDice,
    $numberOfSides->getSide($theProbability->sidesOfDice, 2));
```

The possibilities are endless and the Probability is the same.

```
// output of code 4.32
The probability of getting 2 when you throw the dice is: 0.16666666666667
```

We have seen some connections between discrete mathematical conceptions and programming algorithm. We will see more. In the next section we will explore the relation between the algebraic data set conceptions, such as the Mean, Median and Mode and complex array algorithm.

Skewed Mean, Maximized Median

The idea that National per Capita Income of a country can be manipulated, is not not new to us now. Because it is calculated on the basis of the Mean of a Set of income-inputs, one can skew it quite easily. Keeping that fact in mind, we always think that the Median is more trustworthy.

In one sense, it is true. In another, it is false.

We may think of a natural algorithm where we take income of 10 people and make a set out of it. Of those ten people, eight persons have income less than 5 dollar. But, the other two earn more than 150 dollar. The definition of a Mean of a Set says us that calculating the average of those ten inputs give us an idea of the National per Capita Income.

As a result, the average income of the country becomes nearly 45 dollar; and, we know that the truth has been crucified. Where 80 percent of people earn less than 5 dollar, it cannot be true that the average income of the citizens of that country could be nearly 45 dollar.

Theoretically, choosing the Median is more trustworthy, because the middle value comes around 4 dollar, which is more close to truth value.

Our question is how trustworthy is the Median? Can it not be skewed or manipulated at all?

In this section we will turn over the myths to find out the real truth.

Usually, in a Set of positive integers where the numbers are increasing in an ascending order, it comes out that the Mean and the Median stays close.

Consider a Set of unique and distinct positive integers, like the following one.

In the above Set of values, the Mean and the Median is almost same. In a simple Java program we can check that.

```java
// code 4.33
// Java
// when the number of elements in the array is odd

package fun.sanjibsinha.arrayexamples;
import java.util.Arrays;

public class A23 {

    static double mean;
    static double median;

    // get the mean
    public static double getMean(int[] theArray, int num)
    {
```

```
16          int sum = 0;
17          for (int i = 0; i < num; i++)
18              sum += theArray[i];
19
20          mean = (double)sum / (double)num;
21          return mean;
22      }
23
24      // get the median
25      public static double getMedian(int[] theArray, int num)
26      {
27          //we know that median varies due to the odd and even numbers
28          // let us sort the array first
29          Arrays.sort(theArray);
30          // next check for the even case
31          if (num % 2 != 0){
32              median = (double)theArray[(num / 2)];
33              return median;
34          } else {
35              // check for the odd case
36              median = (double)(theArray[(num - 1) / 2] + theArray[num / 2]) / 2.0;
37              return median;
38          }
39      }
40
41      public static void main(String[] args) {
42          int theArray[] = { 1, 3, 4, 2, 6, 5, 7 };
43          int num = theArray.length;
44          System.out.println("Mean = " + getMean(theArray, num));
45          System.out.println("Median = " + getMedian(theArray, num));
46      }
47 }
```

Running the code will give us this output:

```
1 // output of code 4.33
2 Mean = 4.0
3 Median = 4.0
```

In the above code, the given array was like the following:

```
1 int theArray[] = { 1, 3, 4, 2, 6, 5, 7 };
```

First, we have sorted that array in an ascending order; second, we have counted the array or the set of integers as odd. For that reason, the Mean and the Median has become a whole number, not a fraction.

If the number of the values, which a set contains, is even, the outcome would be in fraction.

We can check that in another Java program.

```java
//code 4.34
// Java
// when the number of elements in the array is even

package fun.sanjibsinha.arrayexamples;
import java.util.Arrays;

public class A23 {

    static double mean;
    static double median;

    // get the mean
    public static double getMean(int[] theArray, int num)
    {
        int sum = 0;
        for (int i = 0; i < num; i++)
            sum += theArray[i];

        mean = (double)sum / (double)num;
        return mean;
    }

    // get the median
    public static double getMedian(int[] theArray, int num)
    {
        //we know that median varies due to the odd and even numbers
        // let us sort the array first
        Arrays.sort(theArray);
        // next check for the even case
        if (num % 2 != 0){
            median = (double)theArray[(num / 2)];
            return median;
        } else {
            // check for the odd case
            median = (double)(theArray[(num - 1) / 2] + theArray[num / 2]) / 2.0;
            return median;
        }
    }

    public static void main(String[] args) {
        int theArray[] = { 1, 3, 4, 2, 6, 5};
        int num = theArray.length;
        System.out.println("Mean = " + getMean(theArray, num));
        System.out.println("Median = " + getMedian(theArray, num));
    }
}
```

The outcome is expected, as we have been told.

```
1 // output of code 4.34
2 Mean = 3.5
3 Median = 3.5
```

Now, we can conclude one truth value from the above observation. If the values belonging to a Set is balanced and in an ascending order, there is no difference between the Mean and the Median.

Unfortunately, the reality bites and it does not come out like this.

Consider a situation where the majority of the values belonging to a Set is increasing in an ordered fashion up to a limit. After that, as it closes to the end, it suddenly behaves in an unordered fashion; the last two numbers are fairly bigger than the rest of the numbers. What will happen?

There will be a huge difference between the Mean and the Median.

In the beginning of this section, we were discussing about the nation's per capita income. We were told that we could not depend on the Mean. Right? We were also told that the Median is more trustworthy, in such cases.

True.

The next Java program will show you the same example that we were told in the beginning of this section.

```java
1 //code 4.35
2 // Java
3
4 package fun.sanjibsinha.arrayexamples;
5
6 import java.util.Arrays;
7
8 public class A23 {
9
10     static double mean;
11     static double median;
12
13     // get the mean
14     public static double getMean(int[] theArray, int num)
15     {
16         int sum = 0;
17         for (int i = 0; i < num; i++)
18             sum += theArray[i];
19
20         mean = (double)sum / (double)num;
21         return mean;
22     }
23
```

```
24      // get the median
25      public static double getMedian(int[] theArray, int num)
26      {
27          //we know that median varies due to the odd and even numbers
28          // let us sort the array first
29          Arrays.sort(theArray);
30          if (num % 2 != 0){
31              median = (double)theArray[(num / 2)];
32              return median;
33          } else {
34              median = (double)(theArray[(num - 1) / 2] + theArray[num / 2]) / 2.0;
35              return median;
36          }
37      }
38
39      public static void main(String[] args) {
40          int theArray[] = { 1, 3, 4, 2, 5, 4, 3, 5, 155, 265};
41          int num = theArray.length;
42          System.out.println("Mean or National Per Capita Income = " + getMean(theArra\
43 y, num));
44          System.out.println("Median = " + getMedian(theArray, num));
45          // the mean or national per capita income is skewed and shows us a wrong imp\
46 ression
47          // about a nation's per capita income, or average citizen's income
48          // here median is more accurate, as 80% of people earn less than or equal to\
49  5 dollar
50          // where the result shows 44.7 dollar
51      }
52 }
```

Watch the outcome, you will be amazed to find how different they are – the Mean and the Median. From this experience, we will tend to believe that we can have our confidence or faith in the Median.

```
1 // output of code 4.35
2 Mean = 44.7
3 Median = 4.0
```

In a country where 80 percent of people have less than or equal to 5 dollars income, calculating the nation's per capita income using the Median is more trustworthy.

At least the above program tells us so, isn't it?

To believe this as 'truth' or a 'proof of a concept', we need to cut into the Median. This guy 'Median' is not an easy guy. Apparently this fellow seems to be normal and we can think, OK, the guy Median is trustworthy.

In the series of finding the true nature of the Median, we need to start with a simple program.

```java
//code 4.36
// Java

package fun.sanjibsinha.arrayexamples;

import java.util.Arrays;

public class FindMedian {

    static double median;
    // get the median
    public static double getMedian(int[] theArray, int num){
        //we know that median varies due to the odd and even numbers
        // let us sort the array first
        Arrays.sort(theArray);
        // checking whether size is even
        if (num % 2 == 0){
            median = (double) (theArray[(num / 2) - 1] + theArray[num / 2]) / 2;
            return median;
        } else{
            // else the size is odd
            median = (double) theArray[num / 2];
            return median;
        }
    }

    public static void main(String[] args) {
        int theArray[] = {3, 2, 3, 4, 2};
        int num = theArray.length + 3;
        System.out.println();
        System.out.println("Median = " + getMedian(theArray, num));
        // 2 2 3 3 4 -> 4 4 4
    }
}
```

As an input array or set of values we have taken an unordered numbers. We know that the value of the Median varies according to the length of the array. If the length is even, we get a Median value. If it is odd, then the Median value changes.

Therefore, we have sorted our array and check it whether that array length is even or odd.

After the sorting has been done, the larger values go the right half section of the array. In the above array, the largest value was 4, so it goes to the far right corner of the array.

Now, in the runtime, we have increased the length of the array by 3 and we call the function to find the Median. What happens? Watch the outcome.

```
1 // output of code 4.36
2 Median = 3.5
```

The Median has become larger than the usual one. It has not increased in a large way, but, we have been able to skew the Median value.

Why?

If you run the code without increasing the length of the array, and calling the function to find the Median, the Median will come out as 3. On the contrary, the Median value has become 3.5.

We are nearing to a bitter truth, the Median is not trustworthy anymore. We can skew it as we have done the same thing to the Mean before.

One thing is certain, we cannot add any number to the length of the array. It depends on the original array length. If the array length is 5, then the number we add, should be less than 5. That is, up to 4 we can add. If it crosses the limit, the Median value goes out of range. Watch the next code:

```java
1 //code 4.37
2 // Java
3
4 package fun.sanjibsinha.arrayexamples;
5
6 import java.util.Arrays;
7
8 public class FindMedian {
9
10     static double median;
11     // get the median
12     public static double getMedian(int[] theArray, int num){
13         //we know that median varies due to the odd and even numbers
14         // let us sort the array first
15         Arrays.sort(theArray);
16         // checking whether size is even
17         if (num % 2 == 0){
18             median = (double) (theArray[(num / 2) - 1] + theArray[num / 2]) / 2;
19             return median;
20         } else{
21             // else the size is odd
22             median = (double) theArray[num / 2];
23             return median;
```

```
24          }
25      }
26
27      public static void main(String[] args) {
28          int theArray[] = {3, 2, 3, 4, 2};
29          int num = theArray.length + 5;
30          System.out.println();
31          System.out.println("Median = " + getMedian(theArray, num));
32          // 2 2 3 3 4 -> 4 4 4
33          // when 5 is added, the array length becomes 10
34          // 2 2 3 3 4 -> 4 4 4 4 4
35      }
36 }
```

Running the code gives us error like the following.

```
1 // output of code 4.37
2 Exception in thread "main" java.lang.ArrayIndexOutOfBoundsException: Index 5 out of \
3 bounds for length 5
4     at fun.sanjibsinha.arrayexamples.FindMedian.getMedian(FindMedian.java:15)
5     at fun.sanjibsinha.arrayexamples.FindMedian.main(FindMedian.java:28)
```

While we skew the Median value we should keep that simple mathematics in our mind.

In the next code, it is more obvious that maximizing the value of the Median is fairly simple. In usual scenario, in the following code, the Median should come out as 3; instead, we have skewed it and made it 4.

```
1 //code 4.38
2 // Java
3
4 package fun.sanjibsinha.arrayexamples;
5
6 import java.util.Arrays;
7
8 public class MaximizingMedian {
9
10      static double median;
11
12      static double getMaxMedian(int[] theArray, int lengthOfArray, int addElement){
13          int size = lengthOfArray + addElement;
14          // sort the array first
15          Arrays.sort(theArray);
16
17          // checking whether size is even
18          if (size % 2 == 0){
```

```java
19              median = (double) (theArray[(size / 2) - 1] +
theArray[size / 2]) / 2;
20              return median;
21          } else{
22              // else the size is odd
23              median = theArray[size / 2];
24              return median;
25          }
26      }
27      public static void main(String[] args) {
28          int[] theArray = {3, 2, 3, 4, 2};
29          int lengthOfArray = theArray.length;
30          int addElement = 4;
31          System.out.print("We can add up to 4 elements to maximize the Median: "
32                  + (int)getMaxMedian(theArray, lengthOfArray, addElement));
33          System.out.println();
34      }
35 }
```

To maximize the Median value we have introduced a function in the above code, where the function fellow takes three parameters; one of them is the variable 'addElement'. We can declare how many integers we want to add with the length of the array to maximize the Median.

Here is the output:

```
1 // output of code 4.38
2 We can add up to 4 elements to maximize the Median: 4
```

We have mentioned that we can add up to 4 elements to maximize the Median, else, it will give us the same error we have faced before.

```java
1 //code 4.39
2 // Java
3
4 package fun.sanjibsinha.arrayexamples;
5
6 import java.util.Arrays;
7
8 public class MaximizingMedian {
9
10     static double median;
11
12     static double getMaxMedian(int[] theArray, int lengthOfArray, int addElement){
13         int size = lengthOfArray + addElement;
14         // sort the array first
15         Arrays.sort(theArray);
16
```

```
17          // checking whether size is even
18          if (size % 2 == 0){
19              median = (double) (theArray[(size / 2) - 1] +
theArray[size / 2]) / 2;
20              return median;
21          } else{
22              // else the size is odd
23              median = theArray[size / 2];
24              return median;
25          }
26      }
27      public static void main(String[] args) {
28          int[] theArray = {3, 2, 3, 4, 2};
29          int lengthOfArray = theArray.length;
30          int addElement = 5;
31          System.out.print("We can add up to 4 elements to maximize the Median: "
32                  + (int)getMaxMedian(theArray, lengthOfArray, addElement));
33          System.out.println();
34      }
35 }
```

We have added 5 elements and we have got the error, same as before.

```
1 // output of code 4.39
2 Exception in thread "main" java.lang.ArrayIndexOutOfBoundsException: Index 5 out of \
3 bounds for length 5
4     at fun.sanjibsinha.arrayexamples.MaximizingMedian.getMaxMedian(MaximizingMedian.\
5 java:16)
6     at fun.sanjibsinha.arrayexamples.MaximizingMedian.main(MaximizingMedian.java:29)
```

The only way to solve this problem is to increase the array elements. When the array length gets larger, we can add more elements to that length and skew the Median size.

The next code tells us the same story.

```
1 //code 4.40
2 // Java
3
4 package fun.sanjibsinha.arrayexamples;
5
6 import java.util.Arrays;
7
8 public class MaximizingMedian {
```

```java
 9
10      static double median;
11
12      static double getMaxMedian(int[] theArray, int lengthOfArray, int addElement){
13          int size = lengthOfArray + addElement;
14          // sort the array first
15          Arrays.sort(theArray);
16
17          // checking whether size is even
18          if (size % 2 == 0){
19              median = (double) (theArray[(size / 2) - 1] + theArray[size / 2]) / 2;
20              return median;
21          } else{
22              // else the size is odd
23              median = theArray[size / 2];
24              return median;
25          }
26      }
27      public static void main(String[] args) {
28          int[] theArray = {3, 2, 3, 4, 2, 4, 5};
29          int lengthOfArray = theArray.length;
30          // we cannot add 5 elements when the number of the array elements is 5
31          // becuase it will give us error as it goes beyond index bound
32          // however we can tackle this problem by increasing the array elements
33          // now we can add up to 6 elements
34          int addElement = 6;
35          System.out.print("We can add up to 6 elements to maximize the Median: "
36                  + (int)getMaxMedian(theArray, lengthOfArray, addElement));
37          System.out.println();
38      }
39 }
```

We have increased the array length adding more elements and we can maximize the Median value more than before.

```
1 // output of code 4.40
2 We can add up to 6 elements to maximize the Median: 5
```

The real fun begins if in an ordered collection of integers, we add only one value that is much bigger than the rest of the elements. Suddenly, the Median becomes much bigger than we have ever imagined.

Remember, with only one bigger value we can skew the Median, and make it much larger.

```java
//code 4.41
// Python 3.6

package fun.sanjibsinha.arrayexamples;

import java.util.Arrays;

public class MaximizingMedian {

    static double median;

    static double getMaxMedian(int[] theArray, int lengthOfArray, int addElement){
        int size = lengthOfArray + addElement;
        // sort the array first
        Arrays.sort(theArray);

        // checking whether size is even
        if (size % 2 == 0){
            median = (double) (theArray[(size / 2) - 1] + theArray[size / 2]) / 2;
            return median;
        } else{
            // else the size is odd
            median = theArray[size / 2];
            return median;
        }
    }
    public static void main(String[] args) {
        int[] theArray = {3, 2, 3, 4, 2, 4, 41};
        int lengthOfArray = theArray.length;
        // we cannot add 5 elements when the number of the array elements is 5
        // becuase it will give us error as it goes beyond index bound
        // however we can tackle this problem by increasing the array elements
        // now we can add up to 6 elements
        int addElement = 6;
        System.out.print("We can add up to 6 elements to maximize the Median: "
                + (int)getMaxMedian(theArray, lengthOfArray, addElement));
        System.out.println();
    }
}
```

In normal circumstance, in the above code, the Median should have been 4. You can find that Median value without any element to its length.

However, in reality, we have just added 6 elements to artificially increase the length and is able to make the Median 41.

```
1 // output of code 4.41
2 We can add up to 6 elements to maximize the Median: 41
```

We can conclude one bitter truth. The Median is not as trustworthy as had believed before.

Isn't it?

In the next section we will cut into more complex algorithm involving array.

Complex Array Algorithm

Before starting this section, let us know that we are going to use a new programming language, called Dart. It is new compared to other programming languages, such as C, C++, PHP, Java, C#, and Python; we have used them before in this book. However, we are going to use Dart, for the first time.

Readers, who have not used Dart before, can stay calm. Dart is a language with which we can build mobile apps, as well as web applications; we can also do server side programming, etc. Dart has been created by Google, therefore, we can conclude that future of Dart is not bleak. Moreover, it has many similarities with Java, and in some cases with Python, so Java or Python programmers will adopt Dart very quickly.

We are going to use Dart to show another thing. What we can do with C, C++, PHP, Java, or Python, we can do with Dart. As a result, we will be introduced to a new general purpose language; that is a benefit.

We will also see one more thing. As any language gets updated and passes into a more better condition gradually, it starts incorporating more features. They are useful, as long as algorithm is concerned. The higher the language is, it comes up with more in-built features that shorten our algorithm, sequence of steps, make developer's life easy.

We can code more in short time.

To reverse an array, we need to write around thirty lines of code, in usual cases. Dart can do that in one line; not only that, Dart can take that array and change it to any other data structure objects, like Set or Map.

Summing up, this book is not for learning Dart, so let us forget this part temporarily, and try to understand how we can understand various complex array algorithm with the help of Dart language. In between we will also use PHP for one example; just for a change.

It is true, array has many limitations; but, it has many advantages, too. That memory can be allocated dynamically in an array, is one of the biggest advantages. This feature of array saves the memory of the system. When memory allocation is not dynamic, the array stores the data in contiguous memory locations. What data type you are using? That determines the amount of storage required. Granted, manipulations of an array may become complex, if you think from the perspective of algorithm; but, an array requires memory space only for the values, the start address and its length. Compare it to Linked list; a Linked List always needs a pointer for every value that is stuck in. It eats up memory for every address, and acquires extra memory for the insertion of data. The Hash table also needs extra allocation of memory.

It is true that many types of data structures need more memory than array, even so, in some cases, we need data structures. We will see those features in the next section. The first program in Dart will help us to find the largest element in an array, after that it finds the second largest element, and, after that, it finds the third largest element. The algorithm does not stop there. It arranges those first, second and the third largest elements in descending order and gives the output.

```
1  //code 4.42
2  // Dart
3
4  import 'dart:math';
5  void main(){
6
7  List<int> myNumbers = List(7);
8  myNumbers[0] = 100;
9  myNumbers[1] = 2;
10 myNumbers[2] = 23;
11 myNumbers[3] = 4;
12 myNumbers[4] = 15;
13 myNumbers[5] = 155;
14 myNumbers[6] = 1;
15 int lengthOfArray = myNumbers.length;
16 DisplayLargestInDescendingOrder(myNumbers, lengthOfArray);
17
18 }
19
20 void DisplayLargestInDescendingOrder(List<int> myNumbers, int lengthOfArray){
21 int first = 0;
22 int second = 0;
23 int third = 0;
24
25 if(((first.isInfinite != false) && (second.isInfinite != false)) && third.isInfinite\
26    != false){
27     print("Three largest elements in descending order: $first, $second and $third");
```

```
28 } else {
29     for(int i = 0; i < myNumbers.length; i++){
30     if(myNumbers[i] > first){
31         third = second;
32         second = first;
33         first = myNumbers[i];
34     }
35     else if(myNumbers[i] > second){
36         third = second;
37         second = myNumbers[i];
38     }
39     else if(myNumbers[i] > third){
40         third = myNumbers[i];
41     }
42     }
43     print("Three largest elements in descending order: $first, $second and $third");
44 }
45 }
```

To run the above program, we have to import the Dart math libraries.

```
1 // output of code 4.42
2 Three largest elements in descending order: 155, 100 and 23
```

Rotating an array clockwise, is one of the most common and complex algorithm involving an array. Actually, it rotates the array to the left by the number of elements. Suppose you have an array like this:

```
1 {1, 2, 3}
```

Now, we will rotate the above array to the left or clockwise by one element. Then it becomes like the following array:

```
1 {2, 3, 1}
```

If we rotate it by 2 elements, it becomes:

```
1 {3, 1, 2}
```

Rotating 3 elements will give us this:

```
1 {1, 2, 3}
```

From the above algorithm, we get a common pattern that we see every day. Yes, we are thinking about a clock. A clock has 12 elements. We will get to that point in a moment. Before that, we need to understand this rotational algorithm in a more efficient way. The next code snippet will give you a better idea about it.

```
1 //code 4.43
2 // Dart
3
```

```
4  void main(){
5  List<int> myNumbers = List(7);
6  myNumbers[0] = 100;
7  myNumbers[1] = 2;
8  myNumbers[2] = 23;
9  myNumbers[3] = 4;
10 myNumbers[4] = 15;
11 myNumbers[5] = 155;
12 myNumbers[6] = 1;
13 int lengthOfArray = myNumbers.length;
14 print("The array before left rotation by two elements: ${myNumbers}");
15 print("The array after rotation.");
16 rotateArrayLeft(myNumbers, 2, lengthOfArray);
17 displayArray(myNumbers, lengthOfArray);
18 }
19
20 void rotateArrayLeft(List<int> myArray, int rotatingNumbers, int arrayLength){
21 for(int i = 0; i < rotatingNumbers; i++){
22      rotateLeftByOne(myArray, arrayLength);
23 }
24 }
25
26 void rotateLeftByOne(List<int> myArray, int arrayLength){
27 int temp = myArray[0], i;
28 for (i = 0; i < arrayLength - 1; i++){
29     myArray[i] = myArray[i + 1];
30 }
31 myArray[i] = temp;
32 }
33
34 void displayArray(List<int> myArray, int arrayLength){
35 for(int i = 0; i < arrayLength; i++){
36     print(myArray[i]);
37 }
38 }
```

Let us first see the output first, then we will try to understand the algorithm.

```
1 // output of code 4.43
2 The array before left rotation by two elements: [100, 2, 23, 4, 15, 155, 1]
3 The array after rotation.
4 23
5 4
6 15
7 155
8 1
```

```
9 100
10 2
```

We have to create a function that will take two inputs – the array and the length of the array. It will give us output of a temporary value by shifting one element. After that we can call that function inside another function that takes three inputs – the array, the length of array, and the number of elements you want to shift to the left. You can dynamically create any length of array and test the above code in any programming language. It will give us the same result.

Based on the same algorithm, we can now create a digital clock in PHP.

```php
1  //code 4.44
2  // PHP
3
4
5
6  class ClockClass {
7
8      public function clockwiseRotatebyOne(&$theDigitalClock, $numberOfHours) {
9          $temp = $theDigitalClock[0];
10         for ($i = 0; $i < $numberOfHours - 1; $i++){
11             $theDigitalClock[$i] = $theDigitalClock[$i + 1];
12         }
13         $theDigitalClock[$i] = $temp;
14     }
15
16
17     public function clockwiseRotate(&$theDigitalClock, $afterThreeHours, $numberOfHo\
18 urs) {
19         for ($i = 0; $i < $afterThreeHours; $i++){
20             $this->clockwiseRotatebyOne($theDigitalClock, $numberOfHours);
21         }
22     }
23
24 /* utility function to print
25 an array */
26     public function displayHour(&$theDigitalClock, $numberOfHours) {
27         for ($i = 0; $i < $numberOfHours; $i++){
28             if($i == 0){
29                 echo "<strong>" . $theDigitalClock[$i] . "</strong>";
30             } else {
31                 echo " " . $theDigitalClock[$i] . " ";
32             }
33         }
34     }
```

```
35 }
36
37 $theDigitalClock = array( 12, 1, 2, 3, 4, 5, 6, 7, 8, 9, 10, 11 );
38 $numberOfHours = sizeof($theDigitalClock);
39 $afterFewHours = 4;
40
41 echo 'The number of hours shown on the clock before it starts :';
42 echo '<pre>';
43 print_r($theDigitalClock);
44 echo '</pre>';
45 echo '<br>';
46
47 $clock = new ClockClass();
48 echo "After {$afterFewHours} hours the clock shows the exact time at the starting po\
49 int : ";
50 echo '<br>';
51 echo "It rotates clockwise shifting the first {$afterFewHours} elements at the last \
52 : ";
53 echo '<br>';
54 echo '<br>';
55 $clock->clockwiseRotate($theDigitalClock, $afterFewHours, $numberOfHours);
56 $clock->displayHour($theDigitalClock, $numberOfHours);
```

While we run the code, first it gives us the hours arranged just like any analog clock. Although the analog clock is an example of discrete mathematical conceptions, it represents contiguous mathematical conceptions that run continuously.

On the other hand the digital clock is the correct example of discrete mathematics. Here it works as a digital clock. As you enter the amount of hours, it gives us the output accordingly.

```
1  // output of code 4.44
2  The number of hours shown on the clock before it starts :
3
4  Array
5  (
6      [0] => 12
7      [1] => 1
8      [2] => 2
9      [3] => 3
10     [4] => 4
11     [5] => 5
12     [6] => 6
13     [7] => 7
14     [8] => 8
15     [9] => 9
16     [10] => 10
```

```
17        [11] => 11
18 )
19
20
21 After 4 hours the clock shows the exact time at the starting point :
22 It rotates clockwise shifting the first 4 elements at the last :
23
24 4 5 6 7 8 9 10 11 12 1 2 3
```

Run the code locally, you will find the starting element in bold point.

According to the Set theory, we know how 'Union' of two sets work. If there is no repeated values, then they join accordingly. We can imagine a situation where, we can add two Sets A and B like this:

```
1 {1, 2} Union {3, 4}
```

It will produce a third Set C like this:

```
1 {1, 2, 3, 4}
```

We can consider them as arrays also. Two arrays, A and B. Now, mathematically we can also do some Union operations on those Sets in reverse order. It means, just as we have added A and B, we can also add B and A. And that Union yields this result:

```
1 {3, 4, 1, 2}
```

Our next algorithm will be to find how we can change this reversing process in a different way. We are going to change (A Union B) to (B Union A) using Dart programming language.

Certainly, there are different solutions available. We follow the next algorithm.

```
1  //code 4.45
2  //Dart
3
4  void main(){
5
6  List<int> arrayOne = List(2);
7  arrayOne[0] = 1;
8  arrayOne[1] = 2;
9
10 List<int> arrayTwo = List(2);
11 arrayTwo[0] = 3;
12 arrayTwo[1] = 4;
13
14 /*
15 arrayOne Union arrayTwo gives us : 1, 2, 3, 4
16 suppose we call it arrayThree
17 from arrayThree we want arrayTwo Union arrayOne, which gives us : 3, 4, 1, 2
```

```
there are different solutions
we can rotate arrayThree by 2 elements to get the same result
we can also follow the following algorithm
*/

List<int> arrayThree = List(4);
arrayThree[0] = 1;
arrayThree[1] = 2;
arrayThree[2] = 3;
arrayThree[3] = 4;

print("The arrayThree is the union of arrayOne and arrayTwo and the output is : ${ar\
rayThree.toString()}");

int num = arrayThree.length;
int element = 2;
element = element % num;
print("We are going to use reversal algorithm, so that arrayThree becomes "
    "the union of arrayTwo and arrayOne.");
print("The new output is : ");
rotatingLeft(arrayThree, element);
displayReversedArray(arrayThree);

}

void reversingTheArray(List<int> arrayThree, int start, int end){
while(start < end){
    int temp = arrayThree[start];
    arrayThree[start] = arrayThree[end];
    arrayThree[end] = temp;
    start += 1;
    end = end -1;
}
}

void rotatingLeft(List<int> arrayThree, int element){
int num = arrayThree.length;
if(element != 0){
    reversingTheArray(arrayThree, 0, (element - 1));
    reversingTheArray(arrayThree, element, (num - 1));
    reversingTheArray(arrayThree, 0, (num - 1));
} else {
    print("Wrong input");
}
}

void displayReversedArray(List<int> arrayThree){
for(int element in arrayThree){
```

```
66      print(element);
67 }
68 }
```

Let us read the comments inside our code. We have clarified our algorithm there.

```
1 // output of code 4.45
2 The arrayThree is the union of arrayOne and arrayTwo and the output
is : [1, 2, 3, 4]
3 We are going to use reversal algorithm, so that arrayThree becomes
the union of arra\
4 yTwo and arrayOne.
5 The new output is :
6 3
7 4
8 1
9 2
```

As we have seen before, there are several solutions available. We just need only 12 lines of code to rotate any array clockwise by one element. The next code snippet will show you how we can do that.

```
 1 //code 4.46
 2 //Dart
 3
 4 void main(){
 5
 6 List<int> anArray = List(4);
 7 anArray[0] = 1;
 8 anArray[1] = 2;
 9 anArray[2] = 3;
10 anArray[3] = 4;
11 print("The array before rotating by one element.");
12 for(int element in anArray){
13      print(element);
14 }
15 print("Rotating the array clockwise just by one element.");
16 justRotate(anArray);
17
18 }
19
20 void justRotate(List<int> someArray){
21 int x;
22 int i;
23 x = someArray.length;
24 for(i = (someArray.length - 1); i > 0; i--){
25      someArray[i] = someArray[i - 1];
26 }
27 someArray[0] = x;
28 for(int element in someArray){
```

```
29      print(element);
30 }
31 }
```

The outcome is quite expected. Rotate the above array clockwise just by one element, and it plucks off the last element from the end and places it at the starting point.

```
 1 // output of code 4.46
 2 The array before rotating by one element.
 3 1
 4 2
 5 3
 6 4
 7 Rotating the array clockwise just by one element.
 8 4
 9 1
10 2
11 3
```

In this section, we have seen many array algorithm, and hopefully those make enough sense to go ahead for more. For us, in the next section, the data structures are awaiting.

Before going to data structures, we should remember one key point – they are not sequential as an array. It has advantages and disadvantages. While we cut into data structures, we will try to use the same algorithm to understand which one is more preferable contextually. No other data structure is able to save memory like array. That it quite evident. However, there are other advantages;and, we will learn them in the coming sections.

I write regularly on Algorithm and Data Structure in

5. Data Structures: Abstractions and Implementation

As we have said in the beginning of the book, Data Structures are the one of the most fundamental and essential building blocks of Computer Science. Any Data Structure can be divided in two distinct parts – Abstract Data Types (ADT) and Implementation. As we progress, we will have elaborate discussion on these features; so, you need not worry at the beginning of this chapter.

We have seen many examples of Array, which is the first step to understand Data Structure. Therefore, we already know that Data Structures are basically different types of manners through which we sort, organize, insert, update, remove or display our data.

Sorting and organizing data in an efficient manner plays a very big role in constructing our data structure. Besides, we need to remember one key aspect of computation; that is, how much time the program takes, and how much memory or space it acquires.

In this part Algorithm plays a vital role. Efficient Algorithm to handle Data Structure is always needed. In this chapter, we also look at that part – time complexity, and memory allocation.

Data Structure, as a whole, is a very big topic and, moreover, every programming language has their own way to use the basic concepts of Data Structure. We will limit our main discussion to C, C++ and Java; although, in many occasions we will talk about Python, Dart, PHP and C#, as well.

To give you an idea about how the whole concepts of the complex entity like Data Structures are constructed, we should look into the Collection Interface first. In Java, the Collection Interface is divided into many branches of sub-interfaces, they are – BeanContext, BeanContextServices, BlockingDeque, BlockingQueue, Deque, List, NavigableSet, Queue, Set, SortedSet, TransferQueue. Let us first talk about the List Interface. AbstractList class implements the List Interface. Next, three more classes – ArrayList, Vector, and AbstractSequentialList classes extends the AbstractList class. Finally the LinkedList class extends the properties and methods of AbstractSequentialList class. However, this list is incomplete.

Actually, there are many implementing classes; they are - AbstractCollection, AbstractList, AbstractQueue, AbstractSequentialList, AbstractSet, ArrayBlockingQueue, ArrayDeque, ArrayList, AttributeList, BeanContextServicesSupport, BeanContextSupport, ConcurrentLinkedDeque, ConcurrentLinkedQueue, ConcurrentSkipListSet, CopyOnWriteArrayList, CopyOnWriteArraySet, DelayQueue, EnumSet, HashSet, JobStateReasons, LinkedBlockingDeque, LinkedBlockingQueue, LinkedHashSet, LinkedList, LinkedTransferQueue, PriorityBlockingQueue, PriorityQueue, RoleList, RoleUnresolvedList, Stack, SynchronousQueue, TreeSet, and Vector.

And this 'Collection' interface has a super-interface – Iterable.

As you see, the list is quite long; understandably, we are not going to cover all these things in a chapter. Maybe, in a different book we can take a more detail look at those interfaces and implementing classes.

In this chapter we will look into the core Collection interface and its implementations that include Set, SortedSet, List, Queue, Deque, Map and SortedMap. Core collection interfaces are the foundation of the Java Collections Framework.

In C or C++, it is thought differently. Other languages have their own constructs.

Before discussing Data Structures, we must have some basic knowledge about how objects act upon one another. How different objects pass messages between themselves. We will also try to manually insert data into a Linked List. This is a List that is linked to each other.

How objects work with each other

We are going to use four, easy-to-understand sample Dart program to see how one object works with other objects. Let us talk about the first program. Suppose each person acquires a mobile application that helps them to enter their tasks. They can categorize the tasks and according to the necessity, they finish their tasks.

To accomplish such simple task, we need to have two classes – Person and the Mobile Application class. Because, one person object acquires one application object, we need an application object inside the Person class. The application object has a blueprint or class that defines what it can do and what it cannot do.

Once a person acquires an application object, she can start doing everything with that object that has been defined in the Mobile Application class.

```
1  //cdoe 5.1
2  //Dart
3
4  void main(){
5
6  var appOne = AppToDo("AppToDo One");
7  var appTwo = AppToDo("AppToDo Two");
8  var john = Person("John");
9  var mac = Person("Mac");
10 john.taskToDo = appOne;
11 mac.taskToDo = appTwo;
12 print("${john.name} gets ${john.taskToDo.name}.");
13 print("${mac.name} gets ${mac.taskToDo.name}");
14 /*
15 John gets AppToDo One.
16 Mac gets AppToDo Two
17 */
18 print("${john.name} is entering tasks.");
19 john.taskToDo.task = "Going to market to get some vegetables";
20 john.taskToDo.type = "Marketing";
21 john.taskToDo.enterTask();
22 // we presume that every task is important
23 john.getTaskFinished(appOne);
24 print("${mac.name} is entering tasks.");
25 mac.taskToDo.task = "Going out with friends";
26 mac.taskToDo.type = "Outing";
27 mac.taskToDo.enterTask();
28 // in some cases, the task may not be so important
29 appTwo.isImportant = false;
30 mac.getTaskFinished(appTwo);
31 }
32
33 class AppToDo{
34
35 String name;
```

```
36 String task;
37 String type;
38 bool isImportant = true;
39
40 AppToDo(String name){
41     this.name = name;
42 }
43
44 void enterTask(){
45     print("I want to finish this task - ${task}. It belongs to this type - ${type}."\
46 );
47 }
48 }
49
50 class Person{
51 String name;
52 AppToDo taskToDo;
53
54 Person(String name){
55     this.name = name;
56 }
57
58 void getTaskFinished(AppToDo taskToDo){
59     this.taskToDo = taskToDo;
60     if(taskToDo.isImportant){
61     print("This task - ${taskToDo.task} is important, and need to be finished.");
62     } else {
63     print("It can be avoided, it is not so important");
64     }
65 }
66 }
```

I hope the explanation makes sense. Each person object is a separate entity, and each application object is also separate entity. However, every separate object has some commonness, and that commonness has been defined in the class.

We can expect the output, now.

```
1 //output of code 5.1
2 John gets AppToDo One.
3 Mac gets AppToDo Two
4 John is entering tasks.
5 I want to finish this task - Going to market to get some vegetables. It belongs to t\
6 his type - Marketing.
7 This task - Going to market to get some vegetables is important, and need to be fini\
8 shed.
```

```
9 Mac is entering tasks.
10 I want to finish this task - Going out with friends. It belongs to this type - Outin\
11 g.
12 It can be avoided, it is not so important
```

The same principle can be adopted for two separate persons. The next code snippet manifests that principle.

```
1 //code 5.2
2 //Dart
3
4 void main(){
5 var alisa = Person("Alica");
6 var john = Person("John");
7
8 alisa.isFollowing(john);
9 john.isNotFollowing(alisa);
10 }
11
12 class Person{
13 String name;
14 Person friend;
15 Person(String name){
16     this.name = name;
17 }
18 void isFollowing(Person friend){
19     this.friend = friend;
20     print("${name} is following ${friend.name}");
21 }
22 void isNotFollowing(Person friend){
23     this.friend = friend;
24     print("${name} is not following back ${friend.name}");
25 }
26 }
```

Here goes the output:

```
1 //output of code 5.2
2 Alica is following John
3 John is not following back Alica
```

We can make the above code more robust and complex. However, we are trying to understand how objects work, just like other primitive data types. There is no doubt that an object is always more powerful than any single primitive data type. If you have some idea about object-oriented-programming, you know that an object encapsulates many dynamic features. An object's power depends solely on the principle that how we have defined that object in its class.

Now, we are more curious about how we can implement this newly acquired knowledge to manipulate a simple Data Structure.

Suppose, we want to insert data into a list, and show them also at the same time. Without taking any help from array, can we do that? Can we write classes that will define such objects that will work with each other to manipulate data in a data structure?

Let us see the next code.

```
1 //code 5.3
2 //Dart
3
4 void main(){
5
6 int countNodes(NodeClass start){
7     int count = 0;
8     NodeClass currentPosiion = start;
9     while(currentPosiion.next != null){
10        currentPosiion = currentPosiion.next;
11        count = count + 1;
12    }
13    return count;
14 }
15
16 var nodeOne = NodeClass(10);
17 print("The value of node 1 is - ${nodeOne.data} and the count is ${countNodes(nodeOn\
18 e)}");
19 var nodeTwo = NodeClass(12);
20 nodeOne.next = nodeTwo;
21 print("The value of node 2 is - ${nodeTwo.data} and the count is ${countNodes(nodeOn\
22 e)}");
23 var nodeThree = NodeClass(122);
24 nodeTwo.next = nodeThree;
25 print("The value of node 3 is - ${nodeThree.data} and the count is ${countNodes(node\
26 One)}");
27 var nodeFour = NodeClass(1122);
28 nodeThree.next = nodeFour;
29 print("The value of node 4 is - ${nodeFour.data} and the count is ${countNodes(nodeO\
30 ne)}");
31 var nodeFive = NodeClass(1226);
32 nodeFour.next = nodeFive;
33 print("The value of node 5 is - ${nodeFive.data} and the count is ${countNodes(nodeO\
34 ne)}");
35 }
```

```
36
37 class NodeClass{
38 int data;
39 NodeClass next;
40 NodeClass(int data){
41     this.data = data;
42 }
43 }
```

We have created a Node Class and with the help of node object we have successfully inserted data into that structure.

```
1 //output of code 5.3
2 The value of node 1 is - 10 and the count is 0
3 The value of node 2 is - 12 and the count is 1
4 The value of node 3 is - 122 and the count is 2
5 The value of node 4 is - 1122 and the count is 3
6 The value of node 5 is - 1226 and the count is 4
```

In the above code, we have inserted data manually. Can we create two separate objects that will manage and show the data?

Yes, we can try to do that in the next program.

```
 1 //code 5.4
 2 //Dart
 3
 4 void main(){
 5
 6 var list = LinkingList();
 7 list.insertData(10);
 8 list.showData();
 9 list.insertData(100);
10 list.insertData(1000);
11 list.insertData(10000);
12 list.insertData(100000);
13 list.insertData(1000000);
14 list.insertData(10000000);
15 list.insertData(100000000);
16 }
17
18 class NodeClass{
19 int data;
20 NodeClass next;
21 }
22
23 class LinkingList{
24 /*
25 this class will insert data into the lists
26 and show the data as well
27 */
```

```
28 /*
29 if our list is empty, the starting point of node, we will call it head, is null
30 however, if the list has at least one value the head is not null
31 */
32 NodeClass head;
33
34 void insertData(int data){
35     var node = NodeClass();
36     node.data = data;
37     // at the beginning
38     node.next = head;
39     if(head == null){
40     head = node;
41     } else {
42     NodeClass currentPosition = head;
43     while(currentPosition.next != null){
44         currentPosition.next = node;
45     }
46     // we take the last value added and print it out
47     print("One value is added to the list. ${node.data}");
48     }
49 }
50 void showData(){
51     NodeClass node = head;
52     // this method will work when the first value is added
53     if(head == null){
54     print("No value has been added in the list. It is empty.");
55     } else {
56     print("One value is added to the list: ${node.data}");
57     }
58 }
59 }
```

Here goes the output, where the node object 'list' has successfully inserted data, and finally, gives us a display of the inserted data.

```
1 //output of code 5.4
2 One value is added to the list: 10
3 One value is added to the list. 100
4 One value is added to the list. 1000
5 One value is added to the list. 10000
6 One value is added to the list. 100000
7 One value is added to the list. 1000000
8 One value is added to the list. 10000000
9 One value is added to the list. 100000000
```

We have tried to understand how in object-oriented-programming languages like C++, Java, or Dart, these Collection interface is being implemented by the implementing classes. Now, we will understand how the core libraries and functions of the Data Structure classes and objects work together.

More Algorithm and Time Complexity

This section will be short. We won't take much time to study a few code snippets, after that we will try to understand how much time it takes to run the program.

At the same time, we will also try to understand the underlying logic, and algorithm.

By this time we are quite familiar with the terms like algorithm and time complexity. We know that our algorithm should be efficient enough to reduce the time to run the code.

We should also remember that, any problem can have many solutions; we need to find the best algorithm.

Okay, let us try to some code in Dart. In the first case, we will try to find the factors of a positive integer. As we know, a positive integer, like 4, has three factors – 1,2 and 4. Factors are the integers that can divide the number. It always starts with 1 and ends with that number.

A prime number is a number that can be divided only by the 1 and the number itself, such as 2, 3, 5, or 7. The list goes on. To find whether a number is prime or not is very easy.

We can start the examination with a prime number like 5. All we need to check that whether all the numbers starting from 2 to 4, can divide 5 or not. If any number can divide 5, then 5 is not prime. Else, 5 is prime. Now, we can easily check whether a number is prime or not.

We will come to that point in a minute. Before that, we will find factors of a number.

```
1  //code 5.5
2  // Dart
3  import 'dart:math';
4  void main(){
5
6  // we will find factors of 36
7  // we can add two factors 1 and 36 itself
8  // time complexity is O(n)
9  List<int> numbers = List();
10 for(int i = 1; i <= 36; i++){
11     if(36 % i == 0){
12     numbers.add(i);
13     }
14 }
15 print("${List.from(numbers)}");
16
17 List<int> moreNumbers = List();
18 moreNumbers.add(1);
```

```
19 for(int i = 1; i <= 18; i++){
20     if(36 % i == 0){
21     moreNumbers.add(i);
22     }
23 }
24 moreNumbers.add(36);
25 print("${List.from(numbers)}");
26
27
28 // in both cases, below, time complexity is O(square root of n)
29 // which is far better than before
30 List<double> nums = List();
31 for(double j = 1; j <= sqrt(36); j ++ ){
32     if(36 % j == 0){
33     nums.add(j);
34     if(j != sqrt(36)){
35         nums.add(36/j);
36     }
37     }
38 }
39 nums..sort();
40 print("${List.from(nums)}");
41
42
43 List<int> moreNums = List();
44 for(int j = 1; j <= sqrt(36); j ++ ){
45     if(36 % j == 0){
46     moreNums.add(j);
47     if(j != sqrt(36)){
48         moreNums.add((36/j).round());
49     }
50     }
51 }
52 moreNums.sort();
53 print("${List.from(moreNums)}");
54
55 List<int> numsMore = List();
56 for(int j = 1; j <= sqrt(35); j++ ){
57     if(35 % j == 0){
58     numsMore.add(j);
59     if(j != sqrt(35)){
60         print("true");
61         numsMore.add((35/j).round());
62     }
63     }
64 }
65 numsMore.sort();
66 print("${List.from(numsMore)}");
67
```

```
68
69 }
```

Let us see the output first.

```
1 // output of code 5.5
2 [1, 2, 3, 4, 6, 9, 12, 18, 36]
3 [1, 2, 3, 4, 6, 9, 12, 18, 36]
4 [1.0, 2.0, 3.0, 4.0, 6.0, 9.0, 12.0, 18.0, 36.0]
5 [1, 2, 3, 4, 6, 9, 12, 18, 36]
6 true
7 true
8 [1, 5, 7, 35]
```

In the first part of code, we will loop through the number itself.

```
1 List<int> numbers = List();
2 for(int i = 1; i <= 36; i++){
3     if(36 % i == 0){
4     numbers.add(i);
5     }
6 }
7 print("${List.from(numbers)}");
```

However, in the next code, we loop to the half of the number.

```
1 List<int> moreNumbers = List();
2 moreNumbers.add(1);
3 for(int i = 1; i <= 18; i++){
4     if(36 % i == 0){
5     moreNumbers.add(i);
6     }
7 }
8 moreNumbers.add(36);
9 print("${List.from(numbers)}");
```

But, the problem, in both cases, we need to the number itself. So the time complexity is big O(n).

Can we reduce the time, to run the program?

Okay, we can check them with the next sample.

```
1 List<double> nums = List();
2 for(double j = 1; j <= sqrt(36); j ++ ){
3     if(36 % j == 0){
4     nums.add(j);
5     if(j != sqrt(36)){
6         nums.add(36/j);
7     }
8     }
9 }
```

```
10 nums..sort();
11 print("${List.from(nums)}");
```

This time, we have succeeded to reduce the time complexity to big O(square root of n). For a big amount of integer, this algorithm fits fine.

In the next code snippets, we will find the prime factors of a positive integer. Factors of any integer can be divided to get the prime factors easily. The factors of 4 is 1, 2 and 4. We cannot divide 1 and 2. The integer 2 is prime. But, we can divide 4 and get 2 multiplied by 2.

Finally, it looks like: 1, 222. We can say the prime factors of 4 is 1 and 222, or we can also say that the prime factors are – 1 and 2 to the power of 3.

Let us check the next code snippets to find out the prime factors of any positive integer by passing the integer as parameter to a function.

```
1  // code 5.6
2  // Dart
3
4  import 'dart:math';
5
6  void main(){
7  getPrimeFactors(444);
8  print("++++++++");
9  findPrimeFactors(444);
10 }
11
12 void getPrimeFactors(int anyInteger){
13
14 /*
15 this is one way where time complexity is close to O(n)
16 for i <- 2 to n
17 for loop starts
18 if n%i == 0
19 if construct starts
20 counter = 0
21 while(n%i == 0)
22 n = n/i
23 count++
24 come out from the while loop
25 print (i, counter)
26 if construct ends
27 for construct ends
28 */
29
30 for(int i = 2; i <= anyInteger; i++){
31     if(anyInteger % i == 0){
32     int counter = 0;
33     while(anyInteger % i == 0){
```

```
34              anyInteger = (anyInteger / i).round();
35              counter++;
36          }
37          // we can say it like this
38          print("${i} to the power ${counter}");
39      }
40 }
41 // we can say it also like this after watching the output
42 print("The prime factors of 444 are 2*2, 3, 37");
43
44 }
45
46 void findPrimeFactors(int anyInteger){
47
48 /*
49 this is one way where time complexity is close to O(square root of n)
50 which is better than the previous solution
51 for i <- 2 to square root of n
52 for loop starts
53 if n%i == 0
54 if construct starts
55 counter = 0
56 while(n%i == 0)
57 n = n/i
58 count++
59 come out from the while loop
60 print (i, counter)
61 if construct ends
62 for construct ends
63 */
64
65 for(int i = 2; i <= sqrt(anyInteger); i++){
66     if(anyInteger % i == 0){
67     int counter = 0;
68     while(anyInteger % i == 0){
69         anyInteger = (anyInteger / i).round();
70         counter++;
71     }
72     // we can say it like this
73     print("${i} to the power ${counter}");
74     }
75 }
76 if(anyInteger != 1){
77     print("${anyInteger} and 1");
78 }
79 // we can say it also like this after watching the output
80 print("The prime factors of 444 are 2*2, 3, 37");
81
82 }
```

As you see, in the first function, due to our algorithm, the time complexity is more. However, we have succeeded to reduce that in the second function.

```
1  // output of code 5.6
2  /home/ss/flutter/bin/cache/dart-sdk/bin/dart --enable-asserts --enable-vm-service:38\
3  103 /home/ss/IdeaProjects/bin/PrimeFactorization.dart
4  Observatory listening on http://127.0.0.1:38103/
5
6  2 to the power 2
7  3 to the power 1
8  37 to the power 1
9  The prime factors of 444 are 2*2, 3, 37
10 ++++++++
11 2 to the power 2
12 3 to the power 1
13 37 and 1
14 The prime factors of 444 are 2*2, 3, 37
15
16 Process finished with exit code 0
```

In the next program, we will try to find whether a positive integer is prime or not.

```
1  // code 5.7
2  // Dart
3
4  void main(){
5  primeOrNot(71);
6  }
7
8  void primeOrNot(int anyPositiveInteger){
9
10 for(int i = 2; i <= (anyPositiveInteger - 1); i++){
11     if(anyPositiveInteger % i == 0){
12     print("${anyPositiveInteger} is not prime");
13     break;
14     } else {
15     print("${anyPositiveInteger} is prime.");
16     break;
17     }
18 }
19
20 }
```

We have passed two positive integers to test whether they are prime or not.

```
1  // output of code 5.7
2  /home/ss/flutter/bin/cache/dart-sdk/bin/dart --enable-asserts --enable-vm-service:37\
3  903 /home/ss/IdeaProjects/bin/PrimeOrNot.dart
4  Observatory listening on http://127.0.0.1:37903/
```

```
5
6  72 is not prime
7
8  Process finished with exit code 0
9
10 /home/ss/flutter/bin/cache/dart-sdk/bin/dart --enable-asserts --
enable-vm-service:32\
11 885 /home/ss/IdeaProjects/bin/PrimeOrNot.dart
12 Observatory listening on http://127.0.0.1:32885/
13
14 71 is prime.
15
16 Process finished with exit code 0
```

In the next section we will start discussing data structures. However, before moving into the data structures, we will see a couple of geometry algorithm, which is important to understand one key feature of data structures in C and C++.

At the same time, we will cut into discrete mathematical concepts of vector space. In Computer Science, Vectors represent a couple of things, such as lists of rows and columns, only rows; sometimes, we can place a vector point with two co-ordinates X and Y and find the direction of the point with respect to a line segment.

This algorithm is used in producing maps, directions, finding area of polygons, and many more things using Vector cross products.

In a map, how do we get the direction of a point? Should we turn right or left? We can move forward also, if that point lies on the same line.

In Geometry, three concepts play vital roles – point, line and plane.

You have probably noticed that, we are talking about these three features, in particular. To understand our points, let us see a figure (Figure 5.1) first.

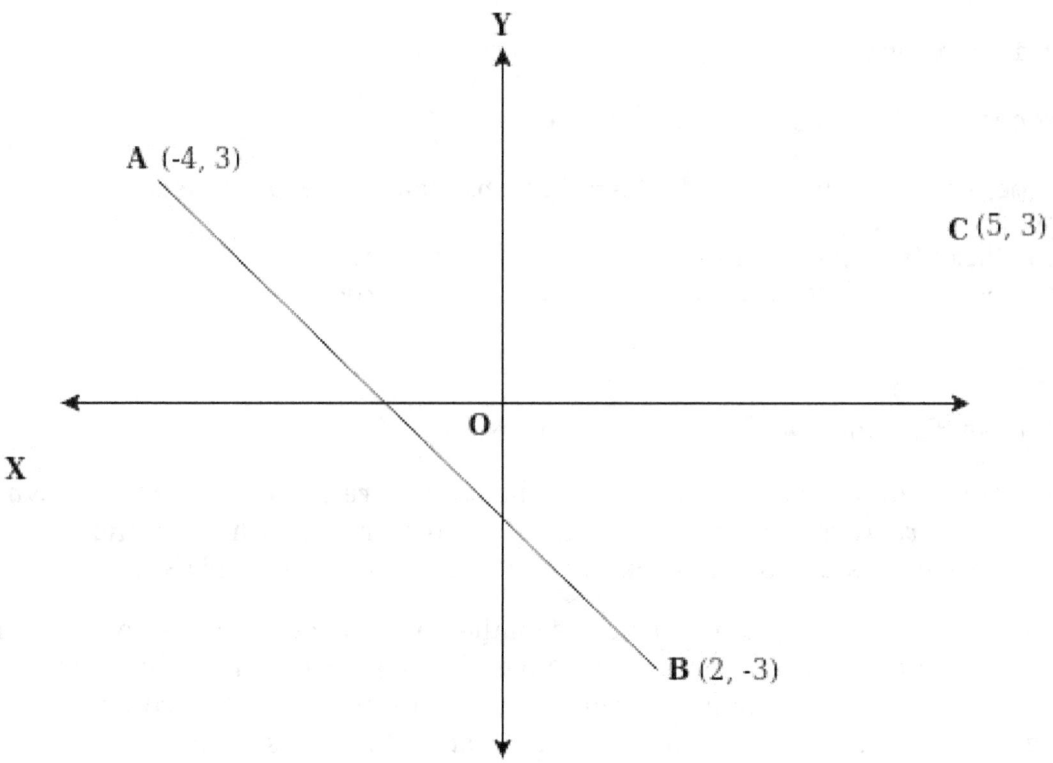

Figure 5.1 – Finding direction. Is C on the left side or right side of the line segment AB

Taking a look at the figure, we can say that the point C is on the left side of the line segment AB. But, is there any formula, to find that in Vector space?

Yes, there are; we can use the Vector cross products. We always calculate the position of any point placing them on the Cartesian plane. We have X and Y co-ordinates. Having the values of two co-ordinates helps us to find the direction of C from the line segment AB.

Suppose we are moving from A to B. Now we want to take turn and reach C. Should we take the left turn, or right turn? Well, the above figure tells us to take the left turn. But, how will we calculate that using co-ordinate system?

In any two-dimensional problem, like this, using Cartesian plane is the best choice, and we have adopted that for the sake of our algorithm.

According to the above figure, co-ordinate values of A is (-4, 3), and the co-ordinate values of B and C are respectively (2, -3) and (5,3).

For the sake of simplicity, if we consider that A lies on the origin O, that is, the co-ordinate values of A changes to (0, 0), then the cross products of B and C help us to determine the exact position of C with respect to B.

If the value of the cross products is greater than 0, or positive, or counter clockwise, then C is on the left side of B. If it is negative, then it is on the right hand side. Finally, if it is 0, then C is on the same line.

The Vector cross products formula is pretty simple. It is just as follows:

```
1 The X co-ordinate value of B * The Y co-ordinate value of C -  The Y co-ordinate val\
2 ue of B * The X co-ordinate value of C
```

According to the figure (assuming A has co-ordinate values (0,0)), the value is 15, which is positive. It proves that C is on the left side of point B. However, we have assumed that the co-ordinate values of A is (0, 0), to look it simple; which is actually not.

To do the real calculation, we need to shift A from its original position to the origin O. The co-ordinate values of A will change from (-4, 3) to (0, 0).

That will also change the co-ordinate values of B and C. The new X co-ordinate value of B will be (X co-ordinate value of B – X co-ordinate value of A), and the new Y co-ordinate value of B will be (Y co-ordinate value of B – Y co-ordinate value of A). The same rule will be applied to the co-ordinate values of C.

In our next Java program, we have calculated that find the direction of C from line segment AB.

```
1  // code 5.8
2  // Java
3
4  package fun.sanjibsinha.classesandobjects;
5
6  class PointClass{
7      double x, y;
8  }
9  public class GetDirection {
10
11     public static void main(String[] args) {
12         PointClass a = new PointClass();
13         a.x = -30;
14         a.y = 25;
15         PointClass b = new PointClass();
16         b.x = 15;
17         b.y = -18;
18         PointClass c = new PointClass();
19         c.x = 13;
20         c.y = 18;
21         // if point a comes to the origin having x and y co-ordinates
22         // both change to 0 and 0
23         // the x and y co-ordinates of b will change
24         b.x = b.x - a.x;
25         b.y = b.y - a.y;
26         // the x and y co-ordinates of c will also change
27         c.x = c.x - a.x;
```

```
28              c.y = c.y - a.y;
29              // to get direction of point c with respect to the
30              // line segment ab, joining points a and b becomes easier
31              // we will use cross products of points b and c
32              double crossProductsOfBAndC = (b.x * c.y) - (b.y * c.x);
33              // the value is 1180.0, which denotes c is on the left
34              if(crossProductsOfBAndC > 0){
35                  System.out.println("The point c is on the left of line ab.");
36              } else if(crossProductsOfBAndC < 0){
37                  System.out.println("The point c is on the right of line ab.");
38              } else {
39                  System.out.println("The point c is on the same line of ab.");
40              }
41          /*
42
43          */
44
45      }
46 }
```

Take a look at the output:

```
1 // output of code 5.8
2 the output is:
3 The point c is on the left of line ab.
4
5 next, let us change all the co-ordinates of c to negative value
6 the output is:
7 The point c is on the right of line ab.
8
9 next, let us change the value of c equal to b
10 the output is:
11 The point c is on the same line of ab.
```

We have already learned how the Vector cross products work to find the direction of the point. So, we are not discussing the algorithm, anymore. We can write our code, in a different way to accomplish a different type of task, considering that we need not shift A.

In the next code snippet, the point A is the origin, having the co-ordinate values (0, 0).

```
1 // code 5.9
2 // Java
3
4 package fun.sanjibsinha.classesandobjects;
5 /*
6 formula = difference between two cross products of two points
```

```
7  if it is counter clockwise it is +ve else -ve
8
9  */
10 class PointA{
11     // for the sake of simplicity we assume that
12     // point A is on the origin
13     double xCoordinate = 0;
14     double yCoordinate = 0;
15 }
16 class PointB{
17     double xCoordinate;
18     double yCoordinate;
19     PointA a;
20     double getNewXCoordinate(PointA a, double xCoordinate){
21         this.xCoordinate = xCoordinate;
22         xCoordinate = xCoordinate * a.yCoordinate - yCoordinate * a.xCoordinate;
23         return xCoordinate;
24     }
25     double getNewYCoordinate(PointA a, double yCoordinate){
26         this.yCoordinate = yCoordinate;
27         yCoordinate = xCoordinate * a.yCoordinate - yCoordinate * a.xCoordinate;
28         return this.yCoordinate;
29     }
30 }
31 class PointC{
32     PointB b;
33     double leftToB = 1.0;
34     double rightToB = -1.0;
35     double onSameLine = 0.0;
36     /*
37     double getNewXCoordinate(){}
38     double getNewYCoordinate(){}
39
40     */
41     double findPosition(PointB b, double xCoordinate, double yCoordinate){
42         this.b = b;
43         double difference;
44         difference = b.xCoordinate * yCoordinate - b.yCoordinate * xCoordinate;
45         if(difference > 0.0){
46             return leftToB;
47         } else if(difference < 0.0){
48             return rightToB;
49         } else {
50             return onSameLine;
51         }
52     }
```

```java
53 }
54
55 public class FindPosition {
56     public static void main(String[] args) {
57         PointB b = new PointB();
58         b.xCoordinate = 5;
59         b.yCoordinate = -6;
60         PointC c = new PointC();
61         System.out.println("On the same line, as c has the same value as b: "
62                 + c.findPosition(b, 5, -6));
63     }
64 }
```

For the sake of simplicity, we have not only kept the co-ordinate values of A as (0, 0); at the same time we make the value of C same as B.

Here is the output:

```
1 // output of code 5.9
2 On the same line, as c has the same value as b: 0.0
```

We are again going to experiment with our code. However, this time we have three different co-ordinate values of A, B and C.

```java
1  // code 5.10
2  // Java
3
4  package fun.sanjibsinha.classesandobjects;
5  /*
6  formula = difference between two cross products of two points
7  if it is counter clockwise it is +ve else -ve
8  */
9  class PointNameA{
10     double xCoordinate;
11     double yCoordinate;
12 }
13 class PointNameB{
14     double xCoordinate;
15     double yCoordinate;
16     PointNameA a;
17     double getNewXCoordinate(PointNameA a, double xCoordinate){
18         this.xCoordinate = xCoordinate;
19         this.a = a;
20         xCoordinate = xCoordinate - a.xCoordinate;
21         return xCoordinate;
22     }
23     double getNewYCoordinate(PointNameA a, double yCoordinate){
24         this.a = a;
25         this.yCoordinate = yCoordinate;
26         yCoordinate = yCoordinate - a.yCoordinate;
```

```java
27            return yCoordinate;
28        }
29 }
30 class PointNameC{
31     double xCoordinate;
32     double yCoordinate;
33     PointNameB b;
34     PointNameA a;
35     PointNameC c;
36     double leftToB = 1.0;
37     double rightToB = -1.0;
38     double onSameLine = 0.0;
39
40     double getNewXCoordinate(PointNameA a, double xCoordinate){
41         this.a = a;
42         this.xCoordinate = xCoordinate;
43         xCoordinate = xCoordinate - a.xCoordinate;
44         return xCoordinate;
45     }
46     double getNewYCoordinate(PointNameA a, double yCoordinate) {
47         this.a = a;
48         this.yCoordinate = yCoordinate;
49         yCoordinate = yCoordinate - a.yCoordinate;
50         return yCoordinate;
51     }
52     double findPosition(PointNameB b, PointNameC c){
53         this.b = b;
54         this.c = c;
55         double difference;
56         difference = b.xCoordinate * c.yCoordinate - b.yCoordinate * c.xCoordinate;
57         if(difference > 0.0){
58             return leftToB;
59         } else if(difference < 0.0){
60             return rightToB;
61         } else {
62             return onSameLine;
63         }
64     }
65 }
66 public class FindPositionMOre {
67     public static void main(String[] args) {
68         PointNameA a = new PointNameA();
69         a.xCoordinate = -3;
70         a.yCoordinate = 6;
71         PointNameB b = new PointNameB();
72         b.getNewXCoordinate(a, 5);
73         b.getNewYCoordinate(a, -8);
74         PointNameC c = new PointNameC();
75         double xOfC = c.getNewXCoordinate(a, 15);
```

```
76          double yOfC = c.getNewYCoordinate(a, 18);
77          System.out.println("The point C is on the left of line segment AB, as the va\
78 lue is positive : "
79                  + c.findPosition(b, c));
80      }
81 }
```

If you run the program, you will get the outcome as follows:

```
1 // output of code 5.10
2 The point C is on the left of line segment AB, as the value is positive : 1.0
```

You can change the co-ordinate values of A, B and C to see how your output changes.

In the next section, we will start with the same problem to understand how data structures in C and C++ works. After that, we will start digging deep into Data Structures and Algorithm in chapter 6.

In the next section, we will have a brief introduction to the Data Structures using the same Vector cross products and finding direction.

Introducing Data Structures

We have already been introduced to data structures before. Of course, we have learned a few operations using Array in various languages, so we can say that the concept of data structures is not completely alien to us.

We need a good way to store, organize and use our data. As times passes by, the nature of data is becoming not only more and more complex, but also it's getting bigger in quantity. More and more people are getting hooked to the Internet, exchanging huge amount of data every day, in various forms; scientific data are getting larger, we need weather data to be processed to get more accurate weather prediction, medical data are becoming humongous; this list is endless.

Therefore, we need more efficient way to sort, organize, and use that data.

Data Structures are all about this. It has a very close relation with Algorithm, because managing such huge amount of data is less tedious if we have more efficient Algorithm, ready at our hand.

While managing such huge humongous data, by sorting, organizing, or using them, one is not only prone to error, but also fail to satisfy one of the most important requirements – time and space. Yes, time complexity really matters, so the space.

In this section we have a short introduction to the Data Structures, but we will actually start the topic in the next chapter. First of all let us have a look at a figure (Figure 5.2) first.

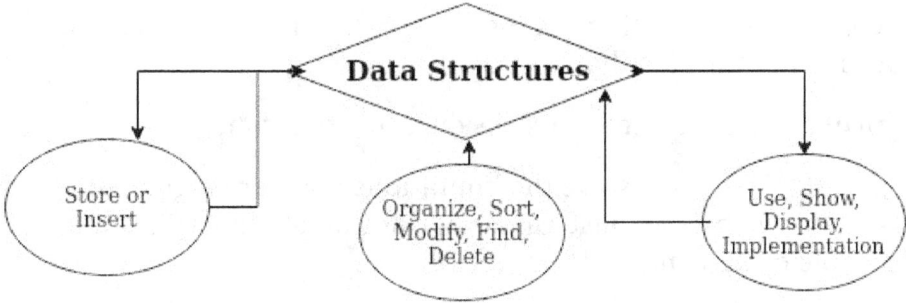

Abstract Data Type

We can write down instructions in Natural Language to define Data Structures and its Operations.

Implementation

We can Implement Data Structures adopting several operations, such as Array, LinkedList, Stack, Queue, Map, etc...

Figure 5.2 – A pictorial representation of Data Structures

We have clearly stated what Data Structures are, in the above figure. We can describe our data structures in our natural language; that is a part of any data structures. It is always good to write it down what we are going to do with our data structures.

Consider a static List or a fixed length List; that is, an array. It is a collection of similar type of data, either integer, double, or string. Moreover, it should have a fixed length while we declare it. Within that range of length, we can insert data, modify data at a specific position, even we can remove a data and make the memory space empty.

Whenever we declare a fixed length List, the memory manager fixes an amount of memory for that list or array. When we write, "int array[4]", it means, memory manager allocates 4 bytes each for individual address, altogether 16 bytes are allocated.

In language like C or C++, if we want to insert one more data, in whatever position we can imagine; the task becomes tedious. First of all, the memory manager has already fixed a space. So we need to create a larger array. Copy the whole array to the new memory space and at the same time empty the old space.

To make an array dynamic, we might think an array with maximum size that particular data type allows us to use. Since the array is a contiguous block of memory, a large space remains unused. Suppose we declare an array of 'n' length. We start with 10 data. Next, as per our need we start adding data to the array. If we add one single data at the very beginning, we need to shift all other data by one space. If the data type is integer, we need not add 4 bytes more at the end in this case particularly because we have kept that space beforehand, after that we need to shift the other data accordingly.

Whatever we do, a large space still remains unused. In terms of memory allocation, this process does not seem friendly.

Since the length of an array is fixed, it works on a constant time.

Now, new languages come up to solve the limitations of older language. Consider the Dart. In Dart, we get two types of List. One is of traditional type – fixed length. Another is growable or dynamic List.

Enough talking, let us see the first code – fixed length List.

```
1 // code 5.11
2 // Dart
3
4 /*
5 The list is a simple ordered group of objects. Creating
6 a List seems easy because Dart core libraries have the necessary support
7 and a List class. There are two types of Lists.
8 */
9 void main(){
10 listFunction();
11 }
12
13 int listFunction(){
14 List<int> nameOfTest = List(3);
15 nameOfTest[0] = 1;
16 nameOfTest[1] = 2;
17 nameOfTest[2] = 3;
18 //there are three methods to capture the list
19 //1. method
20 for(int element in nameOfTest){
21     print(element);
22 }
23 print("-----------");
24 //2. method
25 nameOfTest.forEach((v) => print('${v}'));
26 print("-----------");
27 //3. method
28 for(int i = 0; i < nameOfTest.length; i++){
29     print(nameOfTest[i]);
30 }
31 }
```

The output is quite expected.

```
1 // output of code 5.11
2 1
3 2
4 3
5 -----------
```

```
 6  1
 7  2
 8  3
 9  -----------
10  1
11  2
12  3
```

In Dart, everything is object. Therefore, it is a collection of similar objects. Here it is integer. Next, we will make this list dynamic, and see how it works.

```
 1  // code 5.12
 2  // Dart
 3
 4  void main(){
 5  growableList();
 6  }
 7
 8  Function growableList(){
 9  //1. method
10  List<String> names = List();
11  names.add("Mana");
12  names.add("Babu");
13  names.add("Gopal");
14  names.add("Pota");
15  //there are two methods to capture the list
16  print("-----------");
17  //1. method
18  names.forEach((v) => print('${v}'));
19  print("-----------");
20  //2. method
21  for(int i = 0; i < names.length; i++){
22      print(names[i]);
23  }
24  }
```

Growable Lists are dynamic in nature. We can dynamically add any number of elements and we can also remove it by a simple method: 'names.remove("any name")'. We can also use the key; as this ordered list starts from 0. So we can remove the first name just by passing this key value: 'names.removeAt(0)'. We use the 'removeAt(key)' method for that operation. We can also clear the whole List just by typing: 'names.clear()'. Let us see the output, now.

```
1  // output of code 5.12
2  -----------
3  Mana
4  Babu
5  Gopal
6  Pota
7  -----------
```

```
 8 Mana
 9 Babu
10 Gopal
11 Pota
```

We have a very short introduction to Data Structures. Hopefully, now we understand what are the limitations and advantages of an array. We will discuss them in detail in the first section of the next chapter 6. Comparing array with other Data Structures will help us gain more insights into this complex topic, which is the most fundamental block of Computer Science.

How Calculus and Linear Algebra are Related to this Discourse

Calculus is the branch of mathematics that describes changes in functions. Now, linear algebraic operations start with functions; moreover, computer programming cannot move a step forward without the implementation of functions.

Mathematically, we can define polynomial, rational, trigonometric, exponential, and logarithmic functions, and at the same time, we can review how to evaluate these functions, and we show the properties of their graphs. Is the concept of function used in computer programming same as mathematical functions?

Before finding the answer, let us formally define what is mathematical function. In Mathematics, before defining a function, we need two sets A and B, where where x is an element of A and y is an element of B, is a relation from A to B.

Now, a relation from the set A to the set B defines a relationship between those two sets.

Mathematically, a function is a special type of relation in which each element of the first set is related to exactly one element of the second set.

We call the element of the first set as the input; and, the element of the second set is called the output. Functions are used all the time in mathematics to describe relationships between two sets.

Actually, when we know the input, the output is determined in a function.

We can write a function like this:

```
1 y = f(x)
```

Now, the f(x) can be of any value, such as 'x + 1', or 'x - 1'; in fact, with the addition, subtraction, multiplication or division of any constant value, as we change the value of x, the value of y will change.

The same thing happens in computer programming; a function returns a value. Not always; but it is a general rule that is followed by any programming language.

We may argue that not every function returns a value; there is something called 'void', but that also gives us what? An output.

We can find the area of a square if we know the value of one side. We can find the area of a circle, if we know the value of radius.

Mathematically, when we write y = f(x); it can also be said as 'y equals f of x'. While writing a function like this we refer to x as the independent variable, and y as the dependent variable.

Quite understandably the value of y depends on the value of x.

Now, a function consists of three things, in particular. A set of inputs, a set of outputs and a rule for assigning each input to exactly one output. Mathematically, the set of inputs is called the domain of the function and the set of outputs is called the range of the function.

If the assigning rule of a function is f(x) = 3 – x; and the domain is {1, 2, 3}, then the value of y or the range will be {0, 1, 2}.

Not only we can visualize the function by plotting points (x, y) on coordinate planes, we can write something like this in any programming language.

The code is as follows:

```java
// code 5.13
// Java

package fun.sanjibsinha.functions;

/**
 * a function will take inputs but always return one output
 * mathematically we can write it as y = f(x)
 * here y is output, and f(x) is function
 * the output can be expressed as range and input as domain
 * domain may have multiple values that points to one or more than one range
 */

public class FunctionDemo {
    static int x = 0;
    static int y = 0;

    static int domainOne(int x){
        y = x + 0;
        return y;
    }
    static int domainTwo(int x){
        y = x + 1;
        return y;
    }
    static int domainThree(int x){
        y = x + 2;
        return y;
```

```java
29      }
30      static int domainFour(int x){
31          y = x + 3;
32          return y;
33      }
34      static double domainFive(double x){
35          double y;
36          y = Math.pow(x, 2);
37          return y;
38      }
39      static double domainSix(double x){
40          double y;
41          y = Math.sqrt(x);
42          return y;
43      }
44
45      static double[] xValue = {4, 3, 2, 1};
46
47      static double returnRange(int index){
48          double y = 0;
49          if(xValue[x] == 4){
50              y = xValue[x] + 0;
51              return y;
52          } else if (xValue[x] == 3){
53              y = xValue[x] + 1;
54              return y;
55          } else if (xValue[x] == 2){
56              y = xValue[x] + 2;
57              return y;
58          } else if (xValue[x] == 1){
59              y = xValue[x] + 3;
60              return y;
61          } else if (xValue[x] == 2){
62              y = Math.pow(xValue[x], 2);
63              return y;
64          } else {
65              return y;
66          }
67      }
68
69      public static void main(String[] args) {
70
71          System.out.println("The value of y : " + domainOne(4) + " when x = 4");
72          System.out.println("The value of y : " + domainTwo(3) + " when x = 3");
73          System.out.println("The value of y : " + domainThree(2) + " when x = 2");
74          System.out.println("The value of y : " + domainFour(1) + " when x = 1");
```

```
75          System.out.println("The value of y : " + domainFive(2) + " when x = 2");
76          System.out.println("The value of y : " + domainSix(16) + " when x = 16");
77          System.out.println("*****************");
78          for (int x = 0; x <= 3; x++){
79              System.out.println("The index : " + x + " and the value of set xValue : "
80                      + xValue[x]);
81          }
82          System.out.println();
83          System.out.println("The value of y : " + returnRange(0)
84                  + " when index of xValue = 0");
85          System.out.println("The value of y : " + returnRange(1)
86                  + " when index of xValue = 1");
87          System.out.println("The value of y : " + returnRange(2)
88                  + " when index of xValue = 2");
89          System.out.println("The value of y : " + returnRange(3)
90                  + " when index of xValue = 3");
91          System.out.println("The value of y : " + returnRange(2)
92                  + " when index of xValue = 2");
93
94      }
95 }
```

Let us check the output:

```
1  // output of code 5.13
2  The value of y : 4 when x = 4
3  The value of y : 4 when x = 3
4  The value of y : 4 when x = 2
5  The value of y : 4 when x = 1
6  The value of y : 4.0 when x = 2
7  The value of y : 4.0 when x = 16
8  *****************
9  The index : 0 and the value of set xValue : 4.0
10 The index : 1 and the value of set xValue : 3.0
11 The index : 2 and the value of set xValue : 2.0
12 The index : 3 and the value of set xValue : 1.0
13
14 The value of y : 4.0 when index of xValue = 0
15 The value of y : 4.0 when index of xValue = 1
16 The value of y : 4.0 when index of xValue = 2
17 The value of y : 4.0 when index of xValue = 3
18 The value of y : 4.0 when index of xValue = 2
```

We can see in the above code that the range remains at 4; however, the domain consists more than one values that point to the one output, which is 4. And yes, the domain could have infinite values depending on the permutation and combination of the value of the coefficient.

In some cases, we also need to know how calculus works in computer programming. Consider a car that should have the history of both – velocity and distance. If one is missing, we can calculate the value of the other by using calculus. Therefore, we need to know how to find the velocity from a record of the distance. This part of calculus belongs to differentiation or differential calculus. On the contrary, we also want to compute the distance from a history of the velocity. That is called integration, and it is the goal of integral calculus. We can conclude, differentiation goes from distance to velocity; integration goes from velocity to distance.

However, there is another important factor that we should consider – time. You cannot calculate velocity without time, the rate of speed, etc. At the same time, we also want to know how much time it takes to travel a certain distance. Now, we can guess that from velocity and distance, we can also calculate time.

Let us consider the following code snippet, where we have calculated these factors.

```java
1  // code 5.14
2  // Java
3
4  package fun.sanjibsinha.calculusone;
5
6  public class VelocityClass {
7
8      private float velocity;
9
10     public void setVelocity(int velocity) {
11         this.velocity = velocity;
12     }
13
14     public float getVelocity() {
15         return velocity;
16     }
17
18     public float calculateVelocity(float time, float dis){
19         velocity = dis / time;
20         if((time > 0) && (time < 3)){
21             return velocity;
22         } else if ((time > 3) && (time < 6)){
23             return velocity;
24         } else {
25             return velocity;
26         }
27     }
28 }
29
30
31 package fun.sanjibsinha.calculusone;
32
33 public class DistanceClass {
34
```

```java
    private float distance;

    public void setDistance(int distance) {
        this.distance = distance;
    }

    public float getDistance() {
        return distance;
    }

    public float calculateDistance(float time, float velocity){
        distance = velocity * time;
        if((time >= 0) && (time <= 3)){
            return distance;
        } else if ((time >= 3) && (time <= 6)){
            return distance;
        } else {
            return distance;
        }
    }


}

package fun.sanjibsinha.calculusone;

public class TimeClass {

    private float time;

    public void setTime(int time) {
        this.time = time;
    }

    public float getTime() {
        return time;
    }

    public float calculateTime(float distance, float velocity){
        time = distance / velocity;
        if((velocity > 0) && (velocity < 10)){
            return time;
        } else if ((velocity > 20) && (velocity < 60)){
            return time;
        } else {
            return time;
        }
    }
}
```

```java
package fun.sanjibsinha.calculusone;

public class DemoClass {

    public static void main(String[] args) {
        VelocityClass vel = new VelocityClass();
        TimeClass time = new TimeClass();
        DistanceClass dis = new DistanceClass();
        /**
         * find the velocity from a record of a distance
         * differentiation
         * differential calculus
         */
        time.setTime(5);
        dis.setDistance(80);
        System.out.println("If a car travels " + dis.getDistance() + " kms in "
                + time.getTime() + " hours, its velocity is "
                + vel.calculateVelocity(time.getTime(), dis.getDistance()) + " km pe\
r hour.");

        System.out.println();
        /**
         *compute distance from a history of velocity
         * integration
         * integral calculus
         */
        time.setTime(10);
        vel.setVelocity(40);
        System.out.println("A car with a velocity " + vel.getVelocity() +
                " kms per hour, in " + time.getTime() + " hours travels "
                + dis.calculateDistance(time.getTime(), vel.getVelocity()) + " kms."\
);
        /**
         * we can also time from a history of velocity
         */
        dis.setDistance(100);
        vel.setVelocity(60);
        System.out.println("A car with a velocity of " + vel.getVelocity() + " kms p\
er per hrs, travels" +
                " distance of " + dis.getDistance() + " kms, hence it will reach the\
 " +
                " destination after "
```

```
128                    + time.calculateTime(dis.getDistance(),
vel.getVelocity()) + " hours\
129 .");
130
131     }
132 }
```

Here is the output:

```
1 // output of code 5.14
2 If a car travels 80.0 kms in 5.0 hours, its velocity is 16.0 km per hour.
3
4 A car with a velocity 40.0 kms per hour, in 10.0 hours travels 400.0 kms.
5 A car with a velocity of 60.0 kms per per hrs, travels distance of 100.0 kms, hence \
6 it will reach the  destination after 1.6666666 hours
```

Now we are ready to discuss data structures in detail in the next chapter.

I write regularly on Algorithm and Data Structure in

6. Data Structures in Detail

In this chapter we will discuss every facet of data structures.

Frequently Asked Questions about Data Structures

We show the outline of Frequently Asked Questions about Data Structures in the following way:

```
1 Step 1. Data Structures
2 Step 2. Linear Data Structures
3 Step 3. LinkedList
4 Step 4. Stack
5 Step 5. Queue
6 Step 5. Hierarchical Data Structures
```

While we broadly categorize the above data structures we have kept Java in our mind. It changes with the programming languages. Of course for C it is quite different. However, once you understand the basic concepts,you can transplant the Java code into C++ or vice versa.

Earlier we have seen that any data structure is a way of storing and organizing the data so that it can be used efficiently. It provides a large amount of data efficiently. Efficient algorithm can only be designed with efficient data structures.

Abstract Data Type (ADT)

The first step of designing an efficient data structure is to develop an efficient mathematical model for the data to be stored. After that, we need to choose the methods to access and modify the data. This model with the methods is called Abstract Data Type or ADT.

Through the ADT, we address all the functionalities of the data structures. It tells us what we want to do with the data structures. However, ADT does not tell us anything about the implementation process, memory management, or the algorithm we implement for the data structures.

As we have said earlier, efficient algorithm depends on efficient data structures, we will definitely be interested on which algorithm we should implement; however,in the ADT stage, it is not necessary.

As an example, if we are implementing a dictionary ADT, we may want to implement a "search(word)" method. At the very beginning of the project, we have to specify that; and, what we are doing in that stage is nothing but ADT.

Now, in case of Java, a data structure for implementing an ADT is a structured set of variables for storing data. On the implementation level, an ADT corresponds to a Java Interface, and the data structure implementing the ADT corresponds to a class implementing that interface. We will see to this part in the later section of the book, where we will discuss 'Collection'.

Linear Data Structures

In Linear Data Structures we can arrange elements sequentially so that one element may have next element and the next element may have next elements, and we can extend the sequential order as long as we could extend it.

In this section, our mathematical model of the data is a linear sequence of elements; this sequence has well-defined 'first' and 'last' elements. Every element of a sequence except the first has a unique predecessor while every element except the last has a unique successor. As an example, consider a String 'good'; here, the characters are ordered sequentially. The character 'g' is the first element and has no predecessor. The character 'd' is the last element and has no successor.

The next figure (Figure 6.1) shows the three layers deep linear data structure samples.

Sequential Data Structures

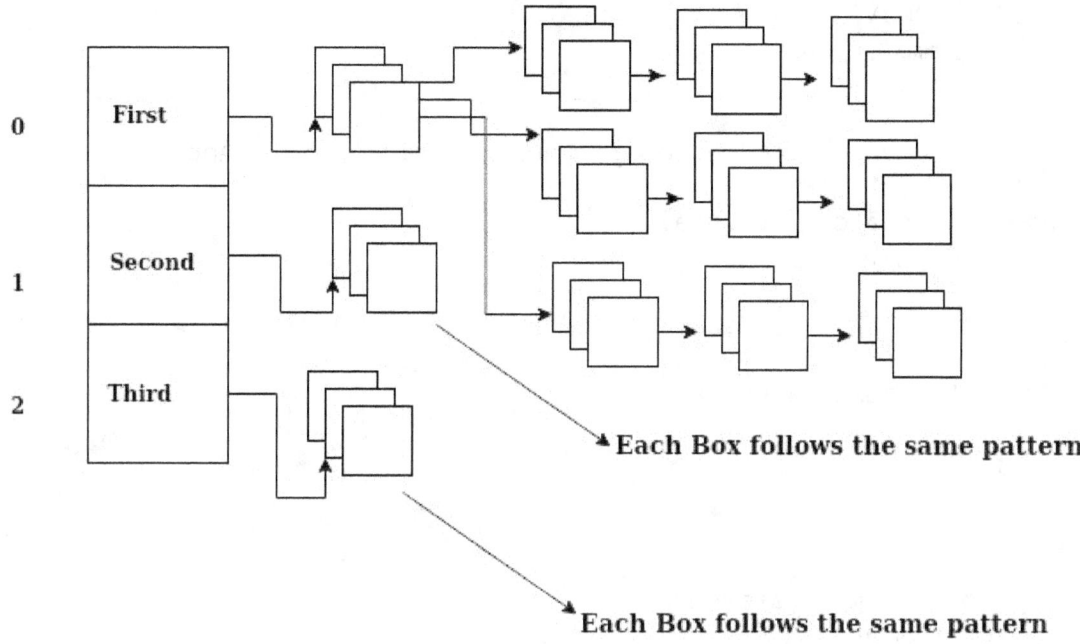

Figure 6.1 – The sequential, or the linear data structure

We can show this linear and sequential data structures using the following code snippets in Java.

```
1 // code 6.1
2 // Java
3 package fun.sanjibsinha;
4
5 public class ArrayExamples {
6
7     /**
8     * each box will contain two boxes
9     */
10    static String[] singleBox = {"First Box", "Second Box", "Third Box"};
11    /**
12    * first box will have white and black box
13    */
14    static String[][] doubleBox = {
15            {"White", "Black", "Empty"},
16            {"Red", "Blue", "Empty"},
17            {"Yellow", "Green", "Empty"}
18    };
19    /**
20    * white box will have three boxes apple, cabbage and mutton
21    */
```

```
22     static String[][][] tripleBox = {
23             {
24                     {"Apple", "Banana", "Guava"}, {"Cabbage", "Potato", "Brinjal"}, {"Mu\
25 tton", "Lamb", "Chicken"}
26             },
27             {
28                     {"Mutton", "Lamb", "Chicken"}, {"Apple", "Banana", "Guava"}, {"C\
29 abbage", "Potato", "Brinjal"}
30             },
31             {
32                     {"Cabbage", "Potato", "Brinjal"}, {"Apple", "Banana", "Guava"}, \
33 {"Mutton", "Lamb", "Chicken"}
34             }
35     };
36
37
38     /**
39      * this is main statement
40      * @param args
41      */
42     public static void main(String[] args) {
43         for (int i = 0; i < singleBox.length; i++){
44             System.out.println(singleBox[i]);
45             for (int j = 0; j < doubleBox.length; j++){
46                 System.out.println(" * " + doubleBox[j][i] + " * ");
47                 /**
48                  * enhanced for loop
49                  */
50                 for (String[][] box : tripleBox) {
51                     System.out.println(" ** " + box[j][0] + " ** ");
52                 }
53             }
54         }
55     }
56 }
```

As the topmost layer or the outermost layer has three boxes, we can arrange the output in three different ways as follows. The first output goes this way:

```
1 // output of code 6.1
2 First Box
3     * White *
4             ** Apple **
5             ** Mutton **
6             ** Cabbage **
7     * Red *
8             ** Cabbage **
```

```
 9              ** Apple **
10              ** Apple **
11      * Yellow *
12              ** Mutton **
13              ** Cabbage **
14              ** Mutton **
15 Second Box
16      * Black *
17              ** Apple **
18              ** Mutton **
19              ** Cabbage **
20      * Blue *
21              ** Cabbage **
22              ** Apple **
23              ** Apple **
24      * Green *
25              ** Mutton **
26              ** Cabbage **
27              ** Mutton **
28 Third Box
29      * Empty *
30              ** Apple **
31              ** Mutton **
32              ** Cabbage **
33      * Empty *
34              ** Cabbage **
35              ** Apple **
36              ** Apple **
37      * Empty *
38              ** Mutton **
39              ** Cabbage **
40              ** Mutton **
41
42 Process finished with exit code 0
```

The sequential order is rearranged if we change the index of the outermost layer from 0 to 1. Watch this part of the above code snippet:

```
1 /**
2               * enhanced for loop
3               */
4               for (String[][] box : tripleBox) {
5                   System.out.println(" ** " + box[j][0] + " ** ");
6               }
```

And the rearranged output is like this:

```
1 // output of code 6.1
2 // rearranging the sequence
3 First Box
4       * White *
```

```
 5              ** Banana **
 6              ** Lamb **
 7              ** Potato **
 8      * Red *
 9              ** Potato **
10              ** Banana **
11              ** Banana **
12      * Yellow *
13              ** Lamb **
14              ** Potato **
15              ** Lamb **
16 Second Box
17      * Black *
18              ** Banana **
19              ** Lamb **
20              ** Potato **
21      * Blue *
22              ** Potato **
23              ** Banana **
24              ** Banana **
25      * Green *
26              ** Lamb **
27              ** Potato **
28              ** Lamb **
29 Third Box
30      * Empty *
31              ** Banana **
32              ** Lamb **
33              ** Potato **
34      * Empty *
35              ** Potato **
36              ** Banana **
37              ** Banana **
38      * Empty *
39              ** Lamb **
40              ** Potato **
41              ** Lamb **
42
43 Process finished with exit code 0
```

We can change this order three times as the outermost layer has three indices or we can imagine it as boxes. The last sequence looks like this:

```
1 // output of code 6.1
2 // rearranging the sequence
3 First Box
4      * White *
5              ** Guava **
6              ** Chicken **
7              ** Brinjal **
```

```
 8      * Red *
 9             ** Brinjal **
10             ** Guava **
11             ** Guava **
12      * Yellow *
13             ** Chicken **
14             ** Brinjal **
15             ** Chicken **
16 Second Box
17      * Black *
18             ** Guava **
19             ** Chicken **
20             ** Brinjal **
21      * Blue *
22             ** Brinjal **
23             ** Guava **
24             ** Guava **
25      * Green *
26             ** Chicken **
27             ** Brinjal **
28             ** Chicken **
29 Third Box
30      * Empty *
31             ** Guava **
32             ** Chicken **
33             ** Brinjal **
34      * Empty *
35             ** Brinjal **
36             ** Guava **
37             ** Guava **
38      * Empty *
39             ** Chicken **
40             ** Brinjal **
41             ** Chicken **
42
43 Process finished with exit code 0
```

Modeling of a Structure

In the Abstract Data Type part, correct modeling of a structure is extremely important. We need to understand why it is important.

In any programming language when we write a code, we actually write some instructions for the computers. Here, human communication through programming language also plays a crucial part. Here when we say humans, we mean programmers. Another programmer will also read the code, and programmers are not computers.

Just because a compiler can understand a given construct there is no guarantee that a programmer can also understand that construct. Therefore, the ADT should be clear and concise. Moreover, it should be human readable and understandable.

Because a human mind has many limitations, any code should be elaborately documented so that the purpose of using any particular algorithm is clear and graspable. Consider a stack algorithm, which handles nested constructs for a compiler. If it is very complicated, human mind cannot follow the structure. It is especially true for the data structures. Deeply nested constructs in a data structure can be incomprehensible; the limitations of human mind cannot comprehend it.

While a construct is ambiguous to a human, at the same time it is clear and comprehensible to a compiler. Consider a simple division algorithm.

```
1 //code 6.2
2 package fun.sanjibsinha;
3
4 public class TestingDemo {
5 //badly written code for humans, although the construct is clear to any compiler
6     public static void main(String[] args) {
7         double a, b, c;
8         a=20;
9         b=10;
10        c=5;
11        System.out.println(a/b/c);
12    }
13 }
14
15 The output is quite obvious: 0.4
```

Although humans cannot follow the construct of division without parentheses, nevertheless the compiler does not complain. It gives us the correct output.

If we wrote this line this way adding the parentheses :

```
1 System.out.println((a / b) / c);
```

The limitations of human mind would not deter it from comprehending correctly.

ArrayList to overcome limitations of Array

Working with array is difficult because they have a fixed size and it is not very easy to add or remove data, always. Arrays are sequentially ordered; for that reason, adding or removing elements from any position between two elements will also involve shifting other values. The whole operation makes the processor overwork, forcing it to overwork to solve the problem.

While the ArrayList is also sequentially ordered, and processor takes the same steps as it does in case of Arrays, nevertheless it is easy to handle because of the ADT.

ArrayList is an ADT that provides a generic class, which has many useful methods to deal with a collection of data. It also supports different data types. Using the ArrayList methods we could easily add, remove, modify any element. Moreover, we could count the size of the list and based on which we could use the looping construct.

An ArrayList is declared as follows:

```
1 ArrayList<T> arrayList = new ArrayList<T>();
```

Here T is the data type, not the primitive data type, but the Wrapper Class. Let us take a look at some implementations.

```
1 //code 6.3
2 //Java
3 package fun.sanjibsinha;
4
5 import java.util.ArrayList;
6
7 public class ArrayListExamples {
8
9     public static void main(String[] args) {
10
11         /**
12         * ArrayList examples
13         * ArrayList is an ADT that provides a generic class, which has many useful m\
14 ethods to deal
15         * with a collection of data. It also supports different data types.
16         * An ArrayList is declared as follows:
17         * ArrayList<T> arrayList = new ArrayList<T>();
18         * Here T is the data type.
19         */
20         ArrayList<String> arrayList = new ArrayList<String>();
21         arrayList.add("index");
22         arrayList.add("about");
23         arrayList.add("contact");
24         arrayList.add("products");
25         arrayList.add("sellers");
26
27         for (int i = 0; i < arrayList.size(); i++){
28             System.out.println(arrayList.get(i));
29         }
30     }
31 }
```

We have added a few elements and the output is quite simple.

```
1 //output of code 6.3
2 index
```

```
3 about
4 contact
5 products
6 sellers
```

Next, we want to remove some elements and give the output to see how it works.

```
1 //code 6.4
2 package fun.sanjibsinha;
3
4 import java.util.ArrayList;
5
6 public class ArrayListExamples {
7
8     public static void main(String[] args) {
9
10        /**
11         * ArrayList examples
12         * ArrayList is an ADT that provides a generic class, which has many useful m\
13 ethods to deal
14         * with a collection of data. It also supports different data types.
15         * An ArrayList is declared as follows:
16         * ArrayList<T> arrayList = new ArrayList<T>();
17         * Here T is the data type.
18         */
19        ArrayList<String> arrayList = new ArrayList<String>();
20
21        //we have added 5 items
22        arrayList.add("index");
23        arrayList.add("about");
24        arrayList.add("contact");
25        arrayList.add("products");
26        arrayList.add("sellers");
27
28        //we have removed 2 items
29        arrayList.remove("products");
30        arrayList.remove("sellers");
31
32        for (int i = 0; i < arrayList.size(); i++){
33            System.out.println(arrayList.get(i));
34        }
35    }
36 }
```

Here goes the output:

```
1 //output of code 6.4
2 index
```

```
3 about
4 contact
```

Next, we are going to modify the first element of the list; we will modify it changing 'index' to 'home'.

```
 1 //code 6.5
 2 package fun.sanjibsinha;
 3
 4 import java.util.ArrayList;
 5
 6 public class ArrayListExamples {
 7
 8     public static void main(String[] args) {
 9
10         /**
11          * ArrayList examples
12          * ArrayList is an ADT that provides a generic class, which has many useful m\
13 ethods to deal
14          * with a collection of data. It also supports different data types.
15          * An ArrayList is declared as follows:
16          * ArrayList<T> arrayList = new ArrayList<T>();
17          * Here T is the data type.
18          */
19         ArrayList<String> arrayList = new ArrayList<String>();
20         //we have added 5 items
21         arrayList.add("index");
22         arrayList.add("about");
23         arrayList.add("contact");
24         arrayList.add("products");
25         arrayList.add("sellers");
26         //we have removed 2 items
27         arrayList.remove("products");
28         arrayList.remove("sellers");
29
30         //we will modify the first index page to home
31         arrayList.set(0, "home");
32
33         for (int i = 0; i < arrayList.size(); i++){
34             System.out.println(arrayList.get(i));
35         }
36     }
37 }
```

We have successfully modified the value. Running the program gives is this output:

```
1 //output of code 6.5
2 home
```

3 about
4 contact

After storing the data, the need to sort them is extremely important. In the final ArrayList code snippet, we will sort our data structures.

```java
//code 6.6
package fun.sanjibsinha;

import java.util.ArrayList;
import java.util.Collections;

public class ArrayListExamples {

    public static void main(String[] args) {

        /**
        * ArrayList examples
        * ArrayList is an ADT that provides a generic class, which has many useful m\
ethods to deal
        * with a collection of data. It also supports different data types.
        * An ArrayList is declared as follows:
        * ArrayList<T> arrayList = new ArrayList<T>();
        * Here T is the data type.
        */
        ArrayList<String> arrayList = new ArrayList<String>();
        //we have added 5 items
        arrayList.add("index");
        arrayList.add("about");
        arrayList.add("contact");
        arrayList.add("products");
        arrayList.add("sellers");
        //we have removed 2 items
        arrayList.remove("products");
        arrayList.remove("sellers");

        //we will change the first index page to home
        arrayList.set(0, "home");

        System.out.println("Unsorted list: ");
        for (int i = 0; i < arrayList.size(); i++){
            System.out.println(arrayList.get(i));
        }
        System.out.println("Now we are going to sort the list: ");
        Collections.sort(arrayList);

        for (int i = 0; i < arrayList.size(); i++){
            System.out.println(arrayList.get(i));
```

```
43              }
44              System.out.println();
45
46              /**
47               * we should use the Wrapper class instead of primitive data type
48               */
49              ArrayList<Double> doubleList = new ArrayList<Double>();
50              doubleList.add(456.45);
51              doubleList.add(12.123);
52              doubleList.add(78945.0258);
53              System.out.println("Unsorted list: ");
54              for (int i = 0; i < doubleList.size(); i++){
55                  System.out.println(doubleList.get(i));
56              }
57              System.out.println("Now we are going to sort the list: ");
58              Collections.sort(doubleList);
59              for (int i = 0; i < doubleList.size(); i++){
60                  System.out.println(doubleList.get(i));
61              }
62          }
63 }
```

In the above code, we have displayed the unsorted output first, after that, we have given the output of the sorted list.

```
1  //output of code 6.6
2  Unsorted list:
3  home
4  about
5  contact
6  Now we are going to sort the list:
7  about
8  contact
9  home
10
11 Unsorted list:
12 456.45
13 12.123
14 78945.0258
15 Now we are going to sort the list:
16 12.123
17 456.45
18 78945.0258
```

We have seen some examples of ArrayList. In the next section, we will see how LinkedList works. We will also learn why LinkedList consumes less memory than ArrayList.

ArrayList or LinkedList, which is faster?

As we have seen that the two most natural ways of storing sequences in computer memory are arrays and linked lists. ArrayList is an ADT that uses all concepts of handling Arrays with more flexibility. That is why, the time complexity is same for the both.

In LinkedList, it does not work that way. We usually model the memory as a sequence of memory cells, each of which has a unique address. An array or ArrayList is a contiguous piece of memory. Each cell of the memory stores one object, which is a part of the sequence stored in an Array or an ArrayList.

In a singly LinkedList two successive memory cells are allocated for each object of the sequence. Two memory cells form a node of a sequence. The first cell stores the object and the second cell stores a reference to the next node of the list.

In the next node there is two memory cells, and the previous node points to the first memory cell of the next node.

In a doubly linked list, the mechanism changes. Then we not only store a reference to the successor of each element, but we need to have a reference to its predecessor. It means each node should have three successive memory cells. We will discuss it in detail later.

At present, we will see how a singly LinkedList works.

```
1  //code 6.7
2  package fun.sanjibsinha.nodepackage;
3
4  public class NodeClass {
5
6      private int dataElement;
7      private NodeClass next;
8
9      public NodeClass(){
10         dataElement = 0;
11         next = null;
12     }
13
14     public NodeClass(int dataInt){
15         this.dataElement = dataInt;
16         this.next = null;
17     }
18
19     public NodeClass(int dataElement, NodeClass node){
20         this.dataElement = dataElement;
21         this.next = node;
22     }
23
24     public void insertAfter(NodeClass node){
```

```
25            NodeClass temporaryNode = this.next;
26            this.next = node;
27            node.next = temporaryNode;
28        }
29
30        public NodeClass nextNode(){
31            return this.next;
32        }
33
34        public void displayDataElement(){
35            System.out.println(this.dataElement);
36        }
37
38 }
39
40
41 package fun.sanjibsinha.nodepackage;
42
43 public class DisplayLinkedList {
44
45     public static void main(String[] args) {
46
47         NodeClass headNode;
48         NodeClass nextNodeOne;
49         NodeClass nextNodeTwo;
50         NodeClass nextNodeThree;
51         NodeClass currentNode;
52
53         headNode = new NodeClass(10);
54
55         nextNodeOne = new NodeClass(120);
56         headNode.insertAfter(nextNodeOne);
57
58         nextNodeTwo = new NodeClass(1200);
59         nextNodeOne.insertAfter(nextNodeTwo);
60
61         nextNodeThree = new NodeClass(12000);
62         nextNodeTwo.insertAfter(nextNodeThree);
63
64         currentNode = headNode;
65         while (currentNode != null){
66             currentNode.displayDataElement();
67             currentNode = currentNode.nextNode();
68         }
69     }
70 }
```

In the above code we have implemented the ADT of a singly LinkedList, where we have only added or inserted next node until it reaches the NULL value.

```
1 //output of code 6.7
2 10
3 120
4 1200
5 12000
```

Now, we have an introduction to Data Structures; we will dig into this matter more in the coming sections.

Collection Framework in programming languages

Every programming language has its own Collection framework. For brevity, in this chapter, we will use two programming languages in particular; they are Java and C++. However, the core ideas are same and implemented widely in every language; we will see to it later.

First of all, we need to understand one thing first. In this book, we are going to learn data structures and algorithm, because they are inter-dependent; and, they are also related to discrete mathematical conceptions.

All together, it is a burden of huge responsibility to organize the data structures and arrange the necessary algorithm to do every kind of operations possible to make an application run successfully. Now, if we get busy in low-level plumbing to organize the data structures using necessary algorithm from the scratch, we cannot concentrate on the other important parts of our programs. Collection framework helps us to get rid of that heavy load of low-level plumbing.

Therefore, every popular high level programming language has its own Collection framework.

As far as Java is concerned, the Collection framework, as an unified structure, consists three core parts; they are interfaces, implementations and algorithm.

Interfaces, as always, represent abstract data types; in object-oriented languages, interfaces generally form a hierarchy and its implementations depend heavily on the data structures and algorithm. When an object implements Collection interface, it uses some methods to perform useful computations, such as searching and sorting. These methods are called algorithm.

We need to understand another core conceptions regarding algorithm; it is polymorphic. It means, we can use the same method on many different data structures. In a moment we will find how it works.

Before going to see the polymorphic implementations of algorithms on different data structures, we must be aware of the benefits of Collection interfaces. In a nutshell, they reduce programming efforts, as we have discussed it earlier, you do not have to do the low-level plumbing. This framework gives you enough freedom to work on other important parts of program, because it supplies high-performance and high-quality implementations of useful data structure and algorithm.

Enough talking, let us see some code snippets to buttress our theory.

Stack and Queue in Java

Stack and Queue are abstract data types or interfaces that extend Collection interface in Java. They have more or less similarities; except the core concept where we remove the elements.

Stack uses 'last in first out' or LIFO method. It means, when we use the remove method, the last element. that has just been inserted, will be popped out first. In Queue, the opposite happens. It works on 'first in first out', or FIFO algorithm.

In this section we will mainly concentrate on Stack and Queue interfaces and on their implementations. In the coming section, we will learn about Deque; it is a double-ended-queue, a linear collection of elements that supports the insertion and removal of elements at both end points. It is the main advantage of Deque. For that reason,the Deque interface is considered to be a richer abstract data type than both Stack and Queue; quite naturally, it implements both stacks and queues at the same time.

Let us start with some Stack algorithms first. In the following program, we will see all the necessary algorithm of stacks.

```
1  //code 6.8
2
3  package fun.sanjibsinha.datastructures;
4
5  import java.util.Stack;
6
7  public class StackExamples {
8
9      public static void main(String[] args) {
10
11         Stack<Integer> lists = new Stack<>();
12         lists.push(10);
13         lists.push(11);
14         lists.push(12);
15         lists.push(13);
16         lists.push(14);
17
18         System.out.println("Here goes all the elements after pushing them.");
19
20         for (int i = 0; i < 5; i++){
21             System.out.println(lists.get(i));
22         }
23
24         System.out.println("The last element of the stack: " + lists.lastElement());
25
```

```
26          System.out.println("Now we are going to remove one element.");
27
28          lists.pop();
29
30          System.out.println("Here goes all the elements after popping one.");
31
32          for (int i = 0; i < 4; i++){
33              System.out.println(lists.get(i));
34          }
35
36          System.out.println("The last element is gone! The last one will always be ou\
37 t first.");
38          System.out.println("For this reason it is called Last in First out (LIFO)");
39
40      }
41 }
```

In the output, we will see how stacks work.

```
1  //output of 6.8
2
3  Here goes all the elements after pushing them.
4  10
5  11
6  12
7  13
8  14
9  The last element of the stack: 14
10 Now we are going to remove one element.
11 Here goes all the elements after popping one.
12 10
13 11
14 12
15 13
16 The last element is gone! The last one will always be out first.
17 For this reason it is called Last in First out (LIFO)
```

Although we do not have to build the Stack algorithms from the scratch, we can have a try to understand the inherent mechanism.

```
1 //code of 6.9
2 package fun.sanjibsinha.datastructures;
3
4 /**
5  * In this example we are going to create our own
6  * Stack class to simulate the Java's in-built methods
7  */
```

```java
public class StackExampleOne {


    final int MAX = 1000;
    int overTheTop;
    //creating an array object with the
    //maximum size of Stack
    int[] max = new int[MAX];

    StackExampleOne(){
        overTheTop = -1;
    }

    boolean pushTheStack(int num){
        if(overTheTop >= (MAX - 1)){
            System.out.println("The Stack has overflowed.");
            return false;
        } else {
            max[++overTheTop] = num;
            System.out.println(num + " pushed into the Stack.");
            return true;
        }
    }

    int popTheStack(){
        if(overTheTop < 0){
            System.out.println("The Stack is underflowed.");
            return 0;
        } else {
            int x = max[overTheTop--];
            return x;
        }
    }

    int peekTheStack(){
        if(overTheTop < 0){
            System.out.println("The Stack is underflowed.");
            return 0;
        } else {
            int x = max[overTheTop];
            return x;
        }
    }

    public static void main(String[] args) {

        StackExampleOne stacks = new StackExampleOne();
        stacks.pushTheStack(10);
        stacks.pushTheStack(100);
```

```
58          stacks.pushTheStack(500);
59          stacks.pushTheStack(600);
60          stacks.pushTheStack(700);
61          System.out.println("Now we are going to use the pop
method.");
62          System.out.println(stacks.popTheStack() + " popped from the
StackClass.");
63
64      }
65 }
```

Watch the output; we have succeeded to create our own stack class.

```
1 //output of 6.9
2
3 10 pushed into the Stack.
4 100 pushed into the Stack.
5 500 pushed into the Stack.
6 600 pushed into the Stack.
7 700 pushed into the Stack.
8 Now we are going to use the pop method.
9 700 popped from the StackClass.
```

Now we can add more functionalities to our Stack class. Watch the following code snippets.

```
1 //code 6.10
2 package fun.sanjibsinha.datastructures;
3
4 /**
5 * In this example we are going to create our own
6 * Stack class to simulate the Java's in-built methods
7 */
8
9 public class StackExampleOne {
10     //we cannot add more than 3 elements
11     final int MAX = 3;
12     int overTheTop;
13     //creating an array object with the
14     //maximum size of Stack
15     int[] max = new int[MAX];
16
17     StackExampleOne(){
18         overTheTop = -1;
19     }
20
21     boolean pushTheStack(int num){
22         if(overTheTop >= (MAX - 1)){
23             System.out.println("The Stack has overflowed.");
24             return false;
25         } else {
```

```java
26                max[++overTheTop] = num;
27                System.out.println(num + " pushed into the Stack.");
28                return true;
29            }
30        }
31
32        int popTheStack(){
33            if(overTheTop < 0){
34                System.out.println("The Stack is underflowed.");
35                return 0;
36            } else {
37                int x = max[overTheTop--];
38                return x;
39            }
40        }
41
42        int peekTheStack(){
43            if(overTheTop < 0){
44                System.out.println("The Stack is underflowed.");
45                return 0;
46            } else {
47                int x = max[overTheTop];
48                return x;
49            }
50        }
51
52    public static void main(String[] args) {
53
54        StackExampleOne stacks = new StackExampleOne();
55        stacks.pushTheStack(10);
56        stacks.pushTheStack(100);
57        stacks.pushTheStack(500);
58        System.out.println("Now we are going to use the pop method.");
59        System.out.println(stacks.popTheStack() + " popped from the StackClass.");
60        System.out.println(stacks.popTheStack() + " popped from the StackClass.");
61        System.out.println(stacks.popTheStack() + " popped from the StackClass.");
62        stacks.pushTheStack(10);
63        stacks.pushTheStack(100);
64        stacks.pushTheStack(500);
65        System.out.println("Now we are going to cross the limit. The Stack" +
66                " is bound to be overflowed.");
67        stacks.pushTheStack(10);
68
69    }
70 }
```

We have added new elements and also set the limit of the stacks. We have also tested whether the stack has been overflowed or not.

```
1 //output of 6.10
2 10 pushed into the Stack.
3 100 pushed into the Stack.
4 500 pushed into the Stack.
5 Now we are going to use the pop method.
6 500 popped from the StackClass.
7 100 popped from the StackClass.
8 10 popped from the StackClass.
9 10 pushed into the Stack.
10 100 pushed into the Stack.
11 500 pushed into the Stack.
12 Now we are going to cross the limit. The Stack is bound to be
overflowed.
13 The Stack has overflowed.
```

We have found that simulating Java's core algorithms is not difficult, we can add more functionalities to our Stack class. We verify the limit to check that no new element can be added.

```
1  //code 6.11
2  package fun.sanjibsinha.datastructures;
3  
4  /**
5   * In this example we are going to create our own
6   * Stack class to simulate the Java's in-built methods
7   */
8  
9  public class StackExampleOne {
10      //we cannot add more than 3 elements
11      final int MAX = 3;
12      int overTheTop;
13      //creating an array object with the
14      //maximum size of Stack
15      int[] max = new int[MAX];
16  
17      StackExampleOne(){
18          overTheTop = -1;
19      }
20  
21      boolean pushTheStack(int num){
22          if(overTheTop >= (MAX - 1)){
23              System.out.println("The Stack has overflowed.");
24              return false;
25          } else {
26              max[++overTheTop] = num;
27              System.out.println(num + " pushed into the Stack.");
28              return true;
```

```java
29              }
30          }
31
32          int popTheStack(){
33              if(overTheTop < 0){
34                  System.out.println("The Stack is underflowed.");
35                  return 0;
36              } else {
37                  int x = max[overTheTop--];
38                  return x;
39              }
40          }
41
42          int peekTheStack(){
43              if(overTheTop < 0){
44                  System.out.println("The Stack is under-flowed.");
45                  return 0;
46              } else {
47                  int x = max[overTheTop];
48                  return x;
49              }
50          }
51
52      public static void main(String[] args) {
53
54          StackExampleOne stacks = new StackExampleOne();
55          stacks.pushTheStack(10);
56          stacks.pushTheStack(100);
57          stacks.pushTheStack(500);
58          System.out.println("Now we are going to use the pop method.");
59          System.out.println(stacks.popTheStack() + " popped from the StackClass.");
60          System.out.println(stacks.popTheStack() + " popped from the StackClass.");
61          System.out.println(stacks.popTheStack() + " popped from the StackClass.");
62          stacks.pushTheStack(10);
63          stacks.pushTheStack(100);
64          stacks.pushTheStack(500);
65          System.out.println("Now we are going to cross the limit. The Stack" +
66                  " is bound to be overflowed.");
67          stacks.pushTheStack(1000);
68          System.out.println(stacks.peekTheStack() + " is the last element." +
69                  " The last element 1000 has not been added.");
70
71      }
72  }
```

Here goes the output:

```
1 //output of 6.11
2 10 pushed into the Stack.
3 100 pushed into the Stack.
4 500 pushed into the Stack.
5 Now we are going to use the pop method.
6 500 popped from the StackClass.
7 100 popped from the StackClass.
8 10 popped from the StackClass.
9 10 pushed into the Stack.
10 100 pushed into the Stack.
11 500 pushed into the Stack.
12 Now we are going to cross the limit. The Stack is bound to be overflowed.
13 The Stack has overflowed.
14 500 is the last element. The last element 1000 has not been added.
```

The Queue interface and its implementations are different, although the algorithm we use have the similarities with the Stack interface.

Let us see one simple Queue implementation, where we have added a few elements. We have kept the code and the output at the same place.

```
1 //code 6.12
2 package fun.sanjibsinha.datastructures;
3
4 import java.util.LinkedList;
5 import java.util.Queue;
6
7 public class QueueExampleOne {
8
9     public static void main(String[] args) {
10
11         Queue<String> letters = new LinkedList<String>();
12         letters.add("A");
13         letters.add("B");
14         letters.add("C");
15         letters.add("D");
16         letters.add("E");
17         letters.add("F");
18         System.out.println(letters);
19     }
20 }
21
22 //ouput of 6.12
23 [A, B, C, D, E, F]
```

We can check whether a Queue has any element or not using this algorithm.

```java
//code 6.13
package fun.sanjibsinha.datastructures;

import java.util.LinkedList;
import java.util.Queue;

public class QueueExampleOne {

    public static void main(String[] args) {

        Queue<String> letters = new LinkedList<String>();
        letters.add("A");
        letters.add("B");
        letters.add("C");
        letters.add("D");
        letters.add("E");
        letters.add("F");
        System.out.println(letters);
        letters.remove();
        System.out.println(letters);
        if(letters.contains("A")){
            System.out.println("The queue contain A.");
        } else {
            System.out.println("The queue does not contain A.");
        }
    }
}


//output 6.13
[A, B, C, D, E, F]
[B, C, D, E, F]
The queue does not contain A.
```

We can convert an array to a queue and use all the queue methods to manipulate that array. This is a big advantage of any Collection framework; because, we can always do this type of conversions.

```java
//code 6.14
package fun.sanjibsinha.datastructures;

import java.util.*;

public class QueueEXampleTwo {

    public static void main(String[] args) {

        //we can convert an array to queue and add more functionality
        String[] arrayNames = {"John", "Json", "Sanjib"};
```

```
12          Queue<String> queueNames = new LinkedList<>();
13          //we are converting array to queue
14          Collections.addAll(queueNames, arrayNames);
15          System.out.println(queueNames);
16          //now we can implement all queue functionality
17          queueNames.remove("Sanjib");
18          System.out.println(queueNames);
19
20      }
21  }
22
23
24  //output 6.14
25  [John, Json, Sanjib]
26  [John, Json]
```

As always, there are same types of algorithms with the different types of algorithms.

```
1  //code 6.15
2  package fun.sanjibsinha.datastructures;
3
4  import java.util.LinkedList;
5  import java.util.Queue;
6
7  public class QueueExampleThree {
8
9      public static void main(String[] args) {
10
11          Queue<String> letters = new LinkedList<String>();
12          letters.add("A");
13          letters.add("B");
14          letters.add("C");
15          letters.add("D");
16          letters.add("E");
17          letters.add("F");
18          System.out.println(letters);
19          //another method of removing
20          letters.poll();
21          System.out.println(letters);
22          //another method of adding
23          letters.offer("G");
24          System.out.println(letters);
25
26      }
27  }
28
29
30  //output 6.15
31  [A, B, C, D, E, F]
```

```
32 [B, C, D, E, F]
33 [B, C, D, E, F, G]
```

Just like Stack, we can also set the limit of a Queue. Crossing that will give you an exception.

```
1  //code 6.16
2  package fun.sanjibsinha.datastructures;
3
4  import java.util.concurrent.*;
5
6  public class QueueExampleFour {
7
8      public static void main(String[] args) {
9
10         BlockingQueue<String> names = new ArrayBlockingQueue<>(2);
11         names.add("John");
12         System.out.println(names);
13         names.add("Json");
14         System.out.println(names);
15         names.add("Sanjib");
16         System.out.println(names);
17     }
18 }
19
20
21 //output 6.16
22
23 [John]
24 [John, Json]
25 Exception in thread "main" java.lang.IllegalStateException: Queue full
26     at java.base/java.util.AbstractQueue.add(AbstractQueue.java:98)
27     at java.base/java.util.concurrent.ArrayBlockingQueue.add(ArrayBlockingQueue.java\
28 :326)
29     at fun.sanjibsinha.datastructures.QueueExampleFour.main(QueueExampleFour.java:14)
```

We can create our own Queue class by implementing the Java Queue interface; however, in this section we are not going to do that. In the coming section, we will check the Deque Abstract data type and see how it uses Stack and Queue at the same time.

Deque, a high-performance Abstract Data Type

We have seen the implementation of the Deque interface before; the Deque is pronounced as 'deck'. In Java, one of the general purpose implementations include

LinkedList. Another is ArrayDeque classes. In terms of efficient operations and flexibility, they can be compared. We will see to them in a minute.

Before that, we will quickly go through a Python code where we will create a double-ended queue or a deque. We have seen an examples of queue, the ordered collection of items. In deque, we have the ordered collection, which has two ends – a front and a rear. One characteristic has made this interface unique in nature – there is no restriction in adding and removing items. New items can be added, either at the front or at the rear.

The same way, we can either remove any item from the front or from the end. In a sense, this hybrid linear data structure provides all the capabilities of stacks and queues under one roof.

Although, it has combination of stacks and queues, it never assumes the LIFO or FIFO orderings that stacks and queues usually posses.

In the following Python code, we have created the Deque class that follows the guideline provided by the interface used in Java.

```
1  //code 6.17
2  //Python
3  # deque example
4
5  class DequeClass:
6
7      def __init__(self):
8          self.elements = []
9
10     def addingToFront(self, element):
11         self.elements.append(element)
12
13     def addingToBack(self, element):
14         self.elements.insert(0, element)
15
16     def removeFromFront(self):
17         self.elements.pop()
18
19     def removeFromBack(self):
20         self.elements.pop(0)
21
22     def isEmptyDeque(self):
23         return self.elements == []
24
25     def sizeOfDequeClass(self):
26         return len(self.elements)
27
28
29 dequeObject = DequeClass()
30 print(dequeObject.isEmptyDeque())
```

```
31 dequeObject.addingToFront("John")
32 dequeObject.addingToFront("Json")
33 dequeObject.addingToBack(4)
34 print(dequeObject.isEmptyDeque())
35 print(dequeObject.sizeOfDequeClass())
36
37 for element in range(0, 1):
38     print(dequeObject.elements)
39
40 dequeObject.addingToFront("Smith")
41 dequeObject.addingToFront(55)
42 dequeObject.addingToBack(40)
43 dequeObject.addingToBack("Web")
44
45 for elements in range(0, 1):
46     print(dequeObject.elements)
47
48 dequeObject.removeFromBack()
49 dequeObject.removeFromFront()
50
51 for elements in range(0, 1):
52     print(dequeObject.elements)
```

The output will tell the story in detail, how we have tested whether the Deque collection is empty or not. We have also added and removed elements at the either ends and shown the output.

```
1 //output 6.17
2 True
3 False
4 3
5 [4, 'John', 'Json']
6 ['Web', 40, 4, 'John', 'Json', 'Smith', 55]
7 [40, 4, 'John', 'Json', 'Smith']
```

In Java, we have performed the same operations, using the ArrayDeque class.

```
1 //code 6.18
2 package fun.sanjibsinha.datastructures;
3
4 import java.util.ArrayDeque;
5
6 public class DequeExampleOne {
7
8     public static void main(String[] args) {
9
10        // ArrayDeque class implements Deque interface
11        ArrayDeque<String> deques = new ArrayDeque<String>();
12        deques.addFirst("John");
13        deques.addLast("Json");
```

```java
14
15            for (String names : deques){
16                System.out.println(deques);
17            }
18
19            deques.addFirst("Smith");
20            deques.addLast("Web");
21
22            for(int i = 4; i >= deques.size(); i--){
23                System.out.println(deques);
24            }
25
26            deques.removeFirst();
27
28            for(int i = 3; i >= deques.size(); i--){
29                System.out.println(deques);
30            }
31
32            deques.removeLast();
33
34            for(int i = 2; i >= deques.size(); i--){
35                System.out.println(deques);
36            }
37        }
38 }
```

The output is almost same as the Python code we have seen before.

```
1 //output 6.18
2 [John, Json]
3 [John, Json]
4 [Smith, John, Json, Web]
5 [John, Json, Web]
6 [John, Json]
```

The next example in Java implementing ArrayDeque class has not done anything new, except that we have given the output in a different way.

```java
1 //code 6.19
2 package fun.sanjibsinha.datastructures;
3
4 import java.util.ArrayDeque;
5 import java.util.Iterator;
6
7 public class DequeExampleTwo {
8
9      public static void main(String[] args) {
10
11          // ArrayDeque class implements Deque interface
12          ArrayDeque<String> deques = new ArrayDeque<String>();
13          deques.addFirst("John");
```

```
14          deques.addLast("Json");
15          deques.addFirst("Smith");
16          deques.addLast("Web");
17
18
19          for (Iterator<String> iter = deques.iterator(); iter.hasNext();  ) {
20              System.out.println(iter.next());
21          }
22
23          System.out.println("After adding two more elements at the end.");
24
25          deques.add("Sanjib");
26          deques.add("Sinha");
27
28          for (Iterator<String> iter = deques.iterator(); iter.hasNext();  ) {
29              System.out.println(iter.next());
30          }
31      }
32 }
```

It is evident in the output.

```
1 //output 6.19
2 Smith
3 John
4 Json
5 Web
6 After adding two more elements at the end.
7 Smith
8 John
9 Json
10 Web
11 Sanjib
12 Sinha
```

As we have said earlier, the ArrayDeque and the LinkedList classes implement Deque interface in different manner. The LinkedList class is the 'list' implementation of the Deque interface; whereas, the ArrayDeque class is the resizable implementation of the same interface.

The basic insertion, removal and retrieval algorithms consist of 'addFirst, addLast, removeFirst, removeLast, getFirst and getLast' methods. As the name suggests, the 'addFirst' method adds an element at the head whereas the 'addLast' method adds an element at the rear.

The 'null' elements are allowed in the LinkedList, but in ArrayDeque, it is not allowed. LinkedList implements all 'list' operations, which adds more flexibility to it.

However, if we compare the efficiency, ArrayDeque is more efficient than LinkedList; because using ArrayDeque, we can add and remove at both ends. Moreover, LinkedList is not a good candidate for iteration.

Again, the advantage of LinkedList is during the iteration, we can remove the current element. According to the size complexity, the LinkedList implementation consumes more memory than ArrayDeque.

As long as data structures are concerned, these implementations are data structures and they always come with their own algorithm.

Here context plays a great role and according to the contexts you should choose the data structures. Comparisons are always there, in every programming language, based on the context, one data structure is preferable than the other.

In C++, the 'std::deque' is considered to be a container that allows fast insertion and deletion at the both ends. The advantage in C++ is, when we add or remove any element at the beginning or the end, it does not make pointers and references invalid to the rest of elements.

Let us first see an example of deque in C++.

```
//code 6.20
#include <iostream>
#include <string>
#include <deque>
using namespace std;

int main()
{
    // Creating a deque container that contains only integers
    std::deque<int> dequeData = {7, 5, 16, 8};

    // let us add an integer to the beginning and rear of the deque
    dequeData.push_front(13);
    dequeData.push_back(25);

    // Iterate and print values of deque
    for(int n : dequeData) {
        std::cout << n << '\n';
    }
}
```

We have created a deque container that contains integers and after that, we have pushed on integer at the beginning and one element at the end.

Therefore we have got this output:

```
//output 6.20
13
7
```

4 5
5 16
6 8
7 25

Now, we can look at this C++ code more closely. We can automatically expand and contract the storage place as needed. In C++ 'std::deque' is compared with 'std::vector', because expansion of deque is cheaper than the expansion of 'std::vector'. The advantage of 'std::deque' is it does not copy the existing elements to a new memory location. The following example shows how it happens.

```cpp
//code 6.21
#include <iostream>
#include <string>
#include <deque>
using namespace std;

int main(int argc, char const *argv[]) {
/* code of indexed sequence containers */
// Creating a deque container that contains only integers
std::deque<int> dequeData = {7, 5, 16};

// Iterating and printing values of deque
for(auto& n : dequeData) {
    std::cout << n << '\n';
}

std::cout << '\n';

dequeData.resize(6);

std::cout << "After we have resized up to 6: ";

// Iterating and printing values of deque
for(auto& n : dequeData) {
    std::cout << n << '\n';
}

std::cout << '\n';
dequeData.resize(2);

std::cout << "After we have resized down to 2: ";

// Iterating and printing values of deque
for(auto& n : dequeData) {
    std::cout << n << '\n';
}

return 0;
}
```

Depending on the resizable nature of expansion and contraction, the above C++ program gives us the following output:

```
1  //output 6.21
2  7
3  5
4  16
5  After we have resized up to 6:
6  7
7  5
8  16
9  0
10 0
11 0
12 After we have resized down to 2:
13 7
14 5
```

Because the 'std::deque' is an indexed sequence container, it is extremely fast in insertion and deletion process.

Moreover, the above example shows us one key aspect of deque in C++, the resizing process, or the insertion and deletion processes does not have any effect on pointers and references to the rest of the elements.

In the mext chapter, we will discuss algorithm and data structure in more detail; stable object-oriented programming languages like Java or C++ always provide reusable functionalities that are known as polymorphic algorithm.

I write regularly on Algorithm and Data Structure in

7. Algorithm, Data Structure, Collection Framework and Standard Template Library (STL)

Algorithm is expressed as a set of steps. By describing the actions at each step we instruct the computer do something. Usually we can use any natural language to describe the actions to perform at each step.

Consider this simple description.

```
1    1. Enter one integer
2    2. Enter another integer
3    3. Compare both integers and return the maximum value
4    4. Compare both integers and return the minimum value
```

In C++ programming language, on one hand, we can create generic functions to find the maximum or minimum value; and, on the other, we can take help from the 'algorithm' template library to find the same values.

Every high level language comes with its own algorithm library. They do so for one reason. Any system of counting or calculation by means of a device like computer involves following a steps or directions. Computer scientists use the word 'algorithm' to describe such as 'set of directions'.

In some cases, these directions could be simple as described above. In most cases, it is much more complex. For complex cases, we need the help of 'algorithm' library. Otherwise, we have to do the low-level plumbing, which is much more time consuming and that takes us away from building other important parts of any application. Historically, the derivation of this word has some interesting facts.

At the beginning of ninth century a mathematician wrote a book called 'Kitab al jabr w'al muqabala' (Rules of Restoration and Reduction). The word 'algebra' comes from the title of the book. This textbook introduced the use of Hindu numerals and included a systematic discussion of fundamental operations on integers.

The word 'algorithm' comes from the name of the mathematician, Abu Ja'far Mohammed ibn Musa al-Khowarizmi.

One of the most famous and well known algorithms is of course Euclid's Algorithm. It is a process for calculating the greatest common divisor (GCD) of two integers.

We can illustrate this algorithm in the following way.

```
1 1. Take two integers x and y
2 2. Divide y by x and get the remainder as r
3 3. Now replace the value of x with the value of r and replace the
value of y with th\
4 e value of x
5 4. Again divide y by x
6 5. This process will continue until we get r = 0
7 6. Once we get r = 0, stop the calculation, x is the GCD
```

Notice that the algorithm is expressed as a set of steps. Each step describes some action to take. The important thing is to describe the actions to be performed clearly and unambiguously.

Let us summarize this introductory part on algorithm in one sentence.

Data go inside the computer as inputs, algorithm takes charge, processing the data and after that the data as outputs come out.

By the way, people often mistake the word 'data' as singular; but, it is actually a plural form of the Latin word 'datum'. Since we have used this word too often in our discourse, and will use in future, therefore, for the curious readers I opened up the Oxford dictionary and searched for the word: datum.

Oxford dictionary defines datum as "A thing given or granted; a thing known or assumed as a fact, and made the basis of reasoning or calculation; a fixed starting-point for a series of measurements etc." It has also made it clear that the plural form of 'datum' is 'data'.

For instance, in Java we have Collection class and in C++ we have containers that manage this data structure part.

We are going to find out how they are related to algorithm.

Introducing Algorithm Library

Now, we have an idea about how algorithm works. For a computer, it is 'set of steps, or directions, or instructions'. For a chef it is a recipe.

Is not it?

In real world, when somebody asks directions to go to a certain place, we always try to help by giving that person a set of directions.

Right?

In the Google map, same thing happens, but in a different way.

There are trillions of algorithms working worldwide, may be more. As time passes by, it will increase. Quite naturally; because the volume of data increases; we need to structure those data in a more organized way. So we need things like 'container classes' in C++ or Collection framework in language like Java. We will discuss them in great detail in this chapter, along with algorithm, and discrete mathematics.

Moreover, it is clear that to avoid low-level plumbing for a huge volume of data we need algorithm libraries. For a small set of data we can manage it by manually, but for a IT product company, it needs very specialized algorithms, to put it eloquently, very complex algorithms that will deliver their complex products successfully.

Let us see two code snippets in C++ to understand why we need algorithm library. It is a component of Standard Template Library (STL). It provides many generic versions of standard algorithms that replace our low-level plumbing.

The first example shows us a simple program where we take two integers from the users and gives the output of the maximum and minimum values.

```
1  // code 7.1
2  #include <iostream>
3  #include <string>
4  using namespace std;
5
6  int Maximum(int a, int b){
7  if(a < b){
8      return b;
9  } else {
10     return a;
11 }
```

```
12 }
13
14 int Minimum(int a, int b){
15 if(a > b){
16     return b;
17 } else {
18     return a;
19 }
20 }
21
22 int EnterAndGet(){
23 std::cout << "Please enter a number (integer): " << '\n';
24 int Recieve;
25 std::cin >> Recieve;
26 return Recieve;
27 }
28
29 int main(int argc, char const *argv[]) {
30 /* code */
31 int valueOne = EnterAndGet();
32 int valueTwo = EnterAndGet();
33 std::cout << "Maximum value: " << Maximum(valueOne, valueTwo) << '\n';
34 std::cout << "Minimum value: " << Minimum(valueOne, valueTwo) << '\n';
35 return 0;
36 }
```

Running the program prompts us to give two integers. We enter two integers, and we get the maximum and the minimum values.

However, we could have tackled the same problem with less lines of code, if we used the C++ algorithms libraries. Let us see the next code snippets.

```
1 // code 7.2
2 #include <iostream>
3 #include <string>
4 #include <algorithm>
5 using namespace std;
6
7 int EnterAndGet(){
8 std::cout << "Please enter a number (integer): " << '\n';
9 int Recieve;
10 std::cin >> Recieve;
11 return Recieve;
12 }
13
14 int main(int argc, char const *argv[]) {
15 /* code */
16 int valueOne = EnterAndGet();
```

```
17 int valueTwo = EnterAndGet();
18 std::cout << "Maximum value: " << max(valueOne, valueTwo) << '\n';
19 std::cout << "Minimum value: " << min(valueOne, valueTwo) << '\n';
20 return 0;
21 }
```

Adding the algorithm header file on the top of our code makes all the difference. Now we can use the max() and min() methods; the libraries take all the load of low-level plumbing. With the less lines of code we get the same result.

In this particular point of our discourse, we need to understand one key concept. Every high level language tries to solve the same problem in their own way using their own framework or libraries.

There are some common algorithmic terms, such as 'sort', 'shuffle', or 'search'.

In Java, the algorithms come from the Collection class and the great majority of the algorithms provided by the Java platform operate on List instances. A few of them also operate on arbitrarily chosen Collection instances.

Let us see one example where we sort a list of alphabets in ascending order.

```
1 // code 7.3
2 //Java
3 package fun.sanjibsinha.chapter7;
4
5 import java.util.Arrays;
6 import java.util.Collections;
7 import java.util.List;
8
9 public class SortExampleOne {
10
11     public static void main(String[] args) {
12
13         List<String> list = Arrays.asList("x", "n", "y", "a", "s", "j");
14         Collections.sort(list);
15         System.out.println(list);
16     }
17 }
```

The algorithm described above takes the form of static methods whose first argument is the collection on which the operation is to be performed. Running the above code gives us the following output:

```
1 //output of 7.3
2
3 [a, j, n, s, x, y]
```

When the volume of the list is small, we can do the low-level plumbing, although it is wise to take help from the Algorithm Library in case of a very large volume of data.

Watch the following code snippets:

```
// code 7.4
package fun.sanjibsinha.chapter7;

import java.util.Arrays;

public class SortExampleTwo {

    public static void main(String[] args) {

        int[] anyArray = {210, 45, 258, 326, -12, 0, 89, 4, 9};
        System.out.println("Before Sorting : ");
        System.out.println(Arrays.toString(anyArray));
        System.out.println("After Sorting : ");
        for (int i = 0; i < anyArray.length; i++){
            int index = i;
            for (int j = i + 1; j < anyArray.length; j++)
                if (anyArray[j] < anyArray[index])
                    index = j;

            int smallerNumber = anyArray[index];
            anyArray[index] = anyArray[i];
            anyArray[i] = smallerNumber;
            System.out.println(anyArray[i]);
        }
    }
}
```

Here goes the output with the elements in ascending order.

```
//output of 7.4
Before Sorting :
[210, 45, 258, 326, -12, 0, 89, 4, 9]
After Sorting :
-12
0
4
9
45
89
210
258
326
```

The above program shows us reordering a List so that its elements are in ascending order according to an ordering relationship. However, to do that we need to hard code from the scratch. It is not necessary. We could have used Java Collection framework and manage to do the same operations by the following code snippets.

```java
// code 7.5
package fun.sanjibsinha.chapter7;
import java.util.Arrays;
import java.util.Collections;
import java.util.List;
public class SortExampleThree {

    public static void main(String[] args) {

        List<Integer> list = Arrays.asList(210, 45, 258, 326, -12, 0, 89, 4, 9);
        Collections.sort(list);
        System.out.println(list);
    }

}

//output of 7.5
[-12, 0, 4, 9, 45, 89, 210, 258, 326]
```

We can do the same thing in C++ programming language. C++ Standard Template Library stands between algorithm and containers (data structure) and manages them wisely. We will discuss them in great detail in this chapter. At the same time we will dig deep into the Collection Framework of Java; as Java does the same thing in its own way.

Comparing these two great programming languages we will have a better understanding of how algorithm and data structures are related.

Let us see the same code snippets in C++.

```cpp
// code 7.6
#include <algorithm>
#include <array>
#include <iostream>

int main()
{
    std::array<int, 9> standardArray = {210, 45, 258, 326, -12, 0, 89, 4, 9}

    // sort using the default operator
    std::sort(standardArray.begin(), standardArray.end());
    for (auto autoVariable : standardArray) {
        std::cout << autoVariable << " ";
    }
    std::cout << '\n';

    // sort using a standard library compare function object
    std::sort(standardArray.begin(), standardArray.end(),
```

```
          std::greater<int>());
19        for (auto autoVariable : standardArray) {
20            std::cout << autoVariable << " ";
21        }
22        std::cout << '\n';
23 }
```

As you see in the above code snippets, the std::sort() method by default takes two arguments-the beginning point and the end point. After that, it puts the list in ascending order. We do not have to reinvent the wheel as we did in the Java code snippets (code 7.4). Besides putting a collection of integers in ascending order, we may turn the order inside out. C++ Standard Template Library lets us do that by passing another argument.

```
1 std::sort(standardArray.begin(), standardArray.end(),
std::greater<int>());
```

Therefore, we get the following output, where the unordered list is ordered in ascending and descending orders both.

```
1 //output of 7.6
2 -12, 0, 4, 9, 45, 89, 210, 258, 326
3 326, 258, 210, 89, 45, 9, 4, 0, -12
```

Hopefully we have understood the basic conceptions regarding the algorithm libraries. In this section we have also learned how algorithm and data structures are related.

We will learn more about this in the coming sections.

Different types of Algorithms

There are many types of algorithm; as intermediate learners of computer science, you may have heard about them, and probably used some of them. In this section, we are neither going to learn them by heart, nor we will discuss them one after another.

We simply cannot do that. Even we could do that, we would not even try to do that because most of the examples are available in open source, and they are all over there in the internet.

In my opinion, the best thing we should do is to understand the core conceptions of different types of algorithms, and after that we can try to apply them to solve different types of problems.

We are not going to define algorithm again, we have already learned that 'set of directions' or 'set of steps' is called algorithm. It is true for everything; as long as algorithm is concerned, humans and computers look utterly alike. They all need directions to do something meaningful.

Some of the better known algorithms are Recursive algorithms, dynamic programming algorithms, Brute Force algorithms, etc.

There is no eternal endpoint for learning algorithm; therefore, especially for basic cognitive process to pick up algorithm, the learning curve is really steep. A steep learning curve will always try to shed you from its roof, just like a steep roof sheds snow; if you want to go the top, and want to master the art of writing your own algorithm, you need to work hard to solve different types of problems.

Recursive Algorithm

Semantically, when we say that a function calls itself directly or indirectly, it is called recursion. However, if we want to put it in an algorithmic way, we should write that 'it is a set of directions by which we want to divide a problem and conquer'. We can put it in more eloquent way, 'decrease the problem and conquer'.

We use one function to call itself, and the corresponding functions are known as recursive functions. But there is a drawback or difficulty that is not evident.

First of all, when a function calls itself, it will call itself endlessly if we do not stop it. Therefore, there should be a mechanism to stop it. Otherwise, it might make things look like eternal looping and cause run time error. We need a base case, so that the mechanism called 'calling itself' should progress towards the base case.

The second most important things are 'space, speed and time'. When a function calls itself again and again, it takes place in the stack. The final code or program might end up as a slow program. We will discuss the pros and cons after we get our head around the recursive algorithm a little bit. Let us try to understand how it works, first.

Suppose using a function we want to print 2 and 1. We can do that two ways-one is iterative way, using loop construct. The another way is the recursive way, allowing the the function to call itself. Consider the code snippet below.

```
1 //code 7.7
2 void printNumber(int n){
3 if (n == 0) { //this is the base case towards which the method proceeds
4     return;
5 }
6 System.out.println(n);
7 printNumber(n - 1);
8 }
```

If we call the method "printNumber(2)", what is going to happen? Let us try to understand the core conception of recursion. When we call the above method, passing the integer parameter 2, three clones are made. The original call should give us 2 as output. But it has made a recursive call creating a clone of the function as the value of 'n' is now equal to 1. This call should give us 1 as output. After that, it makes another recursive call and makes the value of 'n' equal to 0.

However, that is our base case, and we are making progress towards that base case where we have made a condition so that it goes away and stops calling the function. When we reach the base case, that is the output of 'n' is equal to 0, the 'if' condition is true and it just returns. If there were no 'base case', the stacks would be overflowed. There would be a run time error. The 'if' condition or the base case prevents the recursive call from being made again and again.

In our following code snippets we will see some simple examples of recursive functions; then we will move towards the lesser known world of recursion to the unknown world of recursion, solving more complex problems.

The first C++ code snippet will give us a glimpse of recursion in its simplest version. We will move forward to the base case from a given number, and at the same time, we will rearrange the order.

```
1  //code 7.8
2  #include <iostream>
3  #include <string>
4  #include <cmath>
5  #include <cstdlib>
6  #include <sstream>
7  #include <numeric>
8  #include <string>
9  #include <vector>
10 #include <cstddef>
11 #include <limits>
12 #include <algorithm>
13
14 void factorialExampleOne(int n){
15     if(n < 1){
16         return;
17     } else {
18         std::cout << n << "\n";
19         factorialExampleOne(n - 1);
20         std::cout << n << "\n";
21     }
22 }
23
24 int main(int argc, char const *argv[]) {
25
26 std::cout << "Hello World." << "\n";
27 factorialExampleOne(3);
28 return 0;
29 }
```

We will move from 3 to 1 and vice versa. Here is the output:

```
1 //output of 7.8
2 Hello World.
3 3
4 2
5 1
6
7 1
8 2
9 3
```

In the next code snippet, we will manipulate the output by squaring the numbers; it is a test case, it shows that you can do many types of manipulations for your own advantage.

```
1  //code 7.9
2  #include <iostream>
3  #include <string>
4  #include <cmath>
5  #include <cstdlib>
6  #include <sstream>
7  #include <numeric>
8  #include <string>
9  #include <vector>
10 #include <cstddef>
11 #include <limits>
12 #include <algorithm>
13
14 using namespace std;
15
16 void factorialExampleTwo(int n){
17     if(n < 1){
18         return;
19     } else {
20         //pass any integer and get the squared value in descending order
21         cout << n * n << "\n";
22         factorialExampleTwo(n - 1);
23         //reversing the order of the squared integers
24         cout << n * n << "\n";
25     }
26 }
27
28 int main(int argc, char const *argv[]) {
29
30     int n = 4;
31     cout << "Hello World." << "\n";
32     factorialExampleTwo(n);
33     return 0;
34
35 }
```

The output is quite expected. We have the squared values of the output.

```
1  //output of 7.9
2  Hello World.
3  16
4  9
5  4
6  1
7  
8  1
9  4
10 9
11 16
```

The manipulation of integers could cause run time error and make the stack overflow if your base case is wrong. Therefore, that should be the most important part when you call a function recursively.

We can call a recursive function indirectly, too. The next code snippet in C++ shows you a simple example.

```
1  //code 7.10
2  #include <iostream>
3  #include <string>
4  #include <cmath>
5  #include <cstdlib>
6  #include <sstream>
7  #include <numeric>
8  #include <string>
9  #include <vector>
10 #include <cstddef>
11 #include <limits>
12 #include <algorithm>
13 
14 using namespace std;
15 
16 void factorialExampleThree(int n){
17     //cout << "Calling recursion. \n";
18     if(n < 1){
19         return;
20     }else{
21         cout << n << "\n";
22         cout << "Calling recursion. \n";
23         factorialExampleThree(n - 1);
24         //cout << "Calling recursion. \n";
25     }
26     //cout << "Calling recursion. \n";
27 }
28 
29 void AnotherRecursion(){
```

```
30      cout << "Enter a positive even integer to see more recursion.
\n";
31      int a = 0;
32      cin >> a;
33      if(a % 2 == 0){
34          factorialExampleThree(a);
35      } else {
36          cout << "Wrong input!";
37      }
38 }
39
40 int main(int argc, char const *argv[]) {
41
42      int n = 4;
43      cout << "Hello Recursive functions." << "\n";
44      factorialExampleThree(n);
45      cout << "Hello Another Recursive functions." << "\n";
46      AnotherRecursion();
47      return 0;
48
49 }
```

While calling another recursion, we can test whether that integer is even or odd. Based on that, we can make some more recursive calls.

```
 1 //output of 7.10
 2 Hello Recursive functions.
 3 4
 4 Calling recursion.
 5 3
 6 Calling recursion.
 7 2
 8 Calling recursion.
 9 1
10 Calling recursion.
11 Hello Another Recursive functions.
12 Enter a positive even integer to see more recursion.
13 8
14 8
15 Calling recursion.
16 7
17 Calling recursion.
18 6
19 Calling recursion.
20 5
21 Calling recursion.
22 4
23 Calling recursion.
24 3
25 Calling recursion.
```

26 2
27 Calling recursion.
28 1
29 Calling recursion.

Probably you have already noticed that the fee levied for the use of stack memory is enormous. It happens for the memory allocation and re-allocation. When any function is called from main(), the memory is usually allocated to it on the stack, for the recursive calls different copy of local variables or clone is created for each function call. This process continues till the process reaches the base case.

When the same problem is solved using the iterative methods, it consumes less memory, but usually the length of code is bigger than the recursive one. However, for a small problem like finding factors, we cannot even feel the difference.

```
//code 7.11
#include <iostream>
#include <string>
#include <cmath>
#include <cstdlib>
#include <sstream>
#include <numeric>
#include <string>
#include <vector>
#include <cstddef>
#include <limits>
#include <algorithm>

using namespace std;

static int i;

void findFactors(int n, int i){
    // Checking if the number is less than the input
    if (i <= n) {
        if (n % i == 0) {
            cout << i << " ";
        }
        findFactors(n, i + 1);
    }
}

void findidngFactors(int f){
    for(i = 1; i <= f; i++){
        if(f % i == 0){
            cout << i << "\n";
        }
    }
}

```

```
36 int main(int argc, char const *argv[]) {
37
38     cout << "Enter any integer to check factors. \n";
39     int p = 0;
40     cin >> p;
41     findidngFactors(p);
42     cout << "*****";
43     cout << "\n";
44     findFactors(p, 1);
45
46     return 0;
47
48 }
```

Both the functions give us the same output. Whatever number you pass through the functions, it will give you the same output. There is only one difference. The same thing does not take place in the memory region.

```
1 //output of 7.11
2 Enter any integer to check factors.
3 119
4 *****
5 1
6 7
7 17
8 119
9 *****
10 1 7 17 119
```

Some problems, such as tree traversals, or Tower of Hanoi is inherently recursive. Of course the same problems can be solved iterative way with the help of data structures. If you compare the lines of code then recursion takes less and looks cleaner.

In the next problem, we will find the prime factors of any integer. Usually any prime number has only two factors-1, and the number itself. For that reason, they are called prime numbers. Other integers has more than one factors.

Consider a number-6; it has factors, such as 1, 2, 3, and 6. The integer 6 is divisible by all those factors. In this list, not all factors are prime. Only 2 and 3 are prime factors.

In the next code snippet, we will find only the prime factors of any integer, using recursion.

```
1 //code 7.12
2 #include <iostream>
3 #include <string>
4 #include <cmath>
5 #include <cstdlib>
```

```cpp
 6 #include <sstream>
 7 #include <numeric>
 8 #include <string>
 9 #include <vector>
10 #include <cstddef>
11 #include <limits>
12 #include <algorithm>
13
14 using namespace std;
15
16 void findPrimeFactors(int x)
17 {
18     int a;
19     for(a = 2; a <= x; a++)
20     {
21         if(x % a == 0){
22             cout << a << " ";
23             findPrimeFactors(x / a);
24             break;
25         }
26     }
27 }
28
29 int main(int argc, char const *argv[]) {
30     int number;
31     cout << "\n" << "Enter a number: " << "\n";
32     cin >> number;
33     findPrimeFactors(number);
34     cout << "\n\n";
35
36     return 0;
37
38 }
```

We have used a loop counter to call the function recursively. We could have written the same code in shorter space if we did not use the loop counter. Instead we could have pass another parameter through the same function.

```
 1 //output of 7.12
 2 Enter a number:
 3 81
 4 3 3 3 3
 5 Enter a number:
 6 564
 7 2 2 3 47
 8 Enter a number:
 9 45689
10 7 61 107
```

As you have noticed, to prevent the infinite recursion, we always provide a condition, or base case. The next code snippet, in Java, will give us factorials of any integer.

By using comments, we have pointed out the termination call.

```
1 //code 7.13
2 package fun.sanjibsinha.recursive;
3
4 public class AlgoRecursiveOne {
5
6     static int getFactorial(int f) {
7         if (f != 0)  // termination condition, base case
8             return f * getFactorial(f - 1); // recursive call
9         else
10            return 1;
11    }
12
13    public static void main(String[] args) {
14
15        int number = 4, result;
16        result = getFactorial(number);
17        System.out.println(number + " factorial = " + result);
18
19    }
20
21 }
22 //output of 7.13
23 4 factorial = 24
```

To get the factorial of 4 we do not have to write a long line of code. It has been managed in a shorter space. However, as the number gets bigger, the output acts like a beggar. The 'int' data type has a limit. It is overflowed.

In that case, we can use the 'long', the bigger version of 'int' data type.

```
1 //code 7.14
2 package fun.sanjibsinha.recursive;
3
4 import java.util.Scanner;
5
6 public class AlgoRecursiveOne {
7
8     static long i;
9
10    static long getFactorial(long f) {
11        if (f != 0)  // termination condition, base case
12            return f * getFactorial(f - 1); // recursive call
13        else
14            return 1;
15    }
```

```
16
17      public static void main(String[] args) {
18
19          Scanner sc = new Scanner(System.in);
20          System.out.printf("Enter any positive integer to know its factorial: ");
21          i = sc.nextLong();
22          long result;
23          result = getFactorial(i);
24          System.out.println(i + " factorial = " + result);
25
26      }
27
28 }
29
30
31 //output of 7.14
32 12 factorial = 479001600
33 20 factorial = 2432902008176640000
```

With the help of recursion, we can solve such problems quite easily. Moreover, we need to write less line of code than we write when we solve the same problems iterative way.

We need to understand one key concept here. Whenever we call a function an active record is maintained. The active record of each call includes spaces in the stack for many further operations. Remember, between calling a function and returning the value, there are several moments; parameters of methods, local variables, returned addresses;so many things are there. And they all want spaces in the stack. When a function is called, its active record is pushed into the stack, but after that, many things happen.

When a function calls recursively, the stacks get busy with many such operations. This overhead of many operations in the stack, makes any recursion slow. It also uses more memory. Keeping all these barriers that impede free movement of memory, we still need recursion.

Why? We will see in a minute.

We are going to compare two code snippets one after another. In the first one, we get the factorials using iterative way.

```
1 //code 7.15
2 package fun.sanjibsinha.recursive;
3
4 public class AlgoRecursiveTwo {
5
6     static int getFactorial(int f) {
7         if (f == 0){
8             return 1;
```

```
 9            }
10            int tmp = f;
11            for (int k = f-1; k>=1; k--){
12                tmp = tmp * k;
13            }
14            return (tmp);
15        }
16
17        public static void main(String[] args) {
18            int newNumber = 4, result;
19            result = getFactorial(newNumber);
20            System.out.printf("Factorial of " + newNumber + " = " + result);
21            System.out.printf("");
22        }
23 }
24
25
26 //output of 7.15
27 Factorial of 4 = 24
```

Now take a look at the same code, written in recursive way.

```
 1 //code 7.16
 2 package fun.sanjibsinha.recursive;
 3
 4 public class AlgoRecursiveThree {
 5
 6     static int getFactorial(int f) {
 7         if (f == 0){
 8             return 1;
 9         } else {
10             return (f * getFactorial(f - 1));
11         }
12     }
13
14
15     public static void main(String[] args) {
16         int newNumber = 4, result;
17         result = getFactorial(newNumber);
18         System.out.printf("Factorial of " + newNumber + " = " + result);
19         System.out.printf("");
20
21     }
22 }
23
24
25 //output of 7.16
26 Factorial of 4 = 24
```

The advantage of using recursion is its shortness, cleanliness, and moreover, it is closer to our discrete mathematical definitions. If you think and model your code keeping the mathematical conceptions in your mind, then recursion is close to your definition.

It is more evident when we use recursion in finding the Fibonacci series. Mathematically, the Fibonacci is defined as the following:

```
1 Fibonacci of 1 or 2 is 1
2 Fibonacci of F (for F > 2) is Fibonacci of (F - 1) + Fibonacci of (F
 - 2)
```

If we want to find the Fibonacci series using recursion, it is not only the simplest version, but also mathematically similar.

Watch the next line of code snippet.

```
1 //code 7.17
2 package fun.sanjibsinha.recursive;
3
4 public class AlgoFibTwo {
5
6     static int getFibonacci(int f) {
7         if ((f == 1) || (f == 2)){
8             return 1;
9         } else {
10            return (getFibonacci(f - 1) + getFibonacci(f - 2));
11        }
12    }
13
14    public static void main(String[] args) {
15
16        int newNumber = 6, result;
17        result = getFibonacci(newNumber);
18        System.out.printf("Fibonacci series of " + newNumber + " = " + result);
19        System.out.printf("");
20        System.out.printf("");
21    }
22
23 }
24
25
26 //output of 7.17
27
28 Fibonacci series of 6 = 8
```

We can do the same thing using iterative way, but it does not reflect the mathematical conception as the recursion does. The next code snippet shows us the same thing.

```
1  //code 7.18
2  package fun.sanjibsinha.recursive;
3
4  public class AlgoFibOne {
5
6      static int getFibinacci(int f) {
7          int k1, k2, k3;
8          k1 = k2 = k3 = 1;
9          for (int j = 3; j <= f; j++) {
10             k3 = k1 + k2;
11             k1 = k2;
12             k2 = k3;
13         }
14         return k3;
15     }
16
17     public static void main(String[] args) {
18
19         int newNumber = 6, result;
20         result = getFibinacci(newNumber);
21         System.out.printf("Fibonacci series of " + newNumber + " = " + result);
22         System.out.printf("");
23         System.out.printf("");
24     }
25 }
26
27
28 //output of 7.18
29 Fibonacci series of 6 = 8
```

Ability to simulate the mathematical models cannot always give the moral support to the recursions. Because there are many other factors while we program, we need to keep them in our mind.

Maintaining that the recursive versions are slower than the iterative versions, we may still want to adopt it for some reasons. When the code is heavy in iterative versions, it is much simpler to adopt the recursions, it also easier to debug and maintain. Whatever our reasons to adopt the recursions, slowing down the program may cost at the end. We cannot save the memory space, we cannot speed up the execution; yet, in some cases, recursions are essential.

As we progress, we will find that later.

Binary Tree and Data Structure

Binary tree is a specialized representation of data structure. Our main purposes of studying data structure is to organize data in the most efficient manner. Binary tree is used for data storage purposes. A tree is represented by nodes that are connected by edges or pointers.

A binary tree has a special condition, which has also made it very special among other data storage mechanisms. A node of binary tree can have maximum two children. When it has one or two children, we call it a sub-tree. Therefore, each node of a sub-tree might have more sub-trees.

When a node of a tree or a sub-tree does not have any children, it is called leaf node.

While traversing a tree, we always take the leaf node as our end point, or base case for recursion. We can search a binary tree as an ordered array. Besides, we can insert and delete data in any binary tree just like a LinkedList.

As we have just said, a tree and its sub-tree always create a sequence of nodes; this sequence is known as path. This path starts from the top of the node, which is referred as root. Always there is only one root and one path to the other node. It has no duplicate path.

The nodes that are placed below, are called children; and, these children nodes always have nodes above them, which are known as parent nodes.

If we consider a root node as the parent node, then it is said that this node is on the level one. The node just below is placed at level two.

Finally, a tree can be traversed in various manners; they are pre-order, post-order and in-order.

There are different algorithms for each kind of tree traversal. In this section, we will take a brief look at those algorithms of tree traversal.

Tree Traversal Algorithm

As we have just learned, in some cases, recursions are essential. Especially when most of the tree based algorithms are concerned, they can be easily implemented using recursion because a binary tree is a recursive data structure. Although it is wise to learn solving the same problems using without recursion; you can solve the tree based algorithms using iteration, also.

In this section, we will learn tree traversals using recursion and using iteration, both. As the tool of our learning, we have chosen Java as programming language. In the following sections, we will take a brief look at other algorithms as well.

A hierarchical tree structure usually represents a set of linked nodes. We can associate an ADT or abstract data type as it simulates the tree structure. It has a root value and the sub-tree of children may be connected with the parent node.

First of all, let us think about an image of tree structure to understand the concept. We will use this image in the following code snippets also.

```
1 * input:
2 *      1
3 *     / \
```

```
4 *     2       5
5 *    / \       \
6 *   3   4       6
7 *
8 *  output:  1  2  3  4  5  6
```

In the above input section, the collection of nodes start with the root node. Each node is connected with a list of references to children nodes.

This tree structure can be defined recursively; because each node is a data structure consisting of a value that generates the list of references to children nodes.

Although there are other methods to do the binary tree traversal, but the most popular ways to traverse the trees in Java are the pre-order, post-order, and in-order traversal. In this section, we will take a detailed look at each of the traversal methods.

Generally, when you traverse a tree you have three choices-root, left sub-tree, and right sub-tree. In which order you will traverse the tree decides the nature of the algorithm associated with it.

By default a binary tree is a recursive data structure; firstly, it has similarities with LinkedList, which is also a recursive data structure; secondly, if you remove a node, rest of the structure is also a binary tree like left and right binary tree. For that reason, when a function calls itself, it is easier to traverse from one node to the other.

In this section we will limit our discussion to three types of binary tree traversal algorithms; they are pre-order, post-order and in-order.

A tree can be traversed by our algorithm in several ways. In pre-order traversal, it goes this way: root, left and right. In post-order traversal, it goes this way: left, right and root. The in-order traversal traverses the nodes this way: left, root and right.

We have seen how LinkedList works, therefore creating nodes is not difficult. We can start visiting the root node first, then we can move towards the left sub-tree and after that we can proceed towards the right sub-tree.

We should start with the Node class, because a tree has nodes. After that we might use recursion to generate more nodes. The advantage of node is it has left or right pointers that point either to the left side or right side.

To do the pre-order tree traversal, we can use a method like 'preOrder()' that will call itself by passing the node object; you can give it any name.

Pre Order Traversal

Let us start with a pre-order tree traversal code snippet, which will give us a clear picture how we can implement our algorithm. By dissecting that code, we will learn how pre-order tree traversal algorithm works. In the first code snippet, we will see how we can traverse the tree without using recursion. We start traversing the tree with the root node, after that we visit the left sub-tree and next, we visit the right sub-tree.

Each sub-tree is also visited pre-order way. That means it starts from the root of the sub-tree, then it goes to the left sub-tree and the above process continues until we reach a leaf node.

The pattern of traversal tells us one thing very clearly; this tree traversal is a good candidate for recursion. After visiting the root node, we can recursively visit the left sub-tree and then, we can visit the right sub-tree recursively again.

Still recursion is not the only way. We can do the traversal using iteration also. The following code snippet shows that example.

```
1 //code 7.19
2
3 package fun.sanjibsinha.chapter7.binarytree.preordertraversal;
4
5 // we need to use the Stack Collection framework
6 import java.util.Stack;
7
8 public class BinaryTreeWithoutRecursion {
9
10     static class TreeNodeClass {
11         String data;
12         BinaryTreeWithoutRecursion.TreeNodeClass left, right;
13
14         TreeNodeClass(String value) {
15             this.data = value;
16             left = right = null;
17         }
18
19         boolean isLeaf() {
20             return left == null ? right == null : false;
21         }
22
23     }
24
25     // root of the binary tree from where we start our journey
26     BinaryTreeWithoutRecursion.TreeNodeClass root;
27
28     /**
29     * this method will visit tree nodes without recursion.
30     */
31     public void VisitTreeWithoutRecursion() {
32         Stack<BinaryTreeWithoutRecursion.TreeNodeClass> nodes = new Stack<>();
33         nodes.push(root);
34
```

```java
35            while (!nodes.isEmpty()) {
36                BinaryTreeWithoutRecursion.TreeNodeClass current = nodes.pop();
37                System.out.printf("%s ", current.data);
38
39                if (current.right != null) {
40                    nodes.push(current.right);
41                }
42                if (current.left != null) {
43                    nodes.push(current.left);
44                }
45            }
46        }
47
48 }
49
50 package fun.sanjibsinha.chapter7.binarytree.preordertraversal;
51
52 /**
53  * In our example: A B C D E F
54      A
55     / \
56    B   E
57   / \   \
58  C   D   F
59
60  */
61
62 public class PreOrderTreeTraversalWithoutRecursion {
63
64     public static void main(String[] args) {
65
66         // construct the binaryTree object to traverse without recursion
67         BinaryTreeWithoutRecursion binaryTree = new BinaryTreeWithoutRecursion();
68         BinaryTreeWithoutRecursion.TreeNodeClass root = new BinaryTreeWithoutRecursi\
69 on.TreeNodeClass("A");
70         binaryTree.root = root;
71         binaryTree.root.left = new BinaryTreeWithoutRecursion.TreeNodeClass("B");
72         binaryTree.root.left.left = new BinaryTreeWithoutRecursion.TreeNodeClass("C"\
73 );
74
75         binaryTree.root.left.right = new BinaryTreeWithoutRecursion.TreeNodeClass("D\
76 ");
77         binaryTree.root.right = new
```

```
                BinaryTreeWithoutRecursion.TreeNodeClass("E");
78              binaryTree.root.right.right = new
BinaryTreeWithoutRecursion.TreeNodeClass("\
79 F");
80
81              // the binaryTree object will traverse the tree without
recursion
82              binaryTree.VisitTreeWithoutRecursion();
83              System.out.println();
84
85
86          }
87 }
```

The output is quite expected here, in the comments section we have declared how it will look like.

```
1 //output of 7.19
2
3 A B C D E F
4
5 Process finished with exit code 0
```

In general, recursion implicitly uses a Stack data structure. In recursion when we reach the base point, it starts unwinding. For that reason, in the above code, we have used the Stack data structure to traverse the tree without using recursion.

In a tree, the leaf node is the base point. Reaching that point node becomes null, and we reach the base point. To simulate the recursion we need to apply Stack explicitly, instead of implicitly. Let us watch the above code snippets to understand what happens inside.

First, this part where we have defined and declared the static 'TreeNodeClass':

```
 1 static class TreeNodeClass {
 2          String data;
 3          BinaryTreeWithoutRecursion.TreeNodeClass left, right;
 4
 5          TreeNodeClass(String value) {
 6              this.data = value;
 7              left = right = null;
 8          }
 9
10          boolean isLeaf() {
11              return left == null ? right == null : false;
12          }
13
14      }
15
16      // root of the binary tree from where we start our journey
17      BinaryTreeWithoutRecursion.TreeNodeClass root;
```

We want three 'node' objects, and we name them as 'left', 'right', and 'root'. We also need a 'String' data type variable to store our values. The advantage of making the class static is it will run the program faster.

The only problem of using iteration lies in its length of code. We cannot make it as concise and readable as we can do using recursion.

Let us try to do the same pre-order tree traversal in recursive way. Comparing these two code snippets will give us a good idea about why binary tree traversal is usually done recursively.

```
1  //code 7.20
2
3  package fun.sanjibsinha.chapter7.binarytree.preordertraversal;
4
5  public class BinaryTreeWithRecursion {
6
7      static class TreeNodeClass {
8          String data;
9          TreeNodeClass left;
10         TreeNodeClass right;
11
12         TreeNodeClass(String value) {
13             this.data = value;
14             left = right = null;
15         }
16
17         boolean isLeaf() {
18             return left == null ? right == null : false;
19         }
20
21     }
22
23     // root of the binary tree from where we start our journey
24     BinaryTreeWithRecursion.TreeNodeClass root;
25
26     /**
27      * the public method to traverse and display the nodes
28      * by calling the recursive function
29      */
30     public void traversingPreOrderByCallingItself() {
31         traversingPreOrderByCallingItself(root);
32     }
33
34     /**
35      * traversing the binary tree by calling itself
36      */
37     private void traversingPreOrderByCallingItself(BinaryTreeWithRecursion.TreeNodeC\
38 lass node) {
```

```
39            if (node == null) {
40                return;
41            }
42            System.out.printf("%s ", node.data);
43            traversingPreOrderByCallingItself(node.left);
44            traversingPreOrderByCallingItself(node.right);
45       }
46
47 }
48
49
50 package fun.sanjibsinha.chapter7.binarytree.preordertraversal;
51
52 /**
53  * In our example: A B C D E F
54 A
55 / \
56 B   E
57 / \   \
58 C   D   F
59
60 */
61
62 public class PreOrderTreeWithRecursion {
63
64      public static void main(String[] args) {
65
66          // construct the binaryTree object to traverse without recursion
67          BinaryTreeWithRecursion binaryTree = new BinaryTreeWithRecursion();
68          BinaryTreeWithRecursion.TreeNodeClass root = new BinaryTreeWithRecursion.Tre\
69 eNodeClass("A");
70          binaryTree.root = root;
71          binaryTree.root.left = new BinaryTreeWithRecursion.TreeNodeClass("B");
72          binaryTree.root.left.left = new BinaryTreeWithRecursion.TreeNodeClass("C");
73
74          binaryTree.root.left.right = new BinaryTreeWithRecursion.TreeNodeClass("D");
75          binaryTree.root.right = new BinaryTreeWithRecursion.TreeNodeClass("E");
76          binaryTree.root.right.right = new BinaryTreeWithRecursion.TreeNodeClass("F");
77
78          System.out.println();
79          binaryTree.traversingPreOrderByCallingItself();
80          System.out.println();
```

```
81
82      }
83 }
```

If you are a Java developer, you have probably guessed why we have used the pritf() method:

```
1 System.out.printf("%s ", node.data);
```

We want to store the data to build the structure. Until we reach the base case or leaf node, the function traversingPreOrderByCallingItself() calls itself and keeps adding the value to the node tree. Therefore, the output will be same as before.

```
1 //output of 7.20
2
3 A B C D E F
4
5 Process finished with exit code 0
```

Now what are the main differences between the iteration and recursion? For the pre-order tree traversal algorithm, things were a little bit complicated. We needed a Stack of node first, then we pushed the tree root in the Stack. After doing that we keep pushing the right child and left child; at the same time we pop all nodes one by one for each node.

But in recursion the recursive method takes a Node in parameter and and calls itself to add left child and right child. The code snippet, not only looks concise, but it is also more readable.

Post Order Traversal

To visit all the nodes and print their values are known as tree traversal. Just like LinkedList, in pre-order traversal, we start from the root or head node and then we move until we reach the leaf node.

The post-order tree traversal represents just the opposite. Here the root node is visited last. We start from the left sub-tree; then we visit the right sub-tree, and after that we reach the root node.

Therefore, we should use recursion to visit the left sub-tree; then visiting right sub-tree recursively leads us to our final destination-the root node. The post-order tree traversal follows this algorithm.

Let us see the post-order tree traversal using iteration as we have done in the previous case of pre-order traversal.

```
1 //code 7.21
2
3 package fun.sanjibsinha.chapter7.binarytree.postordertraversal;
4
5 import java.util.Stack;
```

```
public class BinaryTreeNotRecursive {

    static class TreeNodeClass {
        String data;
        BinaryTreeNotRecursive.TreeNodeClass left, right;

        TreeNodeClass(String value) {
            this.data = value;
            left = right = null;
        }

        boolean isLeaf() {
            return left == null ? right == null : false;
        }

    }

    // root of the binary tree from where we start our journey
    BinaryTreeNotRecursive.TreeNodeClass root;

    public void postOrderWithoutRecursion() {
        Stack<BinaryTreeNotRecursive.TreeNodeClass> nodes = new Stack<>();
        nodes.push(root);

        while (!nodes.isEmpty()) {
            BinaryTreeNotRecursive.TreeNodeClass current = nodes.peek();

            if (current.isLeaf()) {
                BinaryTreeNotRecursive.TreeNodeClass node = nodes.pop();
                System.out.printf("%s ", node.data);
            } else {

                if(current.right != null){
                    nodes.push(current.right);
                    current.right = null;
                }

                if(current.left != null){
                    nodes.push(current.left);
                    current.left = null;
                }
            }

        }
    }
}
```

```java
package fun.sanjibsinha.chapter7.binarytree.postordertraversal;

/** The binary tree traversal will take place as the following structure
 * With the following output
           A
 *       / \
 *      B   F
 *     / \   \
 *    C   E   G
 *   /   / \
 *  D   H   I
 *
 * output: D C E B H I G F A
 */

public class DisplayPostOrderTraversal {

    public static void main(String[] args) {

        BinaryTreeNotRecursive tree = new BinaryTreeNotRecursive();
        BinaryTreeNotRecursive.TreeNodeClass root = new BinaryTreeNotRecursive.TreeNodeClass("A");
        tree.root = root;
        tree.root.left = new BinaryTreeNotRecursive.TreeNodeClass("B");
        tree.root.left.left = new BinaryTreeNotRecursive.TreeNodeClass("C");
        tree.root.left.left.left = new BinaryTreeNotRecursive.TreeNodeClass("D");

        tree.root.left.right = new BinaryTreeNotRecursive.TreeNodeClass("E");
        tree.root.right = new BinaryTreeNotRecursive.TreeNodeClass("F");
        tree.root.right.right = new BinaryTreeNotRecursive.TreeNodeClass("G");
        tree.root.right.right.left = new BinaryTreeNotRecursive.TreeNodeClass("H");
        tree.root.right.right.right = new BinaryTreeNotRecursive.TreeNodeClass("I");

        System.out.println();
        // post order traversal without recursion
        System.out.println("The nodes of binary tree on post order iterative way...");
        tree.postOrderWithoutRecursion();
```

```
92
93              System.out.println(); // insert new line
94
95
96      }
97 }
```

We have mentioned the output in our comments section. The same output waits to greet us below.

```
1 //output of 7.21
2
3 The nodes of binary tree on post order iterative way...
4 D C E B H I G F A
5
6 Process finished with exit code 0
```

As always, this type of tree traversal can be managed in a better way using recursion. Visiting the left sub-tree leads us to more recursion of right sub-tree, and finally we reach the root node.

The next code snippet shows us how we can do the same operation in a more concise way using recursion.

```
1  //code 7.22
2
3  package fun.sanjibsinha.chapter7.binarytree.postordertraversal;
4
5  public class BinaryTreeRecursive {
6
7      static class TreeNodeClass {
8          String data;
9          BinaryTreeRecursive.TreeNodeClass left, right;
10
11         TreeNodeClass(String value) {
12             this.data = value;
13             left = right = null;
14         }
15
16         boolean isLeaf() {
17             return left == null ? right == null : false;
18         }
19
20     }
21
22     // root of the binary tree from where we start our journey
23     BinaryTreeRecursive.TreeNodeClass root;
24
25     /**
26      * the public method to traverse and display the nodes
27      * by calling the recursive function
```

```java
28      */
29     public void postOrder() {
30         postOrder(root);
31     }
32
33     /**
34      * traversing the binary tree by calling itself
35      */
36     private void postOrder(BinaryTreeRecursive.TreeNodeClass node) {
37         if (node == null) {
38             return;
39         }
40
41         postOrder(node.left);
42         postOrder(node.right);
43         System.out.printf("%s ", node.data);
44     }
45
46
47 }
48
49
50 package fun.sanjibsinha.chapter7.binarytree.postordertraversal;
51
52 /** The binary tree traversal will take place as the following structure
53  * With the following output
54  A
55  *      / \
56  *     B   F
57  *    / \   \
58  *   C   E   G
59  *  /   / \
60  * D   H   I
61  *
62  * output: D C E B H I G F A
63  */
64
65 public class DisplayingPostOrderTraversal {
66
67     public static void main(String[] args) {
68
69         BinaryTreeRecursive tree = new BinaryTreeRecursive();
70         BinaryTreeRecursive.TreeNodeClass root = new BinaryTreeRecursive.TreeNodeCla\
71 ss("A");
72         tree.root = root;
73         tree.root.left = new BinaryTreeRecursive.TreeNodeClass("B");
74         tree.root.left.left = new BinaryTreeRecursive.TreeNodeClass("C");
```

```
75          tree.root.left.left.left = new
BinaryTreeRecursive.TreeNodeClass("D");
76
77          tree.root.left.right = new
BinaryTreeRecursive.TreeNodeClass("E");
78          tree.root.right = new
BinaryTreeRecursive.TreeNodeClass("F");
79          tree.root.right.right = new
BinaryTreeRecursive.TreeNodeClass("G");
80          tree.root.right.right.left = new
BinaryTreeRecursive.TreeNodeClass("H");
81          tree.root.right.right.right = new
BinaryTreeRecursive.TreeNodeClass("I");
82
83          System.out.println();
84
85          // post order traversal recursive way
86          System.out.println("The nodes of binary tree on post order recursive way..."\
87  );
88
89          tree.postOrder();
90
91          System.out.println();
92
93
94      }
95 }
```

Now we can compare the code snippets where we have once used iteration and after that we have used recursion. Still the output is same.

```
1 //output of 7.22
2
3 The nodes of binary tree on post order recursive way...
4 D C E B H I G F A
5
6 Process finished with exit code 0
```

Whenever we use pre-order traversal, the displayed data are different than case when we use post-order traversal. Moreover, it depends on how we want to visit our nodes.

In this section, finally we will use in-order tree traversal, which is different than the previous two cases of tree traversals.

In Order Tree Traversal

When we use in-order tree traversal, we start visiting left sub-tree recursively first. After that, we visit the root and then the right sub-tree. Each node stores a value and we know them as key. In the in-order tree traversal, the output produces sorted key values in an ascending order.

Just like the previous two cases, we will do the in-order tree traversal using iteration first. After that, we will use the recursion.

```java
//code 7.23

package fun.sanjibsinha.chapter7.binarytree.inorder;

import java.util.Stack;

public class InOrderBinaryTreeNotRecursive {

    static class TreeNodeClass {
        String data;
        InOrderBinaryTreeNotRecursive.TreeNodeClass left, right;

        TreeNodeClass(String value) {
            this.data = value;
            left = right = null;
        }

        boolean isLeaf() {
            return left == null ? right == null : false;
        }

    }

    // root of the binary tree from where we start our journey
    InOrderBinaryTreeNotRecursive.TreeNodeClass root;

    public void inOrderWithoutRecursion() {
        Stack<InOrderBinaryTreeNotRecursive.TreeNodeClass> nodes = new Stack<>();
        InOrderBinaryTreeNotRecursive.TreeNodeClass current = root;

        while (!nodes.isEmpty() || current != null) {

            if (current != null) {
                nodes.push(current);
                current = current.left;
            } else {
                InOrderBinaryTreeNotRecursive.TreeNodeClass node = nodes.pop();
                System.out.printf("%s ", node.data);
                current = node.right;
            }

        }
```

```
43     }
44
45
46 }
47
48 package fun.sanjibsinha.chapter7.binarytree.inorder;
49
50 /*
51  *
52  *
53  * input:
54  *      D
55  *     / \
56  *    B   E
57  *   / \   \
58  *  A   C   F
59  *
60  * output: A B C D E F
61  */
62
63 public class PrintingInOrderTraversal {
64
65     public static void main(String[] args) {
66
67         InOrderBinaryTreeNotRecursive tree = new InOrderBinaryTreeNotRecursive();
68         InOrderBinaryTreeNotRecursive.TreeNodeClass root = new InOrderBinaryTreeNotR\
69 ecursive.TreeNodeClass("D");
70         tree.root = root;
71         tree.root.left = new InOrderBinaryTreeNotRecursive.TreeNodeClass("B");
72         tree.root.left.left = new InOrderBinaryTreeNotRecursive.TreeNodeClass("A");
73
74         tree.root.left.right = new InOrderBinaryTreeNotRecursive.TreeNodeClass("C");
75         tree.root.right = new InOrderBinaryTreeNotRecursive.TreeNodeClass("E");
76         tree.root.right.right = new InOrderBinaryTreeNotRecursive.TreeNodeClass("F");
77
78         System.out.println();
79
80         tree.inOrderWithoutRecursion();
81
82         System.out.println();
83
84     }
85 }
```

The inner mechanism of in-order tree traversal is not evident in the output. As we have mentioned earlier the output will be presented in an ascending order.

```
//output of 7.23

A B C D E F

Process finished with exit code 0
```

The main disadvantages of using iteration include the lack of conciseness. For a huge binary tree the lines of code could be too long. Maintaining such huge data could be an issue, yet it is faster than using recursion.

The next code snippet will show how we can use recursion to make the same code look more concise.

```
//code 7.24

package fun.sanjibsinha.chapter7.binarytree.inorder;

public class InOrderBinaryTreeRecursive {

    static class TreeNodeClass {
        String data;
        InOrderBinaryTreeRecursive.TreeNodeClass left, right;

        TreeNodeClass(String value) {
            this.data = value;
            left = right = null;
        }

        boolean isLeaf() {
            return left == null ? right == null : false;
        }

    }

    // root of the binary tree from where we start our journey
    InOrderBinaryTreeRecursive.TreeNodeClass root;

    /**
     * the public method to traverse and display the nodes
     * by calling the recursive function
     */
    public void inOrder() {

        inOrder(root);
    }

    /**
```

```
35      * traversing the binary tree by calling itself
36      */
37     private void inOrder(InOrderBinaryTreeRecursive.TreeNodeClass node) {
38         if (node == null) {
39             return;
40         }
41
42         inOrder(node.left);
43         System.out.printf("%s ", node.data);
44         inOrder(node.right);
45     }
46
47
48 }
49
50
51 package fun.sanjibsinha.chapter7.binarytree.inorder;
52
53 /*
54 *
55 *
56 * input:
57 *      D
58 *     / \
59 *    B   E
60 *   / \   \
61 *  A   C   F
62 *
63 * output: A B C D E F
64 */
65
66 public class PrintInOrderTraversal {
67
68     public static void main(String[] args) {
69
70         InOrderBinaryTreeRecursive tree = new InOrderBinaryTreeRecursive();
71         InOrderBinaryTreeRecursive.TreeNodeClass root = new InOrderBinaryTreeRecursi\
72 ve.TreeNodeClass("D");
73         tree.root = root;
74         tree.root.left = new InOrderBinaryTreeRecursive.TreeNodeClass("B");
75         tree.root.left.left = new InOrderBinaryTreeRecursive.TreeNodeClass("A");
76
77         tree.root.left.right = new InOrderBinaryTreeRecursive.TreeNodeClass("C");
78         tree.root.right = new
```

```
            InOrderBinaryTreeRecursive.TreeNodeClass("E");
79              tree.root.right.right = new
            InOrderBinaryTreeRecursive.TreeNodeClass("F");
80
81              System.out.println();
82
83              tree.inOrder();
84
85              System.out.println();
86          }
87      }
```

If we take a close look at this part of the above code it will give us more insights into the algorithm of recursion.

```
1   /**
2       * the public method to traverse and display the nodes
3       * by calling the recursive function
4       */
5       public void inOrder() {
6
7           inOrder(root);
8       }
9
10      /**
11      * traversing the binary tree by calling itself
12      */
13      private void inOrder(InOrderBinaryTreeRecursive.TreeNodeClass node) {
14          if (node == null) {
15              return;
16          }
17
18          inOrder(node.left);
19          System.out.printf("%s ", node.data);
20          inOrder(node.right);
21      }
```

In the in-order tree traversal, we have recursion this way. However, the post-order algorithm of recursion was different. Let us the same part in the post-order recursive tree traversal.

```
1   /**
2       * the public method to traverse and display the nodes
3       * by calling the recursive function
4       */
5       public void postOrder() {
6           postOrder(root);
7       }
8
```

```
 9      /**
10       * traversing the binary tree by calling itself
11       */
12      private void postOrder(BinaryTreeRecursive.TreeNodeClass node) {
13          if (node == null) {
14              return;
15          }
16
17          postOrder(node.left);
18          postOrder(node.right);
19          System.out.printf("%s ", node.data);
20      }
```

Finally, we will take a look at the pre-order recursive tree traversal algorithm. The position of calling the function itself changes with each recursive tree traversal style.

```
 1 /**
 2      * the public method to traverse and display the nodes
 3      * by calling the recursive function
 4      */
 5      public void traversingPreOrderByCallingItself() {
 6          traversingPreOrderByCallingItself(root);
 7      }
 8
 9      /**
10       * traversing the binary tree by calling itself
11       */
12      private void
traversingPreOrderByCallingItself(BinaryTreeWithRecursion.TreeNodeC\
13 lass node) {
14          if (node == null) {
15              return;
16          }
17          System.out.printf("%s ", node.data);
18          traversingPreOrderByCallingItself(node.left);
19          traversingPreOrderByCallingItself(node.right);
20      }
```

How we use our recursive algorithm is extremely important. Although recursion has many advantages and disadvantages, we need to use this algorithm wisely. We need to understand how it works, we need to keep in our mind one key conception regarding recursive algorithm, which is there must be a base case. Recursive algorithm should have a base case, and in the above examples, we have seen the how we proceed towards the base case where we have a condition to stop the recursion.

The condition checks whether the root is null or not. That was our base case when we had been traversing the tree. Whatever be the style of tree traversal; pre-order, post-order or in-order. We have to maintain the same logic when we use recursion.

We have seen and discussed a small part of algorithm; it is as much as a teaspoon holds. In the coming section we will get more insights about data structure.

Collection Framework in Java

We have already learned that Java Collection Framework has three key components that work together. First one is Interface.

The second one is Implementations; classes that implement interfaces. We get objects from those classes on which algorithmic operations are performed.

The third and the final one is Algorithm. This is the final goal; because algorithms in Java Collection framework are methods that perform useful computations, such as sorting, searching, shuffling, etc. Algorithms are polymorphic; it means, the same method can be used by an Iterator object, and as well as an ListIterator object. We will see those examples in a minute.

We have just said polymorphic algorithm methods. Let us see how add() methods work on different Collection objects.

```
1  //code 7.25
2
3  package fun.sanjibsinha.chapter7.collection;
4
5  /**
6   * in this code snippets we take a brief look at the
7   * Collection framework of Java
8   */
9
10 import java.util.*;
11
12 public class CollectionOverall {
13
14     public static void main(String[] args) {
15
16         // ArrayList Examples where we add elements
17         List arrayList = new ArrayList();
18         arrayList.add("Sanjib");
19         arrayList.add("Json");
20         arrayList.add("John");
21         arrayList.add(10);
22         System.out.println(" ArrayList Elements in tabular format: ");
23         System.out.print("\t" + arrayList);
24
25         // LinkedList Examples where we add elements
26         List linkedList = new LinkedList();
27         linkedList.add("Sanjib");
28         linkedList.add("Json");
29         linkedList.add("John");
```

```
30          linkedList.add(10);
31          System.out.println();
32          System.out.println(" LinkedList Elements in tabular format: ");
33          System.out.print("\t" + linkedList);
34
35          // HashSet Examples where we add elements
36          Set hashSet = new HashSet();
37          hashSet.add("Sanjib");
38          hashSet.add("Json");
39          hashSet.add("John");
40          hashSet.add(10);
41          System.out.println();
42          System.out.println(" Set Elements in tabular format: ");
43          System.out.print("\t" + hashSet);
44
45          // HashMap Examples where we add elements
46          Map hashMap = new HashMap();
47          hashMap.put("Sanjib", "55");
48          hashMap.put("Json", "45");
49          hashMap.put("John", "35");
50          System.out.println();
51          System.out.println(" Map Elements in tabular format: ");
52          System.out.print("\t" + hashMap);
53          System.out.println();
54      }
55
56 }
```

The above code snippets give us the following output; furthermore, from this output, we understand that we can do the same computation using different types of collection objects.

```
1 //output of 7.25
2 ArrayList Elements in tabular format:
3     [Sanjib, Json, John, 10]
4 LinkedList Elements in tabular format:
5     [Sanjib, Json, John, 10]
6 Set Elements in tabular format:
7     [John, 10, Json, Sanjib]
8 Map Elements in tabular format:
9     {John=35, Json=45, Sanjib=55}
```

As we progress, we will learn more about data structure and algorithm through Java Collection framework. We will also find how Java Collection framework unifies its implementations using many discrete mathematical abstractions.

Discrete Mathematical Abstractions and Implementation through Java Collection

We have not forgotten the key discourse of this book. Discrete Mathematics, data structure and algorithm are inter-connected. It is evident when Java Collection Framework introduces Set collection. The Set Collection in Java does not allow duplicate elements, just like mathematical Set abstraction does in the same way. Moreover, Java Set models on discrete mathematical set abstraction.

Let us see an example:

```
1  //code 7.26
2  package fun.sanjibsinha.chapter7.collection;
3
4  import java.util.HashSet;
5  import java.util.Set;
6  import java.util.TreeSet;
7
8  public class SetSortingAlgorithm {
9
10     static int count;
11
12     public static void main(String[] args) {
13
14         int countingDisparateIntegers[] = {100, 256, 18, 605, 78, 5};
15
16         /**
17          * The Set Collection implements discrete mathematical Set abstraction
18          * it does not allow duplicate value like the following list
19          * int countingDisparateIntegers[] = {100, 256, 100, 605, 78, 5};
20          */
21
22         /**
23          * the organization of data can start here
24          * we can use HashSet for displaying the list
25          */
26
27         Set<Integer> hashSet = new HashSet<Integer>();
28         try {
29             for(count = 0; count < 5; count++) {
30                 hashSet.add(countingDisparateIntegers[count]);
31             }
32             System.out.println("Displaying the list of the array elements : ");
33             System.out.println(hashSet);
34
35             /**
36              * we can use TreeSet for sorting algorithm
```

```
37              */
38
39              TreeSet setAfterSorting = new TreeSet<Integer>(hashSet);
40              System.out.println("The list after sorting looks like
this: ");
41              System.out.println(setAfterSorting);
42
43              /**
44              * we can easily pick up the first or last element
45              * after the sorting is over
46              */
47
48              System.out.println("The First element of the generated
list is: " +
49                      (Integer)setAfterSorting.first());
50              System.out.println("The last element of the generated
list is: " +
51                      (Integer)setAfterSorting.last());
52          }
53
54          catch(Exception e) {
55              e.getMessage();
56          }
57      }
58 }
```

We have used sorting algorithm in the above Set Collection. After sorting is over, we have easily picked up the first and the last element.

```
1 //output of 7.26
2 Displaying the list of the array elements :
3 [256, 18, 100, 605, 78]
4 The list after sorting looks like this:
5 [18, 78, 100, 256, 605]
6 The First element of the generated list is: 18
7 The last element of the generated list is: 605
```

We have said earlier that the Set Collection implements discrete mathematical Set abstraction. Let us check it by changing this line of the above code.

```
1 From
2 int countingDisparateIntegers[] = {100, 256, 18, 605, 78, 5};
3 To
4 int countingDisparateIntegers[] = {100, 256, 100, 605, 78, 5};
```

Run the code and you will get the following output, where one '100' is missing.

```
1 Displaying the list of the array elements :
2 [256, 100, 605, 78]
3 The list after sorting looks like this:
4 [78, 100, 256, 605]
```

```
5 The First element of the generated list is: 78
6 The last element of the generated list is: 605
```

In many cases, discrete mathematical abstractions are implemented in data structure and algorithm. In future code snippets, we will see more examples like above, where same things happen, in like manner.

There are more mathematical abstractions wait for us. Map Collection models mathematical abstraction, such as 'function'. Let us see how it works in Map Collection.

```
 1  // code 7.27
 2
 3  package fun.sanjibsinha.chapter7.collection;
 4
 5  import java.util.HashMap;
 6  import java.util.Iterator;
 7  import java.util.Map;
 8  import java.util.Set;
 9
10  /**
11   * Map.Entry is an interface that is implemented by HashMap and Set
12   * We need Iterator interface also to be implemented to work together
13   */
14
15  public class MapEntryAndIteratorInterfaceTogether {
16
17      static int age;
18
19      public static void main(String[] args) {
20
21          // we need to create a HasMap object first
22          HashMap hashMap = new HashMap();
23
24          // adding some key value pairs that represent corresponding ages
25          hashMap.put("Json", 45);
26          hashMap.put("Sanjib", 55);
27          hashMap.put("John", 35);
28
29          // now we need a Set object to implement Map.Entry interface
30          Set setObject = hashMap.entrySet();
31
32          // we need an Iterator object to implement Iterator interface
33          Iterator iteratorObject = setObject.iterator();
34
35          /**
36           * now we want to iterate the key value pair with the help
37           * of iterator object and display them one after another
```

```
38              * in the ascending order after sorting is over
39              */
40
41             System.out.printf("The age of each person in ascending order: ");
42             System.out.println();
43
44             while(iteratorObject.hasNext()) {
45                 Map.Entry mapEntryObject = (Map.Entry)iteratorObject.next();
46                 System.out.print(mapEntryObject.getKey() + " : ");
47                 System.out.println(mapEntryObject.getValue());
48             }
49             System.out.println();
50
51             /**
52             * now we can change the value of any key with the
53             * help of HashMap object
54             */
55
56             age = ((Integer)hashMap.get("John")).intValue();
57             hashMap.put("John", age + 1);
58             System.out.println("John turned " + hashMap.get("John") + " today!");
59
60         }
61 }
```

It gives us the following output, where the key and value pairs work together.

```
1 // output of 7.27
2
3 The age of each person in ascending order:
4 John : 35
5 Json : 45
6 Sanjib : 55
7
8 John turned 36 today!
```

Actually, the Map interface provides a small nested interface called Map.Entry. You have seen in the above code snippets. It is a part of the Collection view methods. The Map interface includes methods or algorithm for all type of basic operations on data structures, such as put, get, remove, etc. Map interface provides bulk operations, such as putAll or clear. There are Collection view algorithms also, keySet, entrySet, and values are among them.

Comparator, Comparable and Iterator

Java Collection framework provides three major interfaces, which have all the qualities of being important and worthy of note. Comparison plays a great role in sorting or shuffling algorithm. In the like manner, iteration is also very important.

We are going to see a few code snippets where these three interfaces (Comparator, Comparable and Iterator) are implemented.

To get elements in sorted order, we can use TreeSet and TreeMap from Java Collection Framework; but, it is the Comparator or the Comparable interface that precisely defines what sorted order means.

Implementing the Comparator and Comparable interfaces, we can have objects that encapsulate ordering. Watch the next code snippet:

```
1 // code 7.29
2
3 package fun.sanjibsinha.chapter7.collection;
4
5 /**
6  * How Comparator and Comparable interfaces are implemented by a class
7  * to sort String and Integer data types provided by List and
8  * ArrayList data structures
9  */
10
11 import java.util.ArrayList;
12 import java.util.Collections;
13 import java.util.Comparator;
14 import java.util.List;
15
16 class Account implements Comparator<Account>, Comparable<Account> {
17
18     private String accountHoldersName;
19     private int accountNumber;
20
21     Account() {
22     }
23
24     Account(String name, int number) {
25         accountHoldersName = name;
26         accountNumber = number;
27     }
28
29     public void setAccountHoldersName(String accountHoldersName) {
30         this.accountHoldersName = accountHoldersName;
31     }
32
33     public String getAccountHoldersName() {
```

```java
34            return accountHoldersName;
35        }
36
37        public void setAccountNumber(int accountNumber) {
38            this.accountNumber = accountNumber;
39        }
40
41        public int getAccountNumber() {
42            return accountNumber;
43        }
44
45        /**
46         * overriding the compareTo() method to sort the name
47         * @param account
48         * @return
49         */
50        public int compareTo(Account account) {
51            return (this.accountHoldersName).compareTo(account.accountHoldersName);
52        }
53
54        /**
55         * overriding the compare() method to sort the account number
56         * @param account
57         * @param anotherAccount
58         * @return
59         */
60        public int compare(Account account, Account anotherAccount) {
61            return account.accountNumber - anotherAccount.accountNumber;
62        }
63 }
64
65 public class ComparatorInterfaceExample {
66
67     public static void main(String[] args) {
68
69         // list of account object
70         List<Account> listOfAccounts = new ArrayList<Account>();
71
72         listOfAccounts.add(new Account("Sanjib", 203));
73         listOfAccounts.add(new Account("Json", 205));
74         listOfAccounts.add(new Account("John", 201));
75         listOfAccounts.add(new Account("Hicky", 204));
76         listOfAccounts.add(new Account("Amubrata", 202));
77
78
79         // sorting the ArrayList
80         Collections.sort(listOfAccounts);
81
```

```
82          /**
83           * printing the sorted names
84           */
85          System.out.println("Printing the sorted names of account holders: ");
86          for(Account account: listOfAccounts){
87              System.out.print(account.getAccountHoldersName() + ", ");
88          }
89
90          /**
91           * sorting the ArrayList with the help of comparator
92           */
93          Collections.sort(listOfAccounts, new Account());
94          System.out.println(" ");
95
96          /**
97           * sorting based on account numbers
98           */
99          System.out.println("Printing the names of account holders based on sorted ac\
100 count" +
101                  " numbers in ascending numbers: ");
102         for(Account account: listOfAccounts)
103             System.out.print(account.getAccountHoldersName() + " : "
104                     + account.getAccountNumber() + ", ");
105     }
106 }
```

First of all, we have sorted the names of the account holders; in similar fashion, we have printed the names of account holders based on sorted account numbers in ascending numbers.

```
1 // output of 7.29
2
3 Printing the sorted names of account holders:
4 Amubrata, Hicky, John, Json, Sanjib,
5 Printing the names of account holders based on sorted account numbers in ascending n\
6 umbers:
7 John : 201, Amubrata : 202, Sanjib : 203, Hicky : 204, Json : 205,
8 Process finished with exit code 0
```

What will happen if inadvertently someone adds a negative account number? Therefore, for the second part of the code where we have implemented Comparator interface method compare(), we should write the logic in this way.

```
1 // code 7.30
2
```

```
3 public int compare(Account account, Account anotherAccount) {
4         /**
5          * Don't do it unless you're absolutely
6          * sure no one will ever have a negative account number!
7          */
8         //return account.accountNumber - anotherAccount.accountNumber;
9         /**
10         * this is more logical approach
11         */
12        return (account.accountNumber < anotherAccount.accountNumber ? -1 :
13               (account.accountNumber == anotherAccount.accountNumber ? 0 : 1));
14    }
15
16 // output of 7.30
17 Printing the sorted names of account holders:
18 Amubrata, Hicky, John, Json, Sanjib,
19 Printing the names of account holders based on sorted account numbers in ascending n\
20 umbers:
21 John : 201, Amubrata : 202, Sanjib : 203, Hicky : 204, Json : 205,
22 Process finished with exit code 0
```

Now, our code is more protected. Why we need to take such protections? It is little bit theoretical and this book is not about only Java Collection Framework. Yet, it is good to know that if an integer is a large positive integer and another integer is a large negative integer, then their subtraction will return a negative integer. To represent the difference of two arbitrary signed integers, a signed integer type is not big enough.

When we implement Comparable or Comparator interfaces, we need to maintain the technical restrictions.

If we want to compare two elements, especially for that type of algorithm, implementing the Comparable interface is always the better choice.

```
1 // code 7.31
2 package fun.sanjibsinha.chapter7.collection;
3
4 import java.util.ArrayList;
5 import java.util.Arrays;
6 import java.util.Collections;
7 import java.util.List;
8
9 class City implements Comparable<City>{
10
11    private String name;
12
```

```java
13      City(String name){
14          if (name == null){
15              throw new NullPointerException();
16          }
17          this.name = name;
18      }
19
20      public String displayName(){
21          return name;
22      }
23
24      public String toString(){
25          return name;
26      }
27
28
29      @Override
30      public int compareTo(City city) {
31          int lastCompare = name.compareTo(city.name);
32          return (lastCompare != 0 ? lastCompare : name.compareTo(city.name));
33      }
34 }
35
36 public class ComparableInterfaceExample {
37
38      public static void main(String[] args) {
39
40          City cityNames[] = {
41                  new City("Berlin"),
42                  new City("Kolkata"),
43                  new City("Munich"),
44                  new City("Paris"),
45                  new City("Mew York"),
46          };
47
48          List<City> names = Arrays.asList(cityNames);
49
50          Collections.sort(names);
51
52          System.out.println("The city names in ascending order: ");
53
54          System.out.println(names.toString());
55
56      }
57 }
```

We can get the city names in ascending order. For the algorithm that is related to sorting and comparing, it is a good choice in Java Collection framework.

```
1 // output of 7.31
2 The city names in ascending order:
3 [Berlin, Kolkata, Mew York, Munich, Paris]
4
5 Process finished with exit code 0
```

Finally we will curtain the Java Collection framework with iteration. It is also a very important part of algorithm and data structure. Java Collection framework handles it quite well by implementing the Iterator interface.

```
1 // code 7.32
2 package fun.sanjibsinha.chapter7.collection;
3
4 import java.util.ArrayList;
5 import java.util.Iterator;
6 import java.util.ListIterator;
7
8 /**
9  * An Iterator is an object that enables you to traverse through a collection
10 * public interface Iterator<E> {
11 *     boolean hasNext();
12 *     E next();
13 *     void remove(); //optional
14 * }
15 * An Iterator object implements either Iterator, or ListIterator interface
16 */
17
18 public class IteratorInterfaceExample {
19
20     public static void main(String[] args) {
21
22         /**
23          * creating an ArrayList that will use iterator object
24          */
25
26         ArrayList arrayList = new ArrayList();
27
28         /**
29          * adding some city names to the array list
30          */
31         arrayList.add("Calcutta");
32         arrayList.add("Allahabad");
33         arrayList.add("Edinburgh");
34         arrayList.add("Berlin");
35         arrayList.add("Detroit");
36         arrayList.add("Fujiyama");
37
38         /**
```

```
39              * we can use iterator to display all the city names now
40              */
41
42             System.out.print("The city names as entered in the list : ");
43             Iterator itratorObject = arrayList.iterator();
44
45             while(itratorObject.hasNext()) {
46                 Object element = itratorObject.next();
47                 System.out.print(element + ", ");
48             }
49             System.out.println();
50
51             /**
52              * ListIterator object can implement the ListIterator interface
53              */
54             ListIterator listIterator = arrayList.listIterator();
55
56             System.out.print("Now we can cycle through the city names forward through li\
57 stIterator : ");
58             System.out.println();
59             while(listIterator.hasNext()) {
60                 Object element = listIterator.next();
61                 listIterator.set(element);
62                 System.out.println(element);
63             }
64
65             System.out.print("Now we can cycle through the city names forward through it\
66 erator : ");
67             itratorObject = arrayList.iterator();
68
69             while(itratorObject.hasNext()) {
70                 Object element = itratorObject.next();
71                 System.out.print(element + ", ");
72             }
73             System.out.println();
74
75             System.out.print("Now we can cycle through the city names forward through li\
76 stIterator : ");
77
78             while(listIterator.hasPrevious()) {
79                 Object element = listIterator.previous();
80                 System.out.print(element + ", ");
81             }
82             System.out.println();
```

```
83     }
84 }
```

To traverse through a collection of elements, we need iteration; and, to do that we need an iterator object that implements the Iterator interface.

```
 1 // output of 7.32
 2 The city names as entered in the list : Calcutta, Allahabad, Edinburgh, Berlin, Detr\
 3 oit, Fujiyama,
 4
 5 Now we can cycle through the city names forward through listIterator :
 6 Calcutta
 7 Allahabad
 8 Edinburgh
 9 Berlin
10 Detroit
11 Fujiyama
12
13 Now we can cycle through the city names forward through iterator : Calcutta, Allahab\
14 ad, Edinburgh, Berlin, Detroit, Fujiyama,
15 Now we can cycle through the city names forward through listIterator : Fujiyama, Det\
16 roit, Berlin, Edinburgh, Allahabad, Calcutta,
17
18 Process finished with exit code 0
```

When we want to iterate through the elements in a collection, and display each element, the easiest way is shown above. Employing an iterator object is the best solution to such algorithmic problems. The iterator object either implements the Iterator interface, or implements ListIterator interface.

We have learned some key concepts about data structure and algorithm; moreover, we have also seen how they model the discrete mathematical abstractions.

In the next section, we will find some more interesting facts about data structure and algorithm through C++ Standard Template Library.

Standard Template Library in C++

We should avoid the practice of being unjust to C++ Standard Template Library, in short, STL. It is a very big topic that we cannot discuss, entirely, in a small section. We can only compare it with Java Collection framework.

C++ STL mainly deals with three main components. They are, Container, Algorithm, and Iterator. However, before moving to the STL, we will try to understand what templates are. In C++, we use templates to create generalized functions and classes.

Why we need generalized functions and classes? For many reasons, of course. But, the foremost among them is through generalized functions and classes, we can use any data types, such as integer, floating point values, characters, etc. The list is not finished yet, we can use also some user defined data.

Theoretically, templates are foundations of generic programming. You can write code in a way, which is independent of any particular type.

Using template we can create a generic class or function. The C++ STL containers, iterators, and algorithms are ideal examples of generic programming. C++ Standard Template Library has been developed using template concept.

For that reason, let us try to understand first, how these template concepts work.

```cpp
// code 7.33
#include <iostream>
#include <string>
#include <cmath>
#include <cstdlib>
#include <sstream>
#include <numeric>
#include <string>
#include <vector>
#include <cstddef>
#include <limits>

using namespace std;

template <typename T>
inline T const& FindMax (T const& c1, T const& c2) {
return c1 < c2 ? c2 : c1;
}

int main(){

    /**
    * We can use two different data types to compare which is maximum
    */

    int num1 = 20;
    int num2 = 10;

    cout << "Find the maximum comparing two values : " << FindMax(num1, num2) << end\
l;

    double d1 = 20.12;
    double d2 = 10.35;

```

```
35      cout << "Find the maximum comparing two values : " <<
FindMax(d1, d2) << endl;
36
37      return 0;
38 }
```

In the above code, we have created a general template method 'FindMax()'. It helps us to find the maximum number. We can pass integers as well as floating point values.

```
1 // output of 7.33
2
3 Find the maximum comparing two values : 20
4 Find the maximum comparing two values : 20.12
```

We can use templates to create not only generalized functions, we can create generalized classes. Now using generalized classes, we can apply any data type, such as int, float, char, etc. In some cases, we can use the template specialization that helps us to use any particular type of data, like char. By this template generalization we can apply special template function for specialization. We will come to that point in a minute, before that let us see how generalization of template classes is used.

```
 1 // code 7.34
 2 #include <iostream>
 3 #include <string>
 4 #include <cmath>
 5 #include <cstdlib>
 6 #include <sstream>
 7 #include <numeric>
 8 #include <string>
 9 #include <vector>
10 #include <cstddef>
11 #include <limits>
12 #include <stdexcept>
13
14 using namespace std;
15
16 /**
17 * We will define class Stack<> and implement generic methods
18 * to push and pop the elements from the stack
19 */
20
21 template <class T>
22
23     class Stack {
24     private:
25         vector<T> elementsToPushAndPop;
26
27     public:
28         void push(T const&);
```

```cpp
29          void pop();
30          T top() const;
31
32          bool empty() const {
33              return elementsToPushAndPop.empty();
34          }
35 };
36
37 template <class T>
38 void Stack<T>::push (T const& elem) {
39 // we can append the copy of the element that we passed
40      elementsToPushAndPop.push_back(elem);
41 }
42
43 template <class T>
44 void Stack<T>::pop () {
45      // if the stack is empty, we can throw an exception
46 if (elementsToPushAndPop.empty()) {
47      throw out_of_range("Stack<>::pop(): empty stack");
48 }
49
50 // then we can remove the last element
51 elementsToPushAndPop.pop_back();
52 }
53
54 template <class T>
55 T Stack<T>::top () const {
56      // if the stack is empty, we can throw an exception
57 if (elementsToPushAndPop.empty()) {
58      throw out_of_range("Stack<>::top(): empty stack");
59 }
60
61 // then we can return copy of last element
62 return elementsToPushAndPop.back();
63 }
64
65 int main(){
66
67      // let us create a stack of integer elements
68      Stack<int> stackIntegers;
69
70      // now we can keep adding the stack
71      stackIntegers.push(500);
72      stackIntegers.push(501);
73
74      cout << stackIntegers.top() << endl;
75      if(stackIntegers.empty()){
76          cout << "The stack is empty." << endl;
77      } else {
78          cout << "The stack is not empty." << endl;
```

```
79     }
80
81
82     return 0;
83 }
```

We have created a general template class of Stack data structure that organizes data by adding value on the top of the table. It can also remove that data as well. A boolean method to create whether the stack is empty or not, is also checked.

```
1 // output of 7.34
2 501
3 The stack is not empty.
```

Now we can add more functionalities to this general template Stack class. It will give you an idea how STL in C++ works behind the scene.

```
1  // code 7.35
2
3  #include <iostream>
4  #include <string>
5  #include <cmath>
6  #include <cstdlib>
7  #include <sstream>
8  #include <numeric>
9  #include <string>
10 #include <vector>
11 #include <cstddef>
12 #include <limits>
13 #include <stdexcept>
14
15 using namespace std;
16
17 /**
18  * We will define class Stack<> and implement generic methods
19  * to push and pop the elements from the stack
20  */
21
22 template <class T>
23
24     class Stack {
25     private:
26         vector<T> elementsToPushAndPop;
27
28     public:
29         void push(T const&);
30         void pop();
31         T top() const;
32
33         bool empty() const {
```

```cpp
34                return elementsToPushAndPop.empty();
35           }
36 };
37
38 template <class T>
39 void Stack<T>::push (T const& elem) {
40 // we can append the copy of the element that we passed
41      elementsToPushAndPop.push_back(elem);
42 }
43
44 template <class T>
45 void Stack<T>::pop () {
46      // if the stack is empty, we can throw an exception
47 if (elementsToPushAndPop.empty()) {
48      throw out_of_range("Stack<>::pop(): empty stack");
49 }
50
51 // then we can remove the last element
52 elementsToPushAndPop.pop_back();
53 }
54
55 template <class T>
56 T Stack<T>::top () const {
57      // if the stack is empty, we can throw an exception
58 if (elementsToPushAndPop.empty()) {
59      throw out_of_range("Stack<>::top(): empty stack");
60 }
61
62 // then we can return copy of last element
63 return elementsToPushAndPop.back();
64 }
65
66 int main(){
67
68      // let us create a stack of integer elements
69      Stack<int> stackIntegers;
70
71      // now we can keep adding the stack
72      stackIntegers.push(500);
73      stackIntegers.push(501);
74
75      cout << stackIntegers.top() << endl;
76      if(stackIntegers.empty()){
77           cout << "The stack is empty." << endl;
78      } else {
79           cout << "The stack is not empty." << endl;
80      }
81
82      // let us remove one element from our stack
83      stackIntegers.pop();
```

```
84
85      // and see the output
86      cout << stackIntegers.top() << endl;
87
88      // after that we can check whether the stack is empty or not
89      if(stackIntegers.empty()){
90          cout << "The stack is empty." << endl;
91      } else {
92          cout << "The stack is not empty." << endl;
93      }
94
95      return 0;
96 }
```

Because we have created generic methods, we can now create Stack object of int data type that will implement a few key algorithms, such as adding, removing, etc.

```
1 // output of 7.35
2
3 501
4 The stack is not empty.
5 500
6 The stack is not empty.
```

The above code snippets give us an idea how STL provides common data structures, such as lists, stacks, arrays, etc. To understand STL properly, we need to learn how to create template classes are created.

The next code snippet gives us a more robust flavor of stack data structure where we have removed all the elements and caught the exception.

```
1 // code 7.36
2
3 #include <iostream>
4 #include <string>
5 #include <cmath>
6 #include <cstdlib>
7 #include <sstream>
8 #include <numeric>
9 #include <string>
10 #include <vector>
11 #include <cstddef>
12 #include <limits>
13 #include <stdexcept>
14
15 using namespace std;
16
17 /**
18  * We will define class Stack<> and implement generic methods
19  * to push and pop the elements from the stack
20  */
```

```cpp
template <class T>

    class Stack {
    private:
        vector<T> elementsToPushAndPop;

    public:
        void push(T const&);
        void pop();
        T top() const;

        bool empty() const {
            return elementsToPushAndPop.empty();
        }
};

template <class T>
void Stack<T>::push (T const& elem) {
// we can append the copy of the element that we passed
    elementsToPushAndPop.push_back(elem);
}

template <class T>
void Stack<T>::pop () {
    // if the stack is empty, we can throw an exception
if (elementsToPushAndPop.empty()) {
    throw out_of_range("Stack<>::pop(): empty stack");
}

// then we can remove the last element
elementsToPushAndPop.pop_back();
}

template <class T>
T Stack<T>::top () const {
    // if the stack is empty, we can throw an exception
if (elementsToPushAndPop.empty()) {
    throw out_of_range("Stack<>::top(): empty stack");
}

// then we can return copy of last element
return elementsToPushAndPop.back();
}

int main(){

    // let us create a stack of integer elements
    Stack<int> stackIntegers;

```

```cpp
71      // now we can keep adding the stack
72      stackIntegers.push(500);
73      stackIntegers.push(501);
74
75      cout << stackIntegers.top() << endl;
76      if(stackIntegers.empty()){
77          cout << "The stack is empty." << endl;
78      } else {
79          cout << "The stack is not empty." << endl;
80      }
81
82      // let us remove one element from our stack
83      stackIntegers.pop();
84
85      // and see the output
86      cout << stackIntegers.top() << endl;
87
88      // after that we can check whether the stack is empty or not
89      if(stackIntegers.empty()){
90          cout << "The stack is empty." << endl;
91      } else {
92          cout << "The stack is not empty." << endl;
93      }
94
95      // and see the output
96      cout << stackIntegers.top() << endl;
97
98      // let us keep removing the stack elements
99      try {
100         // this removes 500
101         stackIntegers.pop();
102         // if we try to remove element again, it will throw an exception
103         // that we can now catch
104         stackIntegers.pop();
105     } catch (exception const& excep) {
106         cerr << "Exception: " << excep.what() << endl;
107         return -1;
108     }
109
110     return 0;
111 }
```

Let us see the output first. After that, we will see why we needed such working experience of creating general template classes and generic methods.

```
1 // output of 7.36
2
3 501
4 The stack is not empty.
```

```
5 500
6 The stack is not empty.
7 500
8 Exception: Stack<>::pop(): empty stack
```

Now, one thing is clear. The Standard Template Library (STL) is a set of C++ template classes that provide common programming data structures and functions, such as lists, stacks, etc. The three major components, container classes, algorithms and iterators work at tandem. In the above examples, we have seen how the components are parameterized.

You approach to understand STL whatever way, in our view, this is the best way. Try to gain the working experience of creating your own general template functions and classes.

Therefore, we will devote more time to understand this conception, after that, we will see a couple of STL examples.

Let us create a simple general template function, as well as a specialized template function.

```
1  // code 7.37
2
3  #include <iostream>
4  #include <string>
5  #include <cmath>
6  #include <cstdlib>
7  #include <sstream>
8  #include <numeric>
9  #include <string>
10 #include <vector>
11 #include <cstddef>
12 #include <limits>
13 #include <stdexcept>
14
15 using namespace std;
16
17 /**
18  * we can use any general template function to pass
19  * any kind of data type as a parameter
20  * we can also use any specialized function that will pass
21  * a certain kind of data type as a parameter
22  */
23
24 // a general template function
25 template<typename T>
26 void templateFucntion(T t) {
27 cout << "A general template function where we can pass any data type : " << t << end\
28 l ;
```

```
29 }
30
31 // a specialized template function where we can pass only string as parameter
32 template<>
33 void templateFucntion(char s) {
34 cout << "A specialized template function where we cannot pass any data type except c\
35 har : " << s << endl ;
36 }
37
38 int main(){
39     templateFucntion(10);
40     templateFucntion(10.14);
41     templateFucntion('A');
42     templateFucntion("A string value....");
43
44     return 0;
45 }
```

The above code snippet is fairly simple. Through the general template function, we can pass any data, like int, float, char, string, even user defined data. However, using specialization makes a key difference. We can now only pass char data.

```
1 // output of 7.37
2
3 A general template function where we can pass any data type : 10
4 A general template function where we can pass any data type : 10.14
5 A specialized template function where we cannot pass any data type except char : A
6 A general template function where we can pass any data type : A string value.…
```

In the same way, we can create general template class and method that will allow to pass any data of our choice.

```
1 // code 7.38
2
3 #include <iostream>
4 #include <string>
5 #include <cmath>
6 #include <cstdlib>
7 #include <sstream>
8 #include <numeric>
9 #include <string>
10 #include <vector>
11 #include <cstddef>
12 #include <limits>
13 #include <stdexcept>
14
```

```
15 using namespace std;
16
17 /**
18  * we can use any general template class to use
19  * any data type
20  */
21
22 template<typename T>
23 class GeneralClass {
24 public:
25     // this is constructor
26     GeneralClass() {
27         cout << "This is constructor of a general class " << endl;
28     }
29     // a general method through which we can pass any data type
30     void generalMethod(T t){
31         cout << "A general template function where we can pass any data type : " << \
32 t << endl;
33     }
34 };
35
36 int main(){
37     // let us create a few different types of objects
38     GeneralClass<int> integerObject;
39     cout << "Let us call the general method to pass an integer value" << endl;
40     integerObject.generalMethod(10);
41     GeneralClass<float> floatObject;
42     cout << "Let us call the general method to pass a float value" << endl;
43     floatObject.generalMethod(10.11);
44     GeneralClass<char> charObject;
45     cout << "Let us call the general method to pass a char value" << endl;
46     charObject.generalMethod('C');
47     GeneralClass<string> strObject;
48     cout << "Let us call the general method to pass a string value" << endl;
49     strObject.generalMethod("Hello World, I an a string!");
50
51
52     return 0;
53 }
```

It appears in the above code, our choice has no limitations. Now we can create an object and call the same method again and again to pass any data.

```
1 // output of 7.38
2
```

```
3 This is constructor of a general class
4 Let us call the general method to pass an integer value
5 A general template function where we can pass any data type : 10
6 This is constructor of a general class
7 Let us call the general method to pass a float value
8 A general template function where we can pass any data type : 10.11
9 This is constructor of a general class
10 Let us call the general method to pass a char value
11 A general template function where we can pass any data type : C
12 This is constructor of a general class
13 Let us call the general method to pass a string value
14 A general template function where we can pass any data type : Hello World, I an a st\
15 ring!
```

In like manner we can also create a specialized template class and method that will allow a certain type of data to be passed.

```
1 // code 7.39
2
3 #include <iostream>
4 #include <string>
5 #include <cmath>
6 #include <cstdlib>
7 #include <sstream>
8 #include <numeric>
9 #include <string>
10 #include <vector>
11 #include <cstddef>
12 #include <limits>
13 #include <stdexcept>
14
15 using namespace std;
16
17 /**
18 * we can use any general template class to use
19 * any data type, but this is special case
20 */
21 template<typename t>
22 class SpecialClass {};
23
24 template<>
25 class SpecialClass<int> {
26 public:
27     // this is constructor
28     SpecialClass() {
29         cout << "This is constructor of a special class for only integer type. " << \
30 endl;
31     }
```

```cpp
32      // a general method through which we can pass any data type
33      void specialMethod(int num){
34          cout << "A special template function where we can pass only integer data typ\
35 e : " << num << endl;
36      }
37 };
38
39 int main(){
40      // let us create a few different types of objects
41      cout << "Let us call the constructor of the special template class, by creating \
42 an object." << endl;
43      SpecialClass<int> integerObject;
44      cout << "Let us call the special method to pass an integer value, we have passed\
45 10" << endl;
46      integerObject.specialMethod(10);
47
48      try {
49          // let us try to pass any other data type
50          cout << "If we pass char, it will give us the ASCII code of that particular \
51 character A." << endl;
52          integerObject.specialMethod('A');
53          cout << "If we pass float, it will change it to the whole number." << endl;
54          integerObject.specialMethod(10.95);
55          /*
56          Details:10.15
57              Default:10.15
58              Decimal:10
59              Hex:0xa
60              Binary:1010
61              Octal:012
62          */
63
64      } catch (exception const& excep) {
65          cerr << "Exception: " << excep.what() << endl;
66          return -1;
67      }
68
69
70      return 0;
71 }
```

A specialized template class that allows only int data type. If you pass a character, it will convert that value to its ASCII equivalent. Watch the output:

```
1 // output of 7.39
2
3 Let us call the constructor of the special template class, by 
creating an object.
4 This is constructor of a special class for only integer type.
5 Let us call the special method to pass an integer value, we have 
passed 10
6 A special template function where we can pass only integer data type
 : 10
7 If we pass char, it will give us the ASCII code of that particular 
character A.
8 A special template function where we can pass only integer data type
 : 65
9 If we pass float, it will change it to the whole number.
10 A special template function where we can pass only integer data type
 : 10
```

We have had enough working experience with the general template classes and functions. Now we can taste of STL. Before using STL, we need to know that container classes mainly manage the data structures part.

Basically, containers store user defined data and primitive data. There are several standard container classes, header files, etc.

In such a small section we cannot elaborate them. We can have a brief look at how they are used. There are sequence containers that implement a special type data structures. The specialty is it can be accessed in sequential manner. It includes vector, list, array, etc. With the new version of C++, something new will be added in the future. Therefore, the list is incomplete.

There are also associative containers that implement a certain type of data structures. Associative containers have set or map; they implement sorted data structures that can be structured in a key and value pair. We will a few examples.

Let us start with 'list'. We will also check different types of STL algorithms that are associated with 'list'.

```
1 // code 7.40
2
3 #include <iostream>
4 #include <string>
5 #include <cmath>
6 #include <cstdlib>
7 #include <list>
8 #include <iterator>
9 #include <stdexcept>
10
11 using namespace std;
12
13 /**
```

```cpp
14  * we want a function to print the elements
15  * that belong to the list
16  */
17
18 void printList(list <int> l)
19 {
20     list <int> :: iterator itr;
21     for(itr = l.begin(); itr != l.end(); ++itr)
22         cout << *itr << ", ";
23     cout << endl;
24 }
25
26 int main()
27 {
28     cout << "Different types of STL Algorithms using List: " << endl;
29     cout << endl;
30
31     list <int> list1, list2;
32
33     // we can apply STL algorithm o print out
34     // in ascending and descending order
35     for (int i = 0; i < 10; ++i)
36     {
37         // place the values in ascending order
38         list1.push_back(i);
39         // place the values in descending order
40         list2.push_front(i);
41     }
42     cout << "First print the list1, in ascending order: " << endl;
43     printList(list1);
44     cout << endl;
45
46     cout << "Then print the list2, in descending order: " << endl;
47     printList(list2);
48     cout << endl;
49
50     // let us print the first value
51     cout << "The first value of list one: ";
52     cout << list1.front() << endl;
53     // let us print the last value
54     cout << "The last value of list one: ";
55     cout << list1.back() << endl;
56
57     // let us print the first value
58     cout << "The first value of list two: ";
59     cout << list2.front() << endl;
60     // let us print the last value
61     cout << "The last value of list two: ";
62     cout << list2.back() << endl;
```

```
63
64      cout << "Let us remove the first element 0 of list one: " << endl;
65      list1.pop_front();
66      printList(list1);
67      cout << endl;
68
69      cout << "Let us remove the last element 0 of list two: " << endl;
70      list2.pop_back();
71      printList(list2);
72      cout << endl;
73
74      cout << "We can reverse the list one making it equal to list two: " << endl;
75      list1.reverse();
76      printList(list1);
77      cout << endl;
78
79      cout << "We can sort the list two making it equal to list one: " << endl;
80      list2.sort();
81      printList(list2);
82
83      return 0;
84
85 }
```

We have implemented a couple of algorithms that show general functionalities, such as sorting, searching, adding, removing, or copying.

```
1 // output of 7.40
2
3 Different types of STL Algorithms using List:
4
5 First print the list1, in ascending order:
6 0, 1, 2, 3, 4, 5, 6, 7, 8, 9,
7
8 Then print the list2, in descending order:
9 9, 8, 7, 6, 5, 4, 3, 2, 1, 0,
10
11 The first value of list one: 0
12 The last value of list one: 9
13 The first value of list two: 9
14 The last value of list two: 0
15 Let us remove the first element 0 of list one:
16 1, 2, 3, 4, 5, 6, 7, 8, 9,
17
18 Let us remove the last element 0 of list two:
19 9, 8, 7, 6, 5, 4, 3, 2, 1,
```

```
20
21 We can reverse the list one making it equal to list two:
22 9, 8, 7, 6, 5, 4, 3, 2, 1,
23
24 We can sort the list two making it equal to list one:
25 1, 2, 3, 4, 5, 6, 7, 8, 9,
```

Hopefully, comments will guide us how STL data structures and algorithms work clasping each other's hands.

Another good sequential container class is 'vector'. It is better than array in one sense. It can automatically adjust its storage capabilities. The following example will show us how it works.

```
1  // code 7.41
2
3  #include <iostream>
4  #include <string>
5  #include <cmath>
6  #include <cstdlib>
7  #include <vector>
8  #include <iterator>
9  #include <stdexcept>
10
11 using namespace std;
12
13 /**
14  * vector container is similar to an array
15  * except that it automatically handles the
16  * storage requirements
17  */
18
19 int main(){
20
21     // let us create a vector to store some names
22     vector<string> vecOne;
23     vector<int> vecTwo;
24     int i;
25     int j;
26
27     // first display the original size of the first container
28     cout << "The vector container size : " << vecOne.size() << endl;
29
30     // then display the original size of the second container
31     cout << "The vector container size : " << vecTwo.size() << endl;
32
33     // let us add a few names into the vector one
34     for (j = 0; j < 5; j++){
35         vecOne.push_back("John");
36         vecOne.push_back("JSON");
```

```
37             vecOne.push_back("Smith");
38             vecOne.push_back("Web");
39             vecOne.push_back("Trace");
40         }
41
42         // let us add a few names into the vector two
43         for (i = 0; i < 5; i++){
44             vecTwo.push_back(i);
45         }
46
47         // display extended size of vector container one
48         cout << "The extended vector size = " << vecOne.size() << endl;
49
50         // display extended size of vector container two
51         cout << "The extended vector size = " << vecTwo.size() << endl;
52
53         // let us access 5 values from the vector one
54         for(j = 0; j < 5; j++) {
55             cout << "The value of vector container one " << j << " = " << vecOne[j] << e\
56 ndl;
57         }
58
59         // let us access 5 values from the vector one
60         for(i = 0; i < 5; i++) {
61             cout << "The value of vector container two " << i << " = " << vecTwo[i] << e\
62 ndl;
63         }
64
65         return 0;
66 }
```

With the help of 'vector' we can definitely solve certain type of problems. The only advantage is with array, we need to do the lower level plumbing. We can avoid them by implementing vector data structures and associated algorithms.

```
 1 // output of 7.41
 2
 3 The vector container size : 0
 4 The vector container size : 0
 5 The extended vector size = 25
 6 The extended vector size = 5
 7 The value of vector container one 0 = John
 8 The value of vector container one 1 = JSON
 9 The value of vector container one 2 = Smith
10 The value of vector container one 3 = Web
11 The value of vector container one 4 = Trace
12 The value of vector container two 0 = 0
13 The value of vector container two 1 = 1
```

```
14 The value of vector container two 2 = 2
15 The value of vector container two 3 = 3
16 The value of vector container two 4 = 4
```

Whatever data structures we implement, or whatever algorithms we use, we need to keep one thing in our mind. Time-complexity is a big factor. In the next example, we will see 'set', and after that 'map'. Both belong to the Associative Container classes. There is an advantage. Because it implements sorted data structures, the search operation takes less time.

In the next chapter we will try to understand how time-complexity works, and why it is necessary in programming.

Before that, in the next examples, let us see how the 'set' data structures from STL sets in with its key algorithms.

```
1  // code 7.42
2
3  #include <iostream>
4  #include <string>
5  #include <cmath>
6  #include <cstdlib>
7  #include <set>
8  #include <iterator>
9  #include <stdexcept>
10
11 using namespace std;
12
13 /**
14  * we will see a lot of set algorithms in this example
15  */
16
17 int main()
18 {
19     // first we need an empty set container
20     set <int, greater <int> > setOne;
21
22     // now we can insert elements in random order
23     // however the numbers are unique
24     setOne.insert(55);
25     setOne.insert(89);
26     setOne.insert(1);
27     setOne.insert(41);
28     setOne.insert(74);
29     setOne.insert(23);
30     setOne.insert(32);
31
32     // to print the set one we need an iterator
33     set <int, greater <int> > :: iterator itr;
34     cout << "The iterator automatically orders the arrangement." <<
```

```
    endl;
35      cout << "The set one is in now descending order : ";
36      for (itr = setOne.begin(); itr != setOne.end(); ++itr)
37      {
38          cout << *itr << ", ";
39      }
40      cout << endl;
41
42      // we can use a special algorithm to reverse the order
43      // to do that we need to assign the values of set one
44      // to another set called set two
45      set <int> setTwo(setOne.begin(), setOne.end());
46      cout << endl;
47
48      // now we can display the value of set two
49      cout << "The set two is in now ascending order : ";
50      for (itr = setTwo.begin(); itr != setTwo.end(); ++itr)
51      {
52          cout << *itr << ", ";
53      }
54      cout << endl;
55
56      // we can remove elements below 41 from set two
57      cout << "Removing values below 41 from set two: " << endl;
58      cout << "Now set two will start from 41: " << endl;
59      cout << "Now set two looks like this: " << endl;
60      setTwo.erase(setTwo.begin(), setTwo.find(41));
61      for (itr = setTwo.begin(); itr != setTwo.end(); ++itr)
62      {
63          cout << *itr << ", ";
64      }
65      cout << endl;
66
67      // we can remove any particular element whose value is 41 in set two
68      setTwo.erase (41);
69      cout << "Erasing 41 from set two" << endl;
70      cout << "Now set two will start from the value after 41 : " << endl;
71      cout << "Now set two looks like this: " << endl;
72      for (itr = setTwo.begin(); itr != setTwo.end(); ++itr)
73      {
74          cout << *itr << ", ";
75      }
76
77      cout << endl;
78
79      cout << "All the algorithms applied on set two have not affected set one : " << \
80 endl;
```

```
81          cout << "Set one remains same, it looks like this: " << endl;
82          for (itr = setOne.begin(); itr != setOne.end(); ++itr)
83          {
84              cout << *itr << ", ";
85          }
86          cout << endl;
87
88          return 0;
89
90  }
```

As we have seen in the above code, there are lots of different types of algorithms applied in 'set'. Moreover, it is implemented as sorted data structures. But we can always change that order, quite easily.

```
1  // output of 7.42
2
3  The iterator automatically orders the arrangement.
4  The set one is in now descending order : 89, 74, 55, 41, 32, 23, 1,
5
6  The set two is in now ascending order : 1, 23, 32, 41, 55, 74, 89,
7  Removing values below 41 from set two:
8  Now set two will start from 41:
9  Now set two looks like this:
10 41, 55, 74, 89,
11 Erasing 41 from set two
12 Now set two will start from the value after 41 :
13 Now set two looks like this:
14 55, 74, 89,
15 All the algorithms applied on set two have not affected set one :
16 Set one remains same, it looks like this:
17 89, 74, 55, 41, 32, 23, 1,
```

As an associative container class, 'map' has also many advantages; with the help of STL algorithms, we can operate on any value through keys.

```
1  // code 7.43
2
3  #include <iostream>
4  #include <string>
5  #include <cmath>
6  #include <cstdlib>
7  #include <map>
8  #include <iterator>
9  #include <stdexcept>
10
11 using namespace std;
12
13 /**
14  * we will see a few map algorithms from STL
```

```cpp
15  * map belongs to the associative containers section
16  * it has key, value pairs
17  */
18
19  int main()
20  {
21      // first we will create an empty map container
22      map<int, int> mapOne;
23
24      // let us insert elements in random order keeping the key in ascending order
25      mapOne.insert(pair<int, int>(1, 56));
26      mapOne.insert(pair<int, int>(2, 89));
27      mapOne.insert(pair<int, int>(3, 2));
28      mapOne.insert(pair<int, int>(4, 64));
29      mapOne.insert(pair<int, int>(5, 14));
30      mapOne.insert(pair<int, int>(6, 35));
31      mapOne.insert(pair<int, int>(7, 75));
32
33      // to display all elements of map one we need iterator
34      map<int, int>::iterator itr;
35      cout << endl;
36      cout << " The map one's key=>value pairs are displayed in tabular form : \n";
37      cout << "\tKEY\tELEMENT\n";
38      for (itr = mapOne.begin(); itr != mapOne.end(); ++itr) {
39          cout << '\t' << itr->first
40              << '\t' << itr->second << '\n';
41      }
42      cout << endl;
43
44      // assigning the elements from mapOne to mapTwo
45      map<int, int> mapTwo(mapOne.begin(), mapOne.end());
46      cout << endl;
47
48      // now we can print all elements of the mapTwo
49      cout << "The map two after having values copied from map one in tabular form : "\
50  << endl;
51      cout << "\tKEY\tELEMENT\n";
52      for (itr = mapTwo.begin(); itr != mapTwo.end(); ++itr) {
53          cout << '\t' << itr->first
54              << '\t' << itr->second << endl;
55      }
56      cout << endl;
57
58      // we can apply the removal algorithm based on key
59      // let us remove all elements below key=>3
60      cout << endl;
61      cout << "The values of map two in tabular form after removal of
```

```
elements less th\
62 an key=3 : " << endl;
63      cout << "\tKEY\tELEMENT\n";
64      mapTwo.erase(mapTwo.begin(), mapTwo.find(3));
65      for (itr = mapTwo.begin(); itr != mapTwo.end(); ++itr) {
66          cout << '\t' << itr->first
67               << '\t' << itr->second << '\n';
68      }
69
70      return 0;
71 }
```

To show the key, value pair properly, we have to use the tabular format. Although we have not use many algorithms, yet hopefully it will give us an idea about how 'map' works.

```
 1 // output of 7.43
 2
 3 The map one's key=>value pairs are displayed in tabular form :
 4      KEY   ELEMENT
 5      1     56
 6      2     89
 7      3     2
 8      4     64
 9      5     14
10      6     35
11      7     75
12
13
14 The map two after having values copied from map one in tabular form :
15      KEY   ELEMENT
16      1     56
17      2     89
18      3     2
19      4     64
20      5     14
21      6     35
22      7     75
23
24
25 The values of map two in tabular form after removal of elements less than key=3 :
26      KEY   ELEMENT
27      3     2
28      4     64
29      5     14
30      6     35
31      7     75
```

So far, we have taken a very brief look at the C++ STL, and before that, we have also seen Java Collection framework in action.

In the next chapter we will try to understand another key concept, time-complexity.

I write regularly on Algorithm and Data Structure in

8. Time Complexity

We have already seen many examples of different kind of data structures and algorithms. We have also found out that to implement such algorithms, we do not have to go through low-level plumbing. Any stable good programming language provides many libraries to avoid such low-level plumbing and different types of algorithms, such as sorting, shuffling, or searching can be done through them.

We have also found out another important fact that tells us about the relationship between algorithms and discrete mathematics. Data structures are discrete structures and hence, the algorithms are all about discrete structures.

Let us consider a simple Java program, where we iterate over two loops at the same time. These outer and inner loops are connected with each other and they finally give us an output.

```
1 //code 8.1
2 package fun.sanjibsinha;
3
4 public class Main {
5
6     static int i, j, totalOne, totalTwo;
7
8     public static void main(String[] args) {
9
10        for (i = 0; i <= 5; i++){
11            totalOne += i;
12            System.out.print("i = " + i);
13            System.out.println("--------");
14            for (j = 0; j <= 5; j++){
15                totalTwo += j;
16                System.out.println("j = " + j);
17            }
18        }
19        System.out.println("The total of outer loop: " + totalOne);
20        System.out.println("The total of inner loop: " + totalTwo);
21    }
22 }
```

And from this very simple program, we get an output like the following:

```
 1  //output of 8.1
 2  i = 0--------
 3  j = 0
 4  j = 1
 5  j = 2
 6  j = 3
 7  j = 4
 8  j = 5
 9  i = 1--------
10  j = 0
11  j = 1
12  j = 2
13  j = 3
14  j = 4
15  j = 5
16  i = 2--------
17  j = 0
18  j = 1
19  j = 2
20  j = 3
21  j = 4
22  j = 5
23  i = 3--------
24  j = 0
25  j = 1
26  j = 2
27  j = 3
28  j = 4
29  j = 5
30  i = 4--------
31  j = 0
32  j = 1
33  j = 2
34  j = 3
35  j = 4
36  j = 5
37  i = 5--------
38  j = 0
39  j = 1
40  j = 2
41  j = 3
42  j = 4
43  j = 5
44  The total of outer loop: 15
45  The total of inner loop: 90
```

You have probably noticed that it is a simple algorithm of finding the total of inner loop and the outer loop.

However, to do that, we need to jump sequentially; each iteration has taken place within a space of discrete data structure.

Any problem has one or more possible solutions. Suppose, we were asked to find the total of the one loop only; we should change the above code to the following code:

```
1 //code 8.2
2 package fun.sanjibsinha;
3
4 public class Main {
5
6     static int i, j, totalOne, totalTwo;
7
8     public static void main(String[] args) {
9
10        for (i = 0; i <= 5; i++){
11            totalOne += i;
12            System.out.print("i = " + i);
13            System.out.println("--------");
14            /*
15            for (j = 0; j <= 5; j++){
16                totalTwo += j;
17                System.out.println("j = " + j + ", ");
18            }
19            */
20        }
21        System.out.println("The total of loop: " + totalOne);
22        // System.out.println("The total of outer loop: " + totalTwo);
23     }
24 }
```

Now, in the changed circumstance, we will come up with this output:

```
1 //output of 8.2
2 i = 0--------
3 i = 1--------
4 i = 2--------
5 i = 3--------
6 i = 4--------
7 i = 5--------
8 The total of loop: 15
```

Now we can also solve this problem another way. By calling the function recursively, we can also solve the same problem. Our problem was, how we could get the total of a series of positive integers that starts from 0 and ends at 5.

It looks like this: total = 0 + 1 + 2 + 3 + 4 + 5; here the end point was chosen as 5. The value of total is 15.

We could have taken the user input and get the total of any big positive integer. Manually it is easy to get the total of a small series. But consider a case, where user gives us an input like 10 to the 6. Now, manually it is not possible to add all the numbers from 0 to that number.

It becomes cumbersome.

Therefore our first algorithm was based on using looping. It easily adds all the numbers, whatever be the end number.

As we have said, any problem might have one or more solutions. Here we can solve the same problem, recursive way.

```
1 //code 8.3
2 package fun.sanjibsinha;
3
4 public class Main {
5
6     static int total;
7
8     static int getTotal(int i){
9         if (i != 0){
10            total = i + getTotal(i - 1);
11            return total;
12        } else {
13            return 0;
14        }
15    }
16
17    public static void main(String[] args) {
18
19        System.out.println("Total : " + getTotal(5));
20
21    }
22 }
```

And we get the same output:

```
1 //output of 8.3
2 Total : 15
```

In the above case, the same jumping of iteration occurs through a discrete structure, but in a different way. It starts from a discrete positive integer 5, and the addition process goes on until we reach the base number by calling the function recursively.

Now we have found that this problem has two solutions. Question is which is desirable? Which algorithm is better than the other?

Here comes the question of time complexity.

Time-Complexity has nothing to do with the execution time.

But it has many things to do with the algorithm. Time-Complexity talks all about the better algorithm. A better algorithm always takes less time to reach the desirable discrete element (here output of a total).

Here we have to iterate over a series of positive integers, to reach our desirable goal. If we could have reached in one iteration, that would be the best algorithm, no doubt.

But it is Utopian.

On the contrary, the worst case will take us to an iteration, that has to traverse each element for an indefinite period of time. In like manner, you may imagine a situation where user gives an input to find whether the integer is prime or not. There are several algorithms to test a number whether it is prime or not. Although there will be one algorithm that is better than other, and takes less time to give you the output. It depends entirely on the size of the input. For a real big integer, one algorithm might take several minutes to complete the operation and for another algorithm, it finishes the operation in a few seconds.

Before trying to understand Time-Complexity, we should remember that actual time requires to execute code is machine dependent; another key thing is network load. But the Time-Complexity has nothing to do with your machine configuration. It is all about better algorithm. That is why, whenever the terms data structures and algorithms appear, time-complexity comes with them.

In this chapter, we will try to understand how time-complexity works. What does the term Big O notation stand for? But before that, we need to understand what does 'order of n' mean?

Order of n, or O(n)

Let us implement an algorithm that will check whether the number or 'n' is prime or not. We know that a prime number is divided by only two numbers, 1 and the number itself and it has no remainder. Consider a prime number 11, it has only two factors 1, and 11. If we divide 11 by 1 and 11, we have no remainders. That is the most basic definition.

Therefore, using a normal looping construct, we can try to check whether that number is prime or not. We can write our algorithm in natural language, this way:

```
1 for each number where integer i starts from 2 to (n - 1)
2 if n % i == 0, then n is not prime
3 else n is prime
```

We can test this algorithm by using a small positive integer like 11. In that case, if we iterate from 2 to (11 − 1), we will see that between 2 to 10, there is no integer that can divide 11 with no remainder. Therefore, 11 is prime. When the value of n is small, our algorithm does not take much time. In fact, that time may appear negligible. Suppose for each iteration, it takes one millisecond or ms. This fraction of second stands for 10 to the power minus 3, that is, if you divide 1 second by 1000, then you get one millisecond.

By the way, as a student of computer science student we should know that one microsecond is 10 to the power minus 6, one nanosecond is 10 to the power of minus 9 and one picosecond is 10 to the power minus 12.

Now, let us assume that each iteration takes one microsecond. When the number of iteration is small, it does take mush time. However, with the increase of iteration, this time also increases. Instead of 11, we want to check a value like 1000003, it will iterate more than one million times. Now our algorithm appears to crumble. Because our algorithm will take huge time to finish the process of iteration.

We can transport this natural language algorithm to a Java code.

```java
//code 8.4

package fun.sanjibsinha.timecomplexity;

import java.util.Scanner;

public class TimeOne {

    static long userInput;

    public static void main(String[] args) {
        Scanner sc = new Scanner(System.in);
        System.out.println("Enter a positive integer to test prime or not: ");
        userInput = sc.nextInt();

        for (long i = 2; i < (userInput - 1); i++){
            if (userInput % i == 0){
                System.out.println(userInput + " is not prime.");
            } else {
                System.out.println(userInput + " is prime.");
            }
        }
    }
}
```

We are not going to run this code; it is just for an example of time-complexity. In the above code you can guess that to reach our goal we need to iterate 'n' number of times. Here 'n' is user's input. It is called 'order of n' or O(n). As the value of 'n' starts increasing, our algorithm starts crumbling. For a value like 10 to power 6 plus 3, it takes huge to time and it simply goes out of our hands.

Therefore, we have to search for a better algorithm to solve the same problem.

Let us take the user's input and instead of iterating over the whole range of that number, we can calculate the square root of that user's input. After that we can iterate up to that value.

It serves our purpose, and at the same time, shortens the length of iteration in a great way. Let us write the code in Java.

```java
//code 8.5

package fun.sanjibsinha.timecomplexity;

import java.util.Scanner;

public class TimeTwo {
    static double userInput;

    public static void main(String[] args) {
        Scanner sc = new Scanner(System.in);
        System.out.println("Enter a positive integer to test prime or not: ");
        userInput = sc.nextInt();

        // 10 to the power 6 + 3 = 1000003
        for (long i = 2; i < (Math.sqrt(userInput)); i++){
            if (userInput % i == 0){
                System.out.println(userInput + " is not prime.");
            } else {
                System.out.println(userInput + " is prime.");
            }
        }
    }
}
```

If we have a user's input like 1000003, our algorithm allows us not to iterate more than 1 million times. On the contrary, it allows us to iterate in and around 1000 times.

We write another short Java code to find the square root of any number.

```java
//code 8.6

package fun.sanjibsinha.timecomplexity;

public class TestClass {

    public static void main(String[] args) {

        System.out.println(Math.sqrt(1000003));
        //1000.001499998875
```

```
11     }
12 }
13
14
15 //output of 8.6
16
17 Square root of 10 to the power of 6 plus 3 is: 1000.001499998875
```

In the above code we can clearly see that the square root of 1000003.

Let us go back to the code 8.5, where we have successfully shortened the length of iteration by calculating the square root of user's input. Reducing the length of iteration means the algorithm takes much less time. Now the running time of our code is not 'order of m', but 'order of square root of n'; it means O(square root of n). It is quite evident that code 8.5 represents much better algorithm than code 8.4 to solve the same problem. Why so? Because, it solves the large test cases in acceptable time. Better algorithm is necessary for better performance.

Here the running time of the program depends on the user's input; and, user's input represents the growth of time which exerts influence on the running time.

As a conclusion to this section, we can say that time-complexity only cares about the 'input'. It also cares about the algorithm that tackles the 'input' in a better way.

Moreover, time-complexity does not care about the machine's hardware configuration. Whether the machine is single processor or multi processor does not matter. What is the network load, is unimportant. The time-complexity really does not care about 32 bit or 64 bit.

Input is the key word for time-complexity. Nothing else.

In the above examples, we have inputs like single integer. It could have been an array, a data structure; is not it? Now, again, we come to the point of the data structures, and algorithms. And, of course, now we also understand how time-complexity is related to them.

Big O Notation

We have already seen how through order of 'n', or 'input', we can represent any algorithm. Consider the code 8.4, where we have to iterate over one million times if 'n' is 1000003. Therefore, the O(n) is the worst case scenario. Any algorithm could not be worse than that O(n).

Big O notation is the most convenient way to express the worst-case scenario for an algorithm. Compare code 8.5 with the previous code 8.4. In code 8.5, the Big O notation is like this: O(square root of n). This algorithm could not be worse than anything. Now, comparing these two worst case scenarios, we can safely tell that the algorithm of code 8.5 is better than code 8.4.

If you are still confused with the definition, do not worry. Everything takes time. The concept of time-complexity is related to algorithm. More you practice, you will be able to get your head around this topic.

Let us try to call back the second code snippet of this chapter. The code 8.2 looks like this:

```
1  package fun.sanjibsinha;
2
3  public class Main {
4      public static void main(String[] args) {
5  int totalOne = 0;
6          for (i = 0; i <= 5; i++){
7              totalOne += i;
8          }
9          System.out.println("The total of loop: " + totalOne);
10     }
11 }
```

For brevity we have trimmed the code omitting the commented parts. When we have declared the variable 'totalOne' to 0, the constant is 1 and the time is also 1. In the next step, the first line of the 'for loop' tells us about two things. First, the constant is more than one, and the same rule applies for the time.

In the next line the algorithm keeps adding the value of iteration for 'n' number of times. Therefore, we have two constants, but the time equals 'n'.

The last line gives us the output. The constant is 1, and the time is also 1.

When we add them up, we get O(n). It happens so, because while summing it up, we remove all the constants.

However, for the code 5.1, where we have used nested loop to get the total of inner loop, this order of 'n' changes to (n * n), that is n squared. Therefore, the Big O notation or the worst case scenario of that algorithm is $O(n^2)$. Although in that code, we have total of the outer loop also. That means, we have O(n) at the same breath. Since there are consecutive statements, we count the statement with maximum complexity, that is $O(n^2)$.

We have got an initial idea of how Big O notation works, and what principles govern it. Many common algorithms we use very often, use the above Big O notation O(n^2). Common algorithms, such as bubble sort, selection sort and insertion sort takes the above Big O notation.

There are many other Big O notations that are related to different types of algorithms. The idea of time-complexity rests on finding the better algorithm to solve a problem.

We should analyze the Big O notations, or worst-case scenarios for the test cases and we will try to find the best solution.

I write regularly on Algorithm and Data Structure in

9. Set, Symmetric Difference and Propositional Logic

Set, Symmetric Difference and Propositional Logic are kind of heart and soul of Discrete Mathematics, as well as Computer Science. These concepts are immersed in data structures and algorithm, too. Without understanding these key concepts, we cannot move forward. Our knowledge of data structures and algorithm will remain incomplete.

In the previous chapters, we have seen a few implementations of Sets in various programming languages. We have also found out that sets are basically statements, just like we use the term statement within the coding paradigm.

Let us write a discrete mathematical Set of even numbers like this:

```
1  A = {2, 4, 6, 8}
```

We can read the Set of this even numbers as a statement – it is an even number. In discrete mathematical concepts, numerical sets are considered as a collection of discrete numbers that will not contain duplicate numbers. Yet, this statement will come into possession of something else if we replace the words 'numbers' with 'things'. We will come to that point in a minute.

If two different sets contain duplicate numbers, the symmetric difference will easily point out those numbers. Set uses XOR symbol to express the inequality, and this Boolean concept is implemented in every programming language.

Here comes Propositional Logic. We cannot find Symmetric Difference of two Sets without implementing Propositional Logic.

Propositional Logic is concerned with statements that are governed by 'truth values'; true and false. These truth values are assigned to analyze these statements either individually or in a composite manner.

These discrete mathematical concepts are not only interrelated, they also help each other clandestinely, within the coding paradigms.

We have found out in the previous chapter, in Java Collection framework, a Set is a Collection that cannot contain duplicate elements. It models the mathematical Set abstraction, Symmetric difference and Propositional logic one behind the other.

The concepts of Propositional logic plays a key role in some special cases, such as where the Set Collection defines behaviors like 'equals' or 'hashCode' operations. Let us consider an example, where we have two Set instances. If we want to compare them, we need to model the discrete mathematical Set abstractions, as well as Symmetric difference and propositional logic. Only if two Set instances are equal, when they contain the same elements.

A simple discrete mathematical example will clarify the concept.

```
1 A = {1, 5, 8, 9} and B = {5, 9, 11, 45}
2 A Symmetric Difference B = {1, 8, 11, 45}
```

Here numbers 1, 8, 11 and 45 are in each Set. However, 5 and 9 are in both Sets.

While we are not going to the details of the discrete mathematical representations, nevertheless we need to understand why implementations of Set abstractions are necessary in Data Structures.

So far, we have seen some mathematical Set implementations with numerical sets. But it could be of 'things'. Even mathematically when we define a Set, we say, a Set is a Collection. Collection of what? Collection of things. And, of course, these things should have a common property. We can imagine a Set of biking gears, such as helmet, gloves, goggles, shoes, etc. In another example of Set we can think of our two eyes – left eye and right eye.

We have already learned the Set notations, so we can write these two examples this way:

```
1 {helmet, gloves, goggles, shoes, ... }
2 {left-eye, right-eye}
```

In the first example, we have used three dots, they are called ellipsis. It means, the biking gear list is endless,or infinite. On the contrary, we have second example, where we have exact two elements.

We call the first one 'infinite set' and the second one is a 'finite set'.

Set abstractions may seem pointless as far as Mathematics is concerned, but this statement is contextual. In many situations Sets can become building blocks of highly complicated mathematical concepts, such as Graph Theory, Abstract Algebra, Linear Algebra, Number theory, etc. Furthermore, Set abstractions are building blocks of Data Structures, of which we are interested at present.

Why Set is important in Data Structures

The Set abstraction has some special characteristics. While we organize our data, we need to implement those special characteristics of Set abstraction. By organizing data we mean creation, retrieval, modification, and removal of data. In such operations, the implementations of Set abstraction comes to our help. Let us try to understand this part.

An element can exist only once in a Set. This Collection does not allow duplication. Particularly, this trait makes Set different from others in Java Collection framework. When we organize our data structures, we can plan it in that way.

We can store unique elements. Since, by default, Set abstraction does not care about order, in some cases, we can take advantage of that character also.

Based on such characteristics, we can store discrete elements without duplication, and we need not care about the order of the elements always. Although Set does not care about order, in some cases, we do not need chaos, but order. In such cases, we have the general-purpose Set implementation 'TreeSet'. It maintains the order of elements based on their values. But implementation of 'TreeSet' comes at a higher cost. It is slower than the other Set implementation 'HashSet', which stores data in a hash table. As long as the order of iteration is concerned, the 'HashSet' implementation does not guarantee that.

Let us take a look at the both implementations.

```
1 //code 9.1
2
3 package chapternine;
4
5 import java.util.HashSet;
6 import java.util.Set;
7 import java.util.TreeSet;
8
9 public class FirstCodeSample {
10
11     public static void main(String[] args) {
12
13         int countingIntegers[] = {25, 44, 78, 1, 65, 3};
14         Set<Integer> hashSet = new HashSet<Integer>();
15         try {
16             for(int i = 0; i < 5; i++) {
17                 hashSet.add(countingIntegers[i]);
18             }
19             System.out.println("HashSet does not sort the order: " + hashSet);
20
21             TreeSet sortedTreeSet = new TreeSet<Integer>(hashSet);
22             System.out.println("TreeSet sort the order based on values :");
23             System.out.println(sortedTreeSet);
24         }
25         catch(Exception e) {}
26     }
27 }
```

We have implemented both, the 'HashSet' and the 'TreeSet'. We can see the difference in the following output:

```
1 //output 9.1
2
3 HashSet does not sort the order: [1, 65, 25, 44, 78]
4 TreeSet sort the order based on values :
5 [1, 25, 44, 65, 78]
```

There is another implementation, called 'LinkedHashSet', which is implemented as a hash table with a linked list running through it. This implementation maintains the order in a different way. As we insert new element, the insertion-order is maintained.

We have started this section with a question, why Set is important in data structures?

A one-line answer is, we can take any Collection containing duplicate elements and convert it to another Collection removing all the duplicate elements. We can do that by implementing the Set discrete mathematical abstraction.

How Symmetric Difference and Propositional Logic combine

The very conception of Symmetric Difference does not exist without the Set abstraction.

Based on that, we can easily implement that abstraction in our Java code.

In general, the symmetric difference of two Sets mean a new Set, where duplication is nonexistent.

```java
1 //code 9.2
2
3 package chapternine;
4
5 import java.util.HashSet;
6 import java.util.Set;
7
8 public class SecondCodeExample {
9
10     public static void main(String[] args) {
11
12         Set<String> uniqueSet = new HashSet<String>();
13         Set<String> duplicateSet    = new HashSet<String>();
14
15         String[] ourArguments = {"I", "saw", "Mary", "I", "left", "Mary", "stayed"};
16         for (String a : ourArguments){
17             if (!uniqueSet.add(a)){
18                 duplicateSet.add(a);
19             }
20         }
21
22         System.out.println("Applying Symmetric Difference abstraction : ");
23         uniqueSet.removeAll(duplicateSet);
24
25         System.out.println("Unique words in unique Set:    " + uniqueSet);
```

```
26         System.out.println("Duplicate words in unique set: " +
duplicateSet);
27
28     }
29 }
```

What kind of output we can expect here? The arguments we have passed possess unique words, as well as duplicate words. We have tried to identify both the unique words, and the duplicate words. After that, we have produced them in the following output.

```
1 //output 9.2
2
3 Applying Symmetric Difference abstraction :
4 Unique words in unique Set:    [left, stayed, saw]
5 Duplicate words in unique set: [I, Mary]
```

We have implemented the symmetric difference abstraction in a different way. Implementing the same abstraction in a different way, may have produced only the discrete words, without duplication.

We can use a few other Set Symmetric Difference; however, we need to understand other Set algebraic operations. To do that, we can write a simple Java code that will show us how the implementation of Set abstraction does not allow duplication.

```
1 //code 9.3
2
3 package chapternine;
4
5 import java.util.HashSet;
6 import java.util.Set;
7
8 public class ThirdCodeExample {
9
10     public static void main(String[] args) {
11
12         Set<String> hashSetExample = new HashSet<String>();
13         hashSetExample.add("Sanjib");
14         hashSetExample.add("Sanjib");
15         hashSetExample.add("Sanjib");
16         hashSetExample.add("Sanjib");
17         hashSetExample.add("Sanjib");
18         System.out.println("HashSet does not allow duplication, we will get one outp\
19 ut: ");
20         System.out.println(hashSetExample);
21     }
22 }
```

The output is quite expected. The Set will not allow duplication. Therefore, repeated entry of same element will not be stored.

```
1 //output 9.3
2
3 HashSet does not allow duplication, we will get one output:
4 [Sanjib]
```

In discrete mathematical paradigms, Set abstraction is basically chaotic, and unordered. But it makes the difference in one area. No duplicate element is allowed in the world of Set. The next code snippet and its output will show you the same property.

```
1 //code 9.4
2
3 package chapternine;
4
5 import java.util.HashSet;
6 import java.util.Set;
7
8 public class ThirdCodeExample {
9
10     public static void main(String[] args) {
11
12         Set<String> hashSetExample = new HashSet<String>();
13         hashSetExample.add("Sanjib");
14         hashSetExample.add("Json");
15         hashSetExample.add("John");
16         hashSetExample.add("Sanjib");
17         hashSetExample.add("Austin");
18         hashSetExample.add("Bob");
19         System.out.println("HashSet is an unordered list: ");
20         System.out.println("HashSet also does not allow duplication; we will get one\
21   Sanjib: ");
22         System.out.println(hashSetExample);
23     }
24 }
25
26
27 //output 9.4
28
29 HashSet is an unordered list:
30 HashSet also does not allow duplication; we will get one Sanjib:
31 [Bob, John, Json, Austin, Sanjib]
```

For the Java enthusiasts we will write the same code again, to show that different types of output can be produced. In fact, every high level language has many ways to produce an output.

```java
//code 9.5

package chapternine;

import java.util.HashSet;
import java.util.Set;

public class ThirdCodeExample {

    public static void main(String[] args) {

        Set<String> hashSetExample = new HashSet<String>();
        hashSetExample.add("Sanjib");
        hashSetExample.add("Json");
        hashSetExample.add("John");
        hashSetExample.add("Sanjib");
        hashSetExample.add("Austin");
        hashSetExample.add("Bob");
        System.out.println("HashSet is an unordered list: ");
        System.out.println("HashSet also does not allow duplication; we will get one\
 Sanjib: ");
        System.out.println(hashSetExample);
        System.out.println();
        for (String name : hashSetExample){
            System.out.println(name);
        }
        System.out.println();
        hashSetExample.forEach(System.out::println);
    }
}

//output 9.5

HashSet is an unordered list:
HashSet also does not allow duplication; we will get one Sanjib:
[Bob, John, Json, Austin, Sanjib]

Bob
John
Json
Austin
Sanjib

Bob
John
Json
Austin
Sanjib
```

When the implementation type is 'HashSet', there is no guarantee that the order will be maintained. However, if we want the list in alphabetical order, we can always use the 'TreeSet' implementation along with the 'HashSet'. Changing the implementation makes our Set abstraction more robust.

```java
1 //code 9.6
2
3 package chapternine;
4
5 import java.util.HashSet;
6 import java.util.Set;
7 import java.util.TreeSet;
8
9 public class FourthCodeExample {
10
11     public static void main(String[] args) {
12
13         Set<String> hashSetExample = new HashSet<String>();
14         hashSetExample.add("Sanjib");
15         hashSetExample.add("Json");
16         hashSetExample.add("John");
17         hashSetExample.add("Sanjib");
18         hashSetExample.add("Austin");
19         hashSetExample.add("Bob");
20         System.out.println("Unordered HashSet output of names: ");
21         System.out.println(hashSetExample);
22         System.out.println();
23         TreeSet sortedTreeSet = new TreeSet<String>(hashSetExample);
24         System.out.println("TreeSet has sorted the order based on values :");
25         System.out.println(sortedTreeSet);
26     }
27 }
28
29
30 //output 9.6
31
32 Unordered HashSet output of names:
33 [Bob, John, Json, Austin, Sanjib]
34
35 TreeSet has sorted the order based on values :
36 [Austin, Bob, John, Json, Sanjib]
```

When a Set is not equal to another Set, in mathematics we use a special symbol. This inequality symbol is a representation of XOR, which is actually inequality on Boolean.

Here, in this part of Set implementation, the Propositional Logic is also implemented. It is a part of Set mathematical abstraction, just like Symmetric Difference.

10. Combinatorics and Counting, Permutation and Combinations

The area of mathematics in which counting is the primarily concern, it is known as Combinatorics. Besides other subjects like statistical physics, it has many applications in Computer Science.

The counting capabilities and other abstractions of Combinatorics is implemented in different ways (algorithm) to obtain results. In like manner, it also studies certain properties of finite structures, like data structures in Computer science.

Primarily, any data structure is related to the abstractions of any finite sets. We can apply different types of permutations on finite sets and that study also plays an important role in the fields of Combinatorics.

We can assume that when different types of permutations are required for data structures, different types of algorithms can also be emerged out from there.

For a single problem where enumeration or counting is required, there can be different types of algorithms. We can approach the problems whatever way. Regardless of how we solve the problems, different algorithms emerge from it.

Furthermore, to know how Combinatorics is associated with data structures and algorithm, we need to know the basic operations that are acted upon on the data structures with the help of different types of algorithms.

Be that as it may, but we cannot ignore these facts.

We have already found that enumeration of a specified data structure is a part of Combinatorics. Arrangements of a certain data structure is also a part of it. We can restructure or rearrange any 'string' value and place the characters in different combinations.

We can check whether a data structure fulfills a certain criteria. If there are several possibilities, we can also check, with the help of algorithms, what is the best structure or solution.

We have just learned that study of Combinatorics deals with different types of permutations on finite sets or data structures.

Therefore, to understand the key abstractions of Combinatorics we need to understand what permutations and combinations are.

Permutation and Combination

When we use the word 'combination', we forget whether 'order' is important or not. We also leave behind another key concept, 'repetition'. When repetition is allowed, the number of combinations increase. When it is not allowed, the number of combination or, in other words, the number of rearrangement reduces.

Consider an example that will make it clear.

Take a word 'forget'. If we go to any thesaurus and try to find what kind of word is it, we find several other words that are close to its meaning.

They are: overlook, drop, neglect, omit, leave out, etc. We can rearrange these group of words in many ways where order is not maintained. When we do not care what order the words are in, we say it a 'combination' of words.

However, when we apply the alphabetical order and rearrange the group of words again, then it comes out like this: drop, neglect, omit, overlook, leave out, etc. When order matters in a combination, it is called permutation. Think about a combination lock. We can choose any three numbers from 0 to 10. If in our case, the combination works in this arrangement '562', we can say that repetition is not allowed in this permutation. If it was like '223', we could have said that repetition is allowed in this permutation.

Take a close look, we will find that any permutation where repetition is allowed, the number of possibilities is nothing but factorial of that number of things that are to be rearranged.

Consider any three things. How many ways we can rearrange them? Finding it is very easy.

1 3 * 2 * 1 = 6

There are 6 ways we can rearrange three elements. If there were 4 elements, the factorial of 4, that is, in 24 ways we could have rearranged those 4 things.

Enough theory; let us dive into our first code where we will find the best algorithm to solve the above problem.

```
 1 // code 10.1
 2
 3 package chapterten;
 4
 5 /**
 6  * permutation is a combination of collections where order matters
 7  * permutation could be with repetition or without
 8  * here we see an example of
 9  * permutations without repetition
10  * if there are 16 things, and if we choose 14
11  * then we cannot choose 14 again
12  * in that case, 15 things remain
13  * no repetitions and order matters
14  */
15
16 /**
```

```
17  * Here is our problem:
18  * what order could 5 balls be in
19  * for 5 balls the possibility is factorial(5)
20  * if we take any otwo out of it
21  * the possibility is factorial(5 - 3)
22  * but the order of 2 out of 5 balls
23  * is factorial(5) / factorial(5 - 3)
24  */
25
26 public class SimplePermutation {
27
28     static int permutationWithoutRepetition(int n){
29         int i = 1;
30         int k = 1;
31         while (i <= n){
32             k *= i;
33             i++;
34         }
35         //we get the factorial of the number we have passed as parameter
36         return k;
37     }
38
39     public static void main(String[] args) {
40
41         /**
42         * the formula of permutation without repetition
43         * is factorial(listOfNumbers)/factorial(listOfNumbers - restOfNumbers)
44         */
45         int listOfNumbers = 5;
46         int restOfNumbers = 3;
47         System.out.println("The list of numbers are (5, 4, 3, 2, 1)");
48         System.out.println("Our first choice has 5 possibilities.");
49         System.out.println("The number of orders 5 numbers could be in: ");
50         System.out.println(permutationWithoutRepetition(5));
51     }
52 }
```

The output is quite expected. When 5 things are to be rearranged, there are 120 possibilities, which is actually the factorial of 5.

```
1 // output of 10.1
2
3 The list of numbers are (5, 4, 3, 2, 1)
4 Our first choice has 5 possibilities.
5 The number of orders 5 numbers could be in:
6 120
```

What we have seen, is a tip of iceberg. In reality, there are hundreds of Combinatorial algorithms that deal with different types of data structures based on finite sets.

We can include even structures that are built from graphs. We will talk about them in a few minutes, but before that, let us see some common examples of Combinatorial algorithms. We can think of generating list of all structures of a given type. In this scenario, we can think of permutation with repetition, or without repetition. We can think of combinations with repetition, or without repetition.

Search algorithms are good examples where Optimization and Approximation algorithms are used to solve such problems. Optimization methods or algorithms also include dynamic programming. On the other hand, Approximation methods include greedy algorithms.

We cannot say that one algorithm is the best solution. There could be a better algorithm than the previously claimed 'best'.

Let us solve a problem and see whether the solution is best or not.

There are five things. We have found out that if there are five things, there could be 120 possibilities. Let us pick any two of them and try to rearrange them in order. However, we cannot repeat the same thing twice. It is a permutation without repetition, still it is little bit different.

If we want to rearrange any two things from that five elements without repetition, what would be the order.

```
// code 10.2

package chapterten;

/**
 * permutation is a combination of collections where order matters
 * permutation could be with repetition or without
 * here we see an example of
 * permutations without repetition
 * if there are 16 things, and if we choose 14
 * then we cannot choose 14 again
 * in that case, 15 things remain
 * no repetitions and order matters
 */

/**
 * Here is our problem:
 * what order could 5 balls be in
 * for 5 balls the possibility is factorial(5)
 * if we take any otwo out of it
 * the possibility is factorial(5 - 3)
 * but the order of 2 out of 5 balls
```

```
23  * is factorial(5) / factorial(5 - 3)
24  */
25
26 public class SimplePermutation {
27
28     static int permutationWithoutRepetition(int n){
29         int i = 1;
30         int k = 1;
31         while (i <= n){
32             k *= i;
33             i++;
34         }
35         //we get the factorial of the number we have passed as parameter
36         return k;
37     }
38
39     public static void main(String[] args) {
40
41         /**
42         * the formula of permutation without repetition
43         * is factorial(listOfNumbers)/factorial(listOfNumbers - restOfNumbers)
44         */
45         int listOfNumbers = 5;
46         int restOfNumbers = 3;
47         System.out.println("The list of numbers are (5, 4, 3, 2, 1)");
48         System.out.println("Our first choice has 5 possibilities.");
49         System.out.println("The number of orders 5 numbers could be in: ");
50         System.out.println(permutationWithoutRepetition(5));
51         System.out.println("Now we need any two numbers from this collection:");
52         System.out.println("The order of 2 numbers out of 5 numbers could be: ");
53 System.out.println(permutationWithoutRepetition(5)/permutationWithoutRepetit\
54 ion(3));
55
56     }
57 }
```

Here is the explanation. When we pick up 2 elements from 5 elements, 3 elements are left behind. The algorithm is quite simple.

```
1 First, find out the factorial of 5.
2 Second, find out the factorial of 3.
3 Third, divide factorial of 5 by factorial of 3.
```

We have done the same thing. And here is the output:

```
// output of 10.2

The list of numbers are (5, 4, 3, 2, 1)
Our first choice has 5 possibilities.
The number of orders 5 numbers could be in:
120
Now we need any two numbers from this collection:
The order of 2 numbers out of 5 numbers could be:
20
```

As we have said earlier, there are hundreds of Combinatorial algorithms. Besides more common 'sorting' and 'searching', we have different types of generating 'permutations and combinations', graphs, and many others.

Our next problem will deal with some kind of generating permutation and combination. How many ways we can rearrange a string? If repetition is allowed, it is obvious that number of rearrangement will be more. How it happens?

A string is a sequence of characters. It is a representation of data structure, an array of characters.

Therefore, it has a length. If repetition is allowed, we can count the length of the string, and safely say that the factorial of that number is the possibility.

But the real trick is in the process of rearrangement.

```java
// code 10.3

package chapterten;

/**
 * When repetition is allowed, we can rearrange the order
 * of a string in various combination
 * since we will keep the order with repetitions,
 * we can call it a permutation of a string
 */

public class StringPermutation {
    // we need a global recursive method
    // that will print all the permutations of the string
    static void arrangeTheStringWithRepetition(String anyString, String anotherStrin\
g){

        // we need to check if the given string is empty
        if (anyString.length() == 0) {
            System.out.print(anotherString + " ");
            return;
        }
```

```java
            for (int i = 0; i < anyString.length(); i++) {

                // reaching to the last character
                char ch = anyString.charAt(i);

                // we can display the rest of the character after
                // excluding the last character
                String restOfTheString = anyString.substring(0, i) +
                        anyString.substring(i + 1);

                // calling the method recursively
                arrangeTheStringWithRepetition(restOfTheString, anotherString + ch);
            }
    }

    public static void main(String[] args) {

        String stringToArrange = "abcd";
        // the given string 'abcd' is of length 4
        // factors of 4 is 4,3,2,1
        // factorial is 24
        // the program will rearrange the string 24 times
        arrangeTheStringWithRepetition(stringToArrange, " ");
        System.out.println();

    }

}


// output of 10.3

abcd  abdc  acbd  acdb  adbc  adcb  bacd  badc  bcad  bcda  bdac  bdca  cabd  cadb  \
cbad  cbda  cdab  cdba  dabc  dacb  dbac  dbca  dcab  dcba
```

In the above code snippet, the string is of length 4.

Therefore, factorial of 4, that is 24 is the number of possibility. The above program rearranges the string 24 ways. However, the condition was repetition could be allowed.

In a given string where the length is 3, we can rearrange that string in 6 ways, which is the factorial of 3. What happens, when repetition is not allowed.

```
// code 10.4


```

```java
package chapterten;

/**
 * When repetition is not allowed to arrange a given string
 * our scope is limited, consider an example
 * for a combination lock, where the given numbers are from
 * 0 to 10, and we are told to choose any three numbers,
 * we cannot use arrangement like 111
 */

public class StringPermutationWithoutRepetition {

    // we need a global method, where we will arrange a string
    // without repeating a sequence more than once
    static void displayingDistinctString(String anyString, String anotherString){

        // we need to check if the given string is empty
        if (anyString.length() == 0) {
            System.out.print(anotherString + " ");
            return;
        }

        // keeping in mind that we have 26 alphabets we need a
        // boolean array of size '26'
        boolean allAlphabets[] = new boolean[26];

        for (int i = 0; i < anyString.length(); i++) {

            // reaching to the last character
            char ch = anyString.charAt(i);

            // we can display the rest of the character after
            // excluding the last character
            String restOfTheString = anyString.substring(0, i) +
                    anyString.substring(i + 1);

            // it will check the repetition, if the character has already been used,
            // it will call the method recursively; else, there will be no recursive\
 call
            if (allAlphabets[ch - 'a'] == false)
                displayingDistinctString(restOfTheString, anotherString + ch);
            allAlphabets[ch - 'a'] = true;
        }
    }

    public static void main(String[] args) {
```

```
50
51              String stringToArrangeWithoutRepeating = "bbc";
52
53              displayingDistinctString(stringToArrangeWithoutRepeating, " ");
54              System.out.println();
55
56       }
57 }
58
59
60 // output of 10.4
61
62 bbc   bcb   cbb
```

To test the above code, we have used a string where one character 'b' has been used twice. As a matter of fact, if repeating is allowed, there could be 6 rearrangements.

Since, repeating is not allowed, we get the above output. Just before, in the code 10.3, we have seen an algorithm where repetition has been allowed, and accordingly we have seen the rearrangements.

We can do the same in a different way. We can rearrange the sequence of characters in such a way so that the string output would be of various orders. Some of them may look similar because we have allowed repetition.

```
 1 // code 10.5
 2
 3 package chapterten;
 4
 5 import java.util.Scanner;
 6
 7 public class StringPermutationWithRepetition {
 8
 9       // we need a global method to swap two characters
10       // and return the string in a sequential array
11
12       static String swappingCharacters(String aString, int i, int j){
13
14          char aCharacter;
15
16          char[] sequentialArray = aString.toCharArray();
17
18          aCharacter = sequentialArray[i];
19
20          sequentialArray[i] = sequentialArray[j];
21
22          sequentialArray[j] = aCharacter;
23
24          return String.valueOf(sequentialArray);
```

```java
    }

    // a method to display every combination of arrangement of the string
    // in order, where repetition is allowed
    static void permuteAStringByRepeating(String aString, int start, int finish){

        if(start == finish){

            System.out.println(aString);

        }
        int i;

        for(i = start; i <= finish; i++){

            aString = swappingCharacters(aString, start, i);

            permuteAStringByRepeating(aString, start + 1, finish);

            aString = swappingCharacters(aString, start, i);

        }

    }

    public static void main(String[] args) {

        Scanner sc = new Scanner(System.in);
        System.out.println("Enter a string to see all possible permutations where re\
petition is allowed: ");
        String enterAString;
        enterAString = sc.next();
        System.out.println("It arranges the string '" + enterAString + "' according \
to the number of factorials" +
                " of its length.");
        permuteAStringByRepeating(enterAString, 0, enterAString.length() - 1);
        System.out.println();
    }
}
```

Since the length of the string is 3, the factorial of 3 would give us the desired number. Factorial of 3 is 6, therefore, we have 6 arrangements in place.

```
 1  // output of 10.5
 2
 3  Enter a string to see all possible permutations where repetition is
allowed:
 4  aab
 5  It arranges the string 'aab' according to the number of factorials
of its length.
 6  aab
 7  aba
 8  aab
 9  aba
10  baa
11  baa
```

There are hundreds of other Combinatorial problems and algorithms. To get our head around them to understand the inner logic, we need practice. Furthermore, we need to keep the issue of time complexity in our mind, at the same time.

I write regularly on Algorithm and Data Structure in

What Next

If you have read the whole book and reach to this point, it is worthy of high praise.

I have tried my best to weave three important components of Computer science Ã¢â‚¬â€œ discrete mathematics, data structure and algorithm. Although they appear to be difficult at first glance, if you understand the key concepts, and understand how these three components are internally related, it no longer seems to be so difficult anymore.

The topic winds through the various programming languages, yet for the intermediate learners that should not be a big issue. Although programming languages have different syntax, the basic structure of every high-level language is same. Especially it is true for discrete mathematics, data structure and algorithm.

The first code repository for this book

The second code repository for this book

```
1  Just click on <sanjib12sinha@gmail.com> to send me an email.
```

Happy reading, best of luck.

www.ingramcontent.com/pod-product-compliance
Lightning Source LLC
Chambersburg PA
CBHW060410220526
45465CB00008B/2828